The Influence of the
Doctrine of Scripture

The Influence of the Doctrine of Scripture

How Beliefs about the Bible Affect the Way It Is Read

Anna Hutchinson

LEXINGTON BOOKS/FORTRESS ACADEMIC
Lanham • Boulder • New York • London

Published by Lexington Books/Fortress Academic
Lexington Books is an imprint of The Rowman & Littlefield Publishing Group, Inc.
4501 Forbes Boulevard, Suite 200, Lanham, Maryland 20706
www.rowman.com

86-90 Paul Street, London EC2A 4NE, United Kingdom

Copyright © 2024 by The Rowman & Littlefield Publishing Group, Inc.

All rights reserved. No part of this book may be reproduced in any form or by any electronic or mechanical means, including information storage and retrieval systems, without written permission from the publisher, except by a reviewer who may quote passages in a review.

British Library Cataloguing in Publication Information Available

Library of Congress Cataloging-in-Publication Data

Names: Hutchinson, Anna, 1992– author.
Title: The influence of the doctrine of scripture : how beliefs about the Bible affect the
   way it is read / Anna Hutchinson.
Description: Lanham : Lexington Books/Fortress Academic, [2024] |
   Includes bibliographical references and index. | Summary: "This book analyses
   how Evangelical Anglicans study the Bible. It explores the relationship between the
   doctrine of Scripture and hermeneutics as it happens 'on the ground', asking how
   Bible beliefs influence and affect the interpretative activity and conclusions that Bible
   readers make"—Provided by publisher.
Identifiers: LCCN 2023051716 (print) | LCCN 2023051717 (ebook) |
   ISBN 9781978714670 (cloth) | ISBN 9781978714687 (epub)
Subjects: LCSH: Bible--Hermeneutics. | Theology, Doctrinal. | Bible—Evidences,
   authority, etc. | Evangelical Church—Doctrines. | Church of England—Doctrines.
Classification: LCC BS476 .H88 2024 (print) | LCC BS476 (ebook) |
   DDC 220.1/3—dc23/eng/20231221
LC record available at https://lccn.loc.gov/2023051716
LC ebook record available at https://lccn.loc.gov/2023051717

♾️ᵀᴹ The paper used in this publication meets the minimum requirements of American
National Standard for Information Sciences—Permanence of Paper for Printed Library
Materials, ANSI/NISO Z39.48-1992.

Contents

Acknowledgments	vii
Chapter 1: Situating the Research	1
Chapter 2: Research Methodology and Design	19
Chapter 3: The Influence of the Doctrine of Scripture: Reading Historically	35
Chapter 4: The Influence of the Doctrine of Scripture: Reading Theologically	55
Chapter 5: The Influence of the Doctrine of Scripture: Reading for Today	73
Chapter 6: The Influence of the Doctrine of Scripture: Some Conclusions	91
Chapter 7: The Influence of Belief: Reading through Doctrine	107
Chapter 8: The Influence of Literature: Reading through Genre	121
Chapter 9: The Influence of Context: Reading Through Experience	139
Chapter 10: The Influence of Education: Comparing Responses	153
Chapter 11: The Influence of the Text: Reading for Transformation	175
Bibliography	193
Index	201
About the Author	205

Acknowledgments

First and foremost, acknowledgment must go to my willing participants for trusting me with their time and their opinions. I am so grateful for you and have become immensely fond of you all as I have thought about what you've said for several years; thank you for being part of this research.

I am greatly indebted to my PhD supervisor, Professor Andrew Davies, for his expertise and guidance. I have been extremely blessed by his professional input and generosity in helping and advising me.

Without critical financial help, this research would not have been possible. My heartfelt thanks go to the St. Christopher's Education Trust, St. Matthias's Trust, The Bible Society, and the University of Birmingham's College of Arts and Law for their financial support and belief in the value and importance of this research.

My research has been nurtured by the camaraderie and insight of some incredibly supportive academics and faithful friends. Thank you to Megan Loumagne, Libby Li, Ben Page, and Tim Glover for your encouragement and understanding. Thank you also to my colleagues at St. Mellitus, particularly Jonny Rowlands, for their encouragement as I have been working on this book and for inspiring me to keep going!

I have also benefitted immensely from the friendship of many whilst this research was undertaken. To Ally, Thomas, Em, Anna, Hannah, Eva, and Ileri—thank you for keeping me sane and loved. Particular thanks to wonderful Lucy, for being my surrogate family and letting me keep a study desk in our lounge.

I also owe acknowledgment to the friends who have patiently indulged me from afar in listening to the ups and downs of my research over the past few years. I am incredibly grateful for the inspiration and love of Bethan, Anna, Ruth, and Joelle.

To my family. Zoe, thank you for reading early draft chapters and offering input; I valued that, and you, so much. Iain and Helen—I'm not convinced either of you actually know what I've been doing the past six years—this book will show you. Thanks for believing in me even though you don't get it! To my parents, Jon and Katherine. I am indebted to you not only for your support on this journey, but for instilling in me a sense of ambition and for being the first to introduce me to the Bible that continues to fascinate. This thesis is dedicated to you both.

Finally, to Danny. This research and book were the biggest commitment of my life, until you. Thank you for encouraging me in the final part; it makes all the difference even when you don't know what to say. You're about to walk through the door and ask if I've finally finished. Yes honey, I'm done!

Chapter 1

Situating the Research

Have you ever been sat in a Bible study and wondered, 'what is going on?' The research in this book was inspired by many such experiences in and around Evangelical Anglican churches and Bible culture. In particular, I found that whilst many readers make certain claims about the Bible (that it is authoritative, true, or relevant), those claims seemed to subtly shift in the face of Bible passages that say things that were found to be uncomfortable or awkward. Belief in a particular nature of Scripture certainly played a part in how the text was interpreted, but it definitely wasn't the whole story.

Christians often profess an explicit doctrine of Scripture using terms such as 'authoritative', 'inerrant', 'inspired', 'God's Word', 'sufficient' and so on, yet frequently seem to hold to a somewhat different implicit doctrine of Scripture that gives meaning and nuance to such assertions through the hermeneutical practices employed in their individual context. One of the key findings of the Anglican 'Bible in the Life of the Church' research project supports this insight: 'A major finding of these investigations is that how Anglicans engage with the Bible turns out to be just as important as its content. This perhaps unnerving claim does not contest the unique place and authority which the Scriptures have in Anglican life, but it does point to the significance, perhaps thus far overlooked, of the contexts in which and processes by which they are heard and read.'[1]

Christians are, in principle, holding to the same general beliefs about the Bible, but the outcomes of these beliefs are related to the processes and contexts of interpretation. To what extent does the doctrine of Scripture prescribe interpretive practice in theory, and how does this match with what happens in reality? How do different contexts affect this dynamic? In particular, might the context of theological education impact the influence the doctrine of Scripture has upon interpretation?

The research in this book was built upon the hypothesis, first and primarily, that the doctrine of Scripture has an influential role in how Evangelical Anglicans interpret the Bible; in other words, that the doctrine of Scripture

2   *Chapter 1*

and interpretation are in some form of affective relationship. Its second hypothesis was that theological education would impact this relationship to some extent. As such, the research was designed in order to answer the following questions:

> What is the role of the Doctrine of Scripture in the reading and interpreting of biblical texts?

> Does this role vary according to theological education?

These dynamics were explored through gathering qualitative data of Evangelical Anglican's reading and interpreting the Bible. The majority of this book focuses on the first question, reviewing the data gathered as a whole. Chapter 10 addresses the second question specifically. So, if you've ever asked in a Bible study or discussion, 'what is going on here?'—this book will show you.

INTENDED AUDIENCE

This book is an adaptation of my PhD thesis and is for a number of audiences. First, it contributes to the growing body of empirical research on Bible reading and is of value for academics conducting research in this field. It provides another window into the interpretative practices of ordinary readers and in particular, seeks to bridge a gap between hermeneutical theory and practice that is often missing in academia.

Second, this book will be of interest to those who serve in ministries where the reading of the Bible takes place. It highlights and breaks down 'what is happening' for such ministry practitioners and invites reflection on the extent to which the participants in this research represent those they minister to in their contexts, which in turn might suggest new avenues for strengthening doctrinal learning or hermeneutical skills.

Third, this book is for the countless Christians I have encountered who have asked questions about what the Bible is, how it should be read, and whether it's being read well. The research presented here gives these readers an opportunity to watch in 'slow motion' the practices and habits that they will undoubtedly be familiar with, and offers an analysis that will help them to appreciate the dynamics of what easily becomes commonplace.

Situating the Research 3

RESEARCH FIELDS

My research stands at the intersection of a number of fields and therefore has a broad disciplinary base. My focus on the doctrine of Scripture draws upon the field of systematic theology, but as this is being examined in relation to interpretation, the research is more at home in the field of hermeneutics. Moreover, the empirical nature of my research situates it alongside studies with methodologies drawn from the social sciences, which has overlaps with the field of practical theology. Additionally, the particular demographic of my research situates it within the field of Evangelical and Anglican studies. Defining this subset of Christians is an important place to start.

DEFINING EVANGELICAL ANGLICANS

It is important at the outset to recognise that Evangelicalism is by nature transdenominational.[2] Therefore, Evangelical Anglicans are one sub-group of the broader 'Evangelical' and 'Anglican' parties. What does it mean to be an Evangelical Anglican? This question is likely to prompt numerous and varied responses from those that class themselves as such, with different emphases on either Evangelicalism or Anglicanism and their respective and combined theology, culture, and history, which is reflected in scholarship.[3]

Quantitative research conducted by Andrew Village recognises three dominant groups within the Church of England: Anglo-Catholic, Broad Church, and Evangelical.[4] According to recent survey research conducted by the Evangelical Alliance, 32 percent of Evangelical respondents attended Anglican churches.[5] The extent to which this is representative is, of course, questionable, but gives an indication that a significant proportion of Evangelicals are Anglicans and vice versa.

How has this group come to exist? The Church of England was formed in 1534 and Evangelicalism did not emerge in England until the eighteenth century, though its roots are discernible in the prior movements of Puritanism and Pietism. The rise of Evangelicals within the Church of England to become a predominant 'party' within the Anglican Communion, as Village attests, has not been a straightforward progression, with debates over the extent to which its trajectory has been a 'hostile takeover or friendly merger'.[6] One of the most significant moments for the relationship between Evangelicalism and the Church of England was the 1966 confrontation between Martin Lloyd-Jones and John Stott at the Second National Assembly of Evangelicals in Westminster. Lloyd-Jones' call for an independent Evangelical denomination was countered by Stott who maintained that Evangelicals belonged

4 *Chapter 1*

in their denominations, demonstrating his own loyalty to the Church of England. A year later, the 1967 Kelle Congress marked a decisive shift for the Evangelical movement within the Church of England.[7] In 2012, *The Economist* reported Peter Brierley's statistic that 40 percent of Anglicans are thought to attend Evangelical parishes,[8] and in 2016 *The Guardian* claimed that 70 percent of those selected for ordination in the Church of England were reported to be Evangelicals.[9] Evangelical Anglicans are a significant group. Graham Kings has identified three strands within this Evangelical Anglican bracket: conservative evangelicals, open evangelicals, and charismatic evangelicals, thus identifying how the target demographic of my research contains breadth.[10]

A more thorough history or exploration of the broader culture and theology of Evangelical Anglicanism is beyond the scope of this book, with the exception of an Evangelical Anglican doctrine of Scripture. What does this group of Christians believe about the Bible?

DEFINING AN EVANGELICAL ANGLICAN DOCTRINE OF SCRIPTURE

The convergence of the Anglican heritage with Evangelicalism creates something of a range of expected beliefs about the Bible. What are the resulting doctrinal commitments that an Evangelical Anglican would likely have with regard to the Bible? This is important to establish in order to have parameters of belief that can be assumed of the participants in the research. Yet, how can expected beliefs about the Bible be established without official doctrines to consult?

Whilst there is much written in the academy on the doctrine of Scripture both in relation to Anglicanism and Evangelicalism and its connection to hermeneutics, this body of literature does not necessarily reflect belief 'on the ground.'[11] Whilst not completely disconnected, the average Bible reader is not consulting scholarship to inform their doctrine of Scripture. With this in mind, the following overview deliberately chooses to consult popular literature which is accessible for a broad audience. Though it is not assumed that all the participants in this research will have read the works cited, this body of literature is more likely to capture the beliefs that such 'ordinary' Evangelical Anglican readers will have been exposed to.[12] There is much written on the doctrine of Scripture, particularly from the Evangelical side,[13] but the voices included below, though not numerous, are specifically Evangelical Anglicans and predominantly British, to reflect my participants. Some of the literature included might seem dated for a contemporary overview, yet the choice to include it is very intentional. Figures like John Stott and J. I. Packer have loomed large over the history and definition of Evangelical Anglicanism, in Britain particularly, and their writings still hold much sway today.

AUTHORITATIVE

The Bible's authority is a key feature of Protestantism, inclusive of Evangelicals and Anglicans. For the Bible to be authoritative means that it is the source of belief and guide for behaviour. Its authority is therefore corporate and individual; corporate concerning doctrine and ecclesial practice and individual concerning personal conduct, choice, and behaviour.

Within Evangelicalism, the Bible's authority has become absolute such that proof of its authority cannot be sought from an external source, which would then become a higher authority. Scripture's authority is thus established from Scripture, and it is founded upon the nature of the Bible as being 'God's Word' and 'God-breathed'.[14] Whilst Anglicans agree with this latter notion, their respect held for tradition recognises that biblical authority is inextricably linked to the people of God, i.e., the church. It is not that biblical authority derives from the church but rather is recognised in and through the church. As McGrath explains,

> For in part, the authority of Scripture rests in the universal acceptance of that authority within the Christian church. . . . We trust the Bible partly because it is trusted by the church. In ascribing authority to Scripture, we are not merely recognising and honouring God's decision to reveal himself to us, nor only the specific form which this took in Jesus Christ; we are also honouring a living tradition, which has remained faithful to the modes of faith and life made known and made possible through Jesus Christ, and mediated through Scripture.[15]

This emphasis on the living tradition of the church is also paired with a slightly more Anglican emphasis upon authority as derived from belief in and commitment to Jesus. It is not only that Jesus himself demonstrated belief in the authority of the Old Testament but that through the Scriptures, one comes to know Jesus. Biblical authority is thus a corollary of Jesus' authority.[16] This is demonstrated by Thompson, who writes 'the link between Jesus the Word of God and Scripture as the word of God is unbreakable and mutually illuminating.'[17]

6 *Chapter 1*

INSPIRED (WORD OF GOD)

Both Evangelicals and Anglicans believe in the inspiration of Scripture as a result of the Bible being the Word of God—the Bible is God's Word because it is inspired, and it is inspired because it is God's Word.

How exactly the process of inspiration is thought to work has tended to be more of a debate amongst Evangelicals; what does inspiration indicate about the level of human autonomy in the writing of the Bible? The most common belief espoused by the majority of Evangelicals and Anglicans is a 'verbal plenary' theory of inspiration which upholds both the autonomy and individuality of the human author whilst maintaining that the text is also entirely what God wanted to say. This belief has sometimes been described using an analogy to the incarnation of Jesus; in the same way that Jesus is both fully human and fully God, the Bible is also fully the work of human authors whilst being fully the words of God.[18] Some have pushed back on this analogy in order to safeguard the uniqueness of the incarnation.[19] Thompson, for example, argues that 'too hasty an appeal to incarnational theology has led to dubious conclusions for the doctrine of Scripture.'[20] Whether or not such an analogy is appealed to, the view that human freedom and divine freedom are not mutually exclusive is common, and that God can work through 'concursive operation' whereby God uses the skills, knowledge, personality, and circumstances of a fallible human to write God's words.[21]

In addition to how inspiration 'works', is the debate about whether such views inevitably lead to affirmations of infallibility and inerrancy. Amongst scholarship there is differing opinion as to what infallibility and inerrancy actually constitute and whether they even differ, though generally speaking, infallibility equates to reliable and trustworthy, whereas inerrancy is stricter and means 'without error'. For some, inerrancy is a necessary consequence of the Bible being God's Word on account of it being inspired,[22] though others, such as Stott, whilst subscribing to the principle, find the language of inerrancy to be unhelpful.[23] For some quarters of the Evangelical party, subscription to such terms is a hallmark of belonging to Evangelicalism. This isn't the case for everyone. In other quarters, that often emphasise the human component of Scripture, inspiration does not result in inerrancy. Sparks offers an example; 'Yet I do not believe that we can so easily overlook that God has chosen to speak to human audiences through human authors in everyday human language. Is it therefore possible that God has selected to speak to human beings through adequate rather than inerrant words, and is it further possible that he did so because human beings are adequate rather than inerrant readers?'[24]

Situating the Research 7

Whether or not inerrancy is affirmed, inspiration means 'a biblical text filled with the spirit, or breath, of God.'[25] The dynamics of this commitment can vary.

SUFFICIENT

The sufficiency of the Bible has typically been a feature of an Anglican doctrine of Scripture, given its history and disassociation from Rome. However, the Bible's sufficiency features as a prominent characteristic of Evangelical doctrines of Scripture. For the Bible to be sufficient means that no further teaching or resource is needed for an understanding of God's character, action, and purposes.

Sometimes sufficiency is framed in relation to salvation; all one needs to know for salvation is contained in the Bible. In the words of Thompson, 'It does not need a supplement in order to accomplish its purpose, whether that supplement is offered by the teaching magisterium of the church, the discoveries and dictates of human reason, or fresh revelation of the Spirit. What has been given to us is enough to make known to us the saving purpose of God in Christ, to warrant faith, and to direct the Christian life.'[26]

On the other hand, the sufficiency of Scripture is sometimes emphasised as a corollary of its authority; if other resources were needed for knowledge of God then Scripture would not be sole authority. This line of thinking is particularly shaped against Church tradition, where any tradition that contributes to an understanding of the Bible, such as the creed, must first be derived from the Bible, in order to maintain Scripture's sufficiency.[27]

Article 6 of the Church of England describes Scripture's sufficiency but interestingly, Stott refutes the Anglican tradition of according also a significant place to the role of tradition and reason.[28] This view is distinctive of the Evangelical Anglican stance. Kings explicates this in relation to his three strands of Evangelical Anglicans—conservative, open, and charismatic. Using a water analogy he claims. 'All three watercourses tend to be uncomfortable with the equality of "scripture", "tradition" and "reason" as Anglican authorities, and are united in preferring to hold to the supreme authority of scripture.'[29] This is perhaps a place of tension for an Evangelical Anglican. Whilst Evangelicalism has often erred on the sufficiency of Scripture to the detriment of tradition, Anglicanism holds a deep appreciation for church tradition:

> Evangelicals have always been prone to read Scripture as if they were the first to do so. The Anglican ethos provides an invaluable corrective to this tendency, by reminding us that others have been there before us, and have read it before

8   *Chapter 1*

us. This process of receiving the scriptural revelation is 'tradition'—not a source of revelation in addition to Scripture, but a particular way of understanding Scripture which the Christian church has recognised as responsible and reliable.[30]

The sufficiency of Scripture is therefore an affirmation of the Bible as sole authority and adequate for knowledge of salvation. The extent to which tradition and other sources of input are actually used in the way the Bible functions is a point of variance amongst Evangelicals and Anglicans. In particular, Kings identifies 'three sub-authorities, under scripture, which are sometimes in danger of becoming supra-authorities and affecting hermeneutics. In the canal [conservative evangelicals], this may be "evangelical tradition", which is sometimes hardened into doctrine; in the river [open evangelicals], these may be "reason" and "church tradition", which can lead astray; and in the rapids [charismatic evangelicals] this may be "experience", which, while live-giving, may be unstable as a foundation.'[31]

UNIT/CONSISTENT

Both Evangelicals and Anglicans believe that both testaments are essential to understanding God's redemptive work and that they faithfully reflect the unchanging character of God throughout salvation history. However, Evangelicals and Anglicans also believe in progressive revelation—that God reveals different truths at different times in history, which explains the need for a New Testament to document the ultimate revelation of God in Jesus. Progressive revelation is affirmed in understanding the New Testament to be the culmination of all that was established in the Old Testament, but Evangelical Anglicans reject the idea that the Old Testament represents Israel's evolving ideas about God that developed and thus overwrote one another as they were built. As Beynon and Sach advise: 'It doesn't matter whether you read about him in Deuteronomy or Habakkuk or Galatians or Revelation. In every one of those books, we're reading about the very same God.'[32] The Old and New Testaments are thus both essential for a full of understanding of God's revelation of himself and his plan for salvation.

Additionally, the Bible's unity and consistency are not just affirmed on theological grounds according to their content but also on account of the entire Bible being 'God's Word'. The unity and consistency of Scripture are hence characteristics of God which must apply to Scripture as his word. Both the content and author of Scripture point to its consistency and unity.

Situating the Research 9

CLEAR

A principle stemming from the Reformation but contested with the rise of biblical criticism, the Bible's clarity is asserted by both Anglicans and Evangelicals. However, this clarity does not mean one can easily understand everything in the Bible or that there is a necessity for all parts of the Bible to be equally clear. The Chicago Statement on Biblical Inerrancy declares, 'We deny that all passages of Scripture are equally clear or have equal bearing on the message of redemption.'[33]

Whilst specialist training and education are needed in order to be able to understand certain aspects of the Bible, it is maintained that even the most basically educated can read the Bible and understand the core message of salvation in order to respond to it. 'The clarity of Scripture is "that quality of the biblical text that, as God's communicative act, ensures meaning is accessible to all who come to it in faith."'[34]

The clarity of Scripture is a much less contested issue amongst Evangelicals and Anglicans, though connected concerns about the role of higher criticism have called into question the ability of the lay reader to understand the Bible properly. However, it is still agreed that the central message of salvation is clear and accessible to all readers and this is ultimately a feature of the Bible being God's written revelation.

AN EVANGELICAL ANGLICAN
DOCTRINE OF SCRIPTURE

The authority, inspiration, sufficiency, consistency, and clarity of Scripture are core features of Evangelical Anglican doctrine of Scripture. Within these commitments are a number of nuances and particularities that result in a spectrum of belief. The Church of England Evangelical Council's 'Basis of Faith' offers a succinct summary of the parameters set out above.

> We receive the canonical books of the Old and New Testaments as the wholly reliable revelation and record of God's grace, given by the Holy Spirit as the true word of God written. The Bible has been given to lead us to salvation, to be the ultimate rule for Christian faith and conduct, and the supreme authority by which the Church must ever reform itself and judge its traditions.[35]

This statement affirms the consistency of the Bible in both testaments, its truthfulness as God's word (inspired), its sufficiency in matters of salvation, and its authority for the church. Though clarity is not mentioned it could be strongly inferred. If the Bible was not clear, then it would be unable to

10 *Chapter 1*

function in the way described. Though perhaps more reflective of the 'conservative' end of the Evangelical Anglican spectrum of belief, this statement sets out what could plausibly be expected for an Evangelical Anglican to believe about the Bible.

HERMENEUTICS

Having specified five key features of an Evangelical Anglican doctrine of Scripture and suggested a range of positions and nuances within a commitment to these five features, they can be further illuminated by connection to their hermeneutic counterparts. That is to say, what it means for the Bible to be authoritative or inspired is seen in the practices and methods that one engages in interpretation.

This is the postulated relationship between the doctrine of Scripture and hermeneutics for Evangelical Anglicans, that doctrine determines hermeneutics, or in the words of Beynon and Sach, 'understanding the nature of the Bible leads us to the right way to approach it.'[36] This means reading the text in light of its divine and human authors. For Thompson, 'This explains why Christians cultivate a specific posture in relation to the Scriptures, not standing over them as critics and judges, deciding for ourselves what is wholesome and true and discarding the remainder.'[37] Whilst recognising that biblical criticism is an essential task of the interpreter, Packer believes it only to be so when 'based on fully biblical presuppositions about that which we are studying.'[38] A reader should therefore interpret the Bible according to the doctrine of Scripture. 'What we expect from Scripture must be determined entirely by what Scripture is, and the purpose for which God has caused it to be written.'[39] This naturally leads to the adoption of certain principles and the rejection of others, as will be seen in chapters 3–6. The doctrine of Scripture is to be a controlling influence in the way the text is read.

However, in connection with this idea is another that sits somewhat at odds with it. Whilst approaching the text with a firm commitment to its inspired and authoritative nature is mandated, there is also a concern that the reader maintains an openness so that the text can be properly heard, and one does not end up reading their own agenda back into the text. Thiselton claims that the ability to be addressed by God and confronted with the truth through Scripture is muted when there is too rigid a framework in place that pigeonholes interpretation into a determined outcome. Scripture is alive and active but 'a word that must always be made to conform to pre-packaged theology has already been tamed and domesticated.'[40] This doctrinal commitment, therefore, is something of a fine balancing act between reading within a belief in the nature of Scripture but reading with an openness to the text's

Situating the Research 11

voice addressing the reader. This begs the question, what does this look like practically? How does a commitment to the descriptors of the Bible's nature above determine hermeneutical approach and method, in theory? Specifically, does the doctrine of Scripture determine that an Evangelical Anglican should read historically (chapter 3), theologically (chapter 4) and with relevance for today (chapter 5)?

HERMENEUTICAL FIELDWORK

Having offered a brief denominational and doctrinal overview, it's helpful to locate my research amongst recent studies that encompass a key cross-section of the fields this research spans: empirical research related to biblical interpretation. In the last twenty years, there have been increasing efforts to understand the Bible reading of 'ordinary readers', the everyday reading and interpretation that Christians do as they look to Scripture for guidance in matters of faith and life. Such studies have been conducted utilising the methods of the social sciences to gather 'data' that reflects the reading habits and practices of Bible-readers 'on the ground'. This growing field is largely the result of changes in hermeneutical theory that began to occur during the mid-twentieth century. Amongst literary critics, focus began to shift from the author to the reader. This 'turn' to the reader, or the 'reader-response' movement recognised the role of the reader in creating a text's meaning. The work of Louise Rosenblatt, who put forward a transactional theory between text and reader,[41] and Stanley Fish, who theorised that it is interpretive communities that define reading practices and interpretation, are significant.[42]

This literary movement was underpinned by developments in philosophical hermeneutics, where the work of Hans-Georg Gadamer arguably dominates.[43] Gadamer proposed that interpretation involves a 'fusion of horizons' between the text's horizon and the reader's horizon, which is their respective 'pre-understanding' according to their historical situatedness. Within contemporary theology, Anthony Thiselton has engaged in widespread inter-disciplinary dialogue between the composite fields of hermeneutics, and placed these insights in relation to the Bible.[44] Thiselton is not alone in this task of utilising hermeneutics for the benefit of biblical interpretation. Many theologians and biblical scholars have sought to engage hermeneutical theory in relation to the Bible.[45] However, the majority of such literature that integrates hermeneutics with the Bible is based on theory. Somewhat ironically, the hermeneutical focus upon the reader does not actually include real readers, but rather a hypothetical or idealised reader. Hermeneutical biblical scholarship has not typically engaged theory with practice by observing how interpretation actually happens.

12   *Chapter 1*

The practical move towards the reality of the 'ordinary' reader first began in the Liberation Theology movement of South America. Interest and value in what the 'ordinary' reader has to offer began here and grew, leading to the Contextual Bible Study (CBS) of Gerald West in South Africa.[46] This dialogue has paved the way for biblical research which prioritises the 'social location' of the reader, recognising that particular facets of one's social location (such as personality,[47] gender,[48] place[49]) informs how one reads and understands the biblical text.

This hermeneutical turn to the reader, both theoretical and practical, in combination with methodological approaches from the social sciences, has led to the growing field of empirical research which attempts to understand what readers actually 'do' when they attempt to interpret the Bible. Reflecting on the lived practices of Christians is a key component of practical theology.[50] In pragmatic terms, Richard Osmer defines the four tasks of practical theology as the descriptive-empirical task which asks, 'what is going on?'; the interpretive task which asks, 'why is this going on?'; the normative task which asks, 'what ought to be going on?'; and the pragmatic task which asks, 'how might we respond?'.[51] Whilst my research has clear and significant overlaps with the field of practical theology, my engagement with the final two tasks, normative and pragmatic, is limited. I seek to understand primarily the dynamics of what is 'going on' in relation to the influence of the doctrine of Scripture upon interpretation, but I will be understanding these dynamics against postulated theories of what is normative (above), rather than seeking to determine what should be normative and what steps are needed to achieve this.

The research in this book is therefore situated amongst what might be termed 'empirical hermeneutics', a field that is indebted to liberation theology, contextual Bible study and the social sciences. It begins with raw data of what readers actually do when they read the Bible and then reflects on these practices in light of theological and hermeneutical theory relating to the doctrine of Scripture and interpretation. My research builds on that of other empirical hermeneutical projects that have provided important insights into ordinary reading practices. What follows is a brief overview of such projects, from which more detailed insights will be drawn in relation to the data I set out in chapters 3–10.

Bible research that focuses on an evangelical demographic in particular began with Brian Malley.[52] His qualitative research was gathered from a church in America through interviews with church members, a survey of the congregation, and observation of the church's services, groups, and practices over a number of years. Taking a cognitive approach, Malley posits that the Biblicist tradition Evangelicals learn and inherit is primarily a set of cognitive skills rather than theological beliefs or behavioural practices/habits. His

Situating the Research 13

dominant cognitive focus therefore doesn't leave room for an exploration of how interpretative activity might be doctrinally underpinned, rather than merely the product of developing a set of cognitive skills.

James Bielo's research[53] is based within the United States with a focus on the nature of group Bible study as a social phenomenon. He offers insights into the social nature of Bible reading and how interpretative practices function within a group. In contrast to Malley's cognitive approach, Bielo investigates Bible study groups from an anthropological perspective, with an interest in understanding the cultural significance of Bible study groups as a social phenomenon in the United States.[54]

Andrew Rogers' UK-based research[55] is some of the most comprehensive within the field of 'ordinary reading'. His comparison of two Evangelical churches in London considers the whole of the church's life and activity. The two churches provide an interesting contrast to one another, with Holder Church's bibliocentrism highlighting how congregational culture impacts the hermeneutics employed in 'ordinary reading'.

Ruth Perrin's research focuses on a millennial Evangelical demographic, and her UK-based focus groups of self-led Bible studies allows for a context in which the interpretative strategies, theological priorities, and attitudes towards Bible reading are articulated, observable, and open to analysis.[56] Her methodology strongly informed my own, described in chapter 2.

Two further empirical hermeneutic projects that don't focus on Evangelicals specifically but have a comparative educational angle offer a helpful background to the educational comparison of my research detailed in chapter 10. First, Andrew Village's study has important statistical analysis to bear upon my own research, considering its scope within the Church of England in the UK.[57] His research is distinct from those above, first, in gathering quantitative data, allowing for a broad research field, and second, in focusing upon an Anglican demographic. His research is therefore the only study to share my demographic, Evangelical Anglicans, though such participants only form a subset of his entire demographic. Second, Mark Powell[58] conducted a small-scale biblical interpretation experiment explicitly contrasting the biblical interpretation of clergy and laity.

A final research project worth noting has neither a focus on Evangelicals nor a comparative element, but nonetheless has significant insight into the dynamics of biblical interpretation of ordinary readers. Andrew Todd's doctoral thesis focuses on the nature of interpretation within the dynamics of conversation in Bible-study groups.[59] With a specific emphasis on linguistic ethnography rooted in discourse analysis, Todd looks at how interpretation evolves in conversation.

14 *Chapter 1*

All the existing research on the dynamics of biblical interpretation lacks explicit consideration of the context of the doctrine of Scripture. Hermeneutical activity is either treated as its own entity and unrelated to the nature of the Bible, or the connection is assumed but not explored. This is what my research will contribute to the field, an understanding of the role of the doctrine of Scripture in interpretation. This book asks, how does the doctrine of Scripture actually 'function' in practice? To what extent does it drive hermeneutical activity? What other factors play a part in this dynamic?

NOTES

1. Clare Amos, ed., *The Bible in the Life of the Church* (New York: Morehouse Publishing, 2013).

2. Alister McGrath, "Evangelical Anglicanism: A Contradiction in Terms?," in *Evangelical Anglicans*, eds. Richard France and Alister McGrath (London: SPCK, 1993), 13.

3. For Evangelicals, see: David Bebbington, *Evangelicalism in Modern Britain: A History from the 1730s to the 1980s* (London: Routledge, 1993); Rob Warner, *Reinventing English Evangelicalism 1966–2001: A Theological and Sociological Study* (Milton Keynes: Paternoster, 2007). For Anglicans, see: Mark Chapman, Sathianathan Clarke, and Martyn Percy, *The Oxford Handbook of Anglican Studies* (Oxford: Oxford University Press, 2015); Scott MacDougall, *The Shape of Anglican Theology: Faith Seeking Wisdom* (Leiden: Brill, 2022). For Evangelical Anglicans, see: Richard Turnball, *Anglican and Evangelical?* (London: Continuum, 2007); Richard France and Alister McGrath, *Evangelical Anglicans* (London: SPCK, 1993).

4. Andrew Village, "English Anglicanism: Construct Validity of a Scale of Anglo-Catholic versus Evangelical Self-Identification," in *Religious Identity and National Heritage*, eds. Francis-Vincent Anthony and Hans-Georg Ziebertz (Boston: Brill, 2012), 93–122.

5. Mandy Robbins and Greg Smith, "Life in the Church," in *21st Century Evangelicals*, ed. Greg Smith (Watford: InstantApostle, 2015), 41.

6. Sam Hailes, "How Evangelicals Took Over the Church of England," *Premier Christianity*, October 26, 2017, https://www.premierchristianity.com/home/how -evangelicals-took-over-the-church-of-england/3081.article. For historical accounts, see: Randle Manwaring, *From Controversy to Co-Existence: Evangelicals in the Church of England 1914–1980* (Cambridge: Cambridge University Press, 1985); Gareth Atkins, "Anglican Evangelicalism," in *The Oxford History of Anglicanism, Vol. II: Establishment and Empire, 1662–1829*, ed. Jeremy Gregory (Oxford: Oxford University Press, 2017); Grayson Carter, "Anglican Evangelicalis," in *The Oxford Handbook of Early Evangelicalism,* ed. Jonathan Yeager (Oxford: Oxford University Press, 2022).

7. Andrew Atherstone, "The Keele Congress of 1967: A Paradigm Shift in Anglican Evangelical Attitudes," *Journal of Anglican Studies* 9, no. 2 (2011): 175–97.

Situating the Research 15

8. Anonymous, "Hot and Bothered," *The Economist*, March 10, 2012, https://www.economist.com/britain/2012/03/10/hot-and-bothered.

9. Harriet Sherwood, "As traditional believers turn away, is this a new crisis of faith?," *The Guardian*, August 14, 2016, https://www.theguardian.com/world/2016/aug/13/church-of-england-evangelical-drive.

10. Graham Kings, *Nourishing Mission: Theological Settings* (Leiden, The Netherlands: Brill, 2022), ch. 8.

11. For example: Vincent Bacote, Laura Miguélez, and Dennis Okholm, *Evangelicals and Scripture: Tradition, Authority, Hermeneutics* (Downers Grove, IL: IVP, 2009); Daniel Trier and Douglas Sweeny, *Hearing and Doing the Word* (London: T&T Clark, 2021); Kevin J. Vanhoozer and Daniel J. Treier, *Theology and the Mirror of Scripture: A Mere Evangelical Account* (London: Apollos, 2016); Francis Watson, "Hermeneutics and the Doctrine of Scripture: Why They Need Each Other," *International Journal of Systematic Theology* 12, no. 2 (2010): 118–43.

12. 'Ordinary' is used here in line with Astley to mean non-scholarly or non-academic, expounded further in chapter 2. See: Jeff Astley, *Ordinary Theology: Looking, Listening and Learning in Theology* (Aldershot: Ashgate, 2002).

13. For example: Peter Adam, *Written For Us: Receiving God's Words in the Bible* (Nottingham: IVP, 2008); John S. Feinberg, *Light in a Dark Place: The Doctrine of Scripture* (Wheaton, IL: Crossway, 2018). On the more 'liberal' end of the spectrum: Rob Bell, *What Is the Bible?* (London: William Collins, 2017).

14. Based on interpretation of 2 Timothy 3:16.

15. Alister McGrath and David Wenham, "Biblical Authority," in *Evangelical Anglicans*, eds. France and McGrath, 30.

16. The inerrancy movement has led to accusations of bibliolatry—that the authority of Scripture is not just derived from God but equal to God. This could be levied at Packer who claims, 'Scripture comes to us, as it were, from Jesus' hand, and its authority and his are so interlocked as to be one' (James Packer, *Truth and Power: The Place of Scripture in the Christian Life* [Wheaton, IL: Harold Shaw Publishers, 1996], 39). Whether an accusation of bibliolatry is valid is beyond the scope of my discussion, rather the point is to note that belief in authority can have different emphases for different thinkers.

17. Mark D. Thompson, *The Doctrine of Scripture: An Introduction* (Wheaton, IL: Crossway, 2022), 43.

18. For example: Peter Enns, *Inspiration and Incarnation: Evangelicals and the Problem of the Old Testament* (Grand Rapids, MI: Baker, 2005).

19. Timothy Ward, *Words of Life: Scripture as the Living and Active Word of God* (Nottingham: IVP, 2009), 74–78.

20. Thompson, *The Doctrine of Scripture*, 24.

21. John Stott, *Evangelical Truth* (Nottingham: Intervarsity Press, 2011), 32; Thompson, *The Doctrine of Scripture*, 82.

22. Thompson, *The Doctrine of Scripture*, 141–56; Ward, *Words of Life*, 130–40.

23. Stott, *Evangelical Truth*, 70–71.

24. Kenton L. Sparks, *God's Word in Human Words: An Evangelical Appropriation of Critical Biblical Scholarship* (Grand Rapids, MI: Baker Academic, 2008), 55.

16   *Chapter 1*

25. Richard Briggs, *Reading the Bible Wisely* (London: SPCK, 2003), 77.

26. Thompson, *The Doctrine of Scripture*, 163.

27. James Packer, *God Has Spoken*, 4th ed. (London: Hodder & Stoughton, 2016), 106–9.

28. Stott, *Evangelical Truth*, 64–65.

29. Kings, *Nourishing Mission*, 144.

30. McGrath and Wenham, 'Biblical Authority,' 28.

31. Kings, *Nourishing Mission*, 144–45 (bracket clarifications added).

32. Nigel Beynon and Andrew Sach, *Dig Deeper: Tools to Unearth the Bible's Treasure* (Leicester: IVP, 2005), 132.

33. 'Chicago Statement on Biblical Inerrancy'.

34. Thompson quoting Thompson, *The Doctrine of Scripture*, 125.

35. "Basis of Faith," Church of England Evangelical Council, accessed August 3, 2023, https://ceec.info/basis-of-faith/.

36. Beynon and Sach, *Dig Deeper*, 28.

37. Thompson, *The Doctrine of Scripture*, 182.

38. Packer, *God Has Spoken*, 86.

39. Ward, *Words of Life*, 174.

40. Anthony Thiselton, "Understanding God's Word Today," in *Obeying Christ in a Changing World: Vol. 1, The Lord Christ*, ed. John Stott (Glasgow: Fountain Books, 1977), 97.

41. Louise Rosenblatt, *The Reader, the Text, the Poem: The Transactional Theory of the Literary Work* (Carbondale: Southern Illinois University Press, 1994).

42. Stanley Fish, *Is There a Text in This Class?: The Authority of Interpretive Communities* (Cambridge, MA: Harvard University Press, 1980).

43. Hans-Georg Gadamer, *Truth and Method*, trans. Garrett Barden and John Cumming (London: Sheed & Ward, 1975).

44. Anthony Thiselton, *Thiselton on Hermeneutics: The Collected Writings and New Essays of Anthony Thiselton* (Aldershot: Ashgate, 2006).

45. For example: Walter Bruggemann, *Texts Under Negotiation: The Bible and Postmodern Imagination* (Minneapolis, MN: Fortress Press, 1993); David Clines, *Interested Parties: The Ideology of Writers and Readers of the Hebrew Bible* (Sheffield: Sheffield Academic Press, 1995).

46. Gerald West, "Locating 'Contextual Bible Study' within Biblical Liberation Hermeneutics and Intercultural Biblical Hermeneutics," *HTS Theological Studies* 70, no. 1 (2014): 1–10, http://dx.doi.org/10.4102/hts.v70i1.2641.

47. For example: Andrew Village, "Biblical Conservatism and Psychological Type," *Journal of Empirical Theology* 29, no. 2 (2016): 137–59, https://doi.org/10.1163/15709256-12341340.

48. For example: Silvia Arzt, "Reading the Bible Is a Gendered Act," *Feminist Theology* 29, no. 10 (2002): 32–39.

49. For example: Louise Lawrence, *The Word in Place: Reading the New Testament in Contemporary Contexts* (London: SPCK, 2009).

50. John Swinton and Harriet Mowat, *Practical Theology and Qualitative Research* (London: SCM Press, 2006), 6.

Situating the Research 17

51. Richard Robert Osmer, *Practical Theology: An Introduction* (Grand Rapids, MI: W. B. Eerdmans, 2008), 4.

52. Brian Malley, *How the Bible Works: An Anthropological Study of Evangelical Biblicism* (Walnut Creek, CA: AltaMira Press, 2004).

53. James Bielo, *Words Upon the Word: An Ethnography of Evangelical Bible Study* (New York: NYU Press, 2009).

54. Ibid., 5–6.

55. Andrew Rogers, *Congregational Hermeneutics* (Surrey: Ashgate, 2015).

56. Ruth Perrin, *The Bible Reading of Young Evangelicals* (Eugene, OR: Pickwick Publications, 2016).

57. Andrew Village, *The Bible and Lay People: An Empirical Approach to Ordinary Hermeneutics* (Hampshire: Ashgate Publishing Limited, 2007).

58. Mark Powell, *Chasing the Eastern Star: Adventures in Biblical Reader-Response Criticism* (Louisville, KY: Westminster John Knox Press, 2001).

59. Andrew Todd, "The Talk, Dynamics and Theological Practice of Bible-Study Groups" (PhD diss., Cardiff University, 2009), https://orca.cf.ac.uk/54856/1/U585245.pdf.

Chapter 2

Research Methodology and Design

Designing research that would provide an insight into the relationship between the doctrine of Scripture and interpretation involved a number of factors. Whilst many different methodologies could explore this connection, I chose to conduct focus groups, where participants would be asked to read a Bible passage and discuss it. The choice to conduct the research in this way was largely based on the successful methodology of Ruth Perrin's research, who gathered rich data that, as far as possible, allowed for organic responses to the Bible.[1] Whilst her research was focused on millennials, I wanted to adapt her model to allow for insights into what influence the doctrine of Scripture exerted upon participant's interpretative practices and conclusions.

FOCUS GROUP RATIONALE

In addition to Perrin's methodology, the decision to conduct focus groups rather than interviews or written reflections was made on a number of grounds. Though individual interviews would have provided rich data on the nature of people's beliefs about Scripture and has the advantage of the researcher being able to probe specifically in order to gather the exact information required, focus groups provide a much more suitable arena for the investigation of this topic.

First, focus groups allow for a more natural context for study of the Bible to occur. The practice of small group Bible studies is familiar to Evangelical Christians and replicates a common activity, which not only adds to the credibility of the research but also reflects the fact that small groups are the arena in which a large majority of Bible interpretation takes place for ordinary readers.[2] As the aim of this research is to understand interpretative practices, creating an environment similar to that in which such interpretative practices would normally take place will produce more authentic and reliable findings. Moreover, in order to ascertain authentic responses to the text, focus groups have the added benefit of allowing participants to explore their own ideas and ask the questions that naturally arise for them in their reading of the text. This allows reading priorities to be identified and the extent to which they are connected to doctrinal beliefs about the Bible.

The second reason focus groups are an appropriate method for this research is the ability to analyse interaction. Focus groups allow people's ideas to sharpen and crystalize in conversation, present areas of agreement and conflict, and can record reaction and response.[3] Analysis focused at the level of interaction allows for the process behind conclusions to be transparent, not just the conclusions themselves. Considering the aim of identifying the controlling influence of the doctrine of Scripture upon interpretation, focus groups provide a forum in which not just interpretative conclusions are offered but the rationale and process behind such conclusions is likely to be made explicit in group interaction. This allows better connections to be made between doctrinal beliefs and interpretation.

Third and finally, there are theological warrants for researching this topic through focus groups. The first of these relates to dispositional accounts of belief which understand belief as 'action-oriented, situation-related, and embedded in the particularities and contingencies of everyday living.'[4] What this means is that the reality of lived belief, as opposed to professed belief, is best identified in practice, particularly in situations that challenge belief. In the view of H. H. Price, summarised by Thiselton, 'the test of a "real" belief, in contrast to what we may merely claim to believe, lies not in whether such a belief lies consciously in the mind, but in the course of action, or in the habituated actions, which proceed from the belief.'[5] In other words, the reality of beliefs about the Bible can be more accurately ascertained in the interpretative challenge a reading experience can present, rather than professed statements that might arise from an interview. By giving participants a text that challenges biblical beliefs in an environment where they would naturally give voice to their thoughts, their doctrine of Scripture can be adequately determined from a focus group setting.

A second theological warrant for the use of focus groups is the social nature of doctrine. McGrath has identified doctrine's role in demarcating group-identity.[6] The doctrine of Scripture is a collective doctrine of the church, but its varying forms differentiate and identify certain sub-groups, particularly within Evangelicalism, such as 'conservatives' from 'liberals'. The social nature of focus groups provides a forum in which such identities will arise, most likely in conflict. One is more likely to assert their 'conservative' biblical beliefs when faced with the 'liberal' alternative, whereas an interview or solo reflection would be less likely to provoke doctrinal reflections connected with social demarcation.

Research Methodology and Design   21

FINDING PARTICIPANTS

The research required two types of participants relating to different levels of theological education, which I will be distinguishing by the terms 'formal' and 'informal'. Formal participants are Christians who have undergone at least a year of recognised theological education, and informal participants are Christians who have not. The language of formal and informal is preferable to educated and non-educated, given that many of the informal participants were educated to degree level or higher, just not in the field of Theology. To refer to them as non-educated would thus mistakenly infer that they are not educated at all. Additionally, the term 'informal' also leaves room for the consideration that though not having a theological qualification, an informal participant might enjoy reading theology books or attending theology lectures and thus share in higher levels of knowledge that would contest the term 'non-educated.' Though scholarship has used the term 'ordinary' to explore the theology of those who haven't undertaken any theological education of an academic or scholarly nature,[7] this would seemingly designate those who have as 'extraordinary readers', which carries unhelpful overtones of this being vastly superior to the other.

I initially decided to recruit informal participants through relevant churches, and formal participants through theological institutions. Recruitment proved to be one of the biggest challenges of the research. Without an incentive to offer for participation, it was difficult to find participants willing to volunteer, especially amongst those currently in theological education who had lots of claims on their time. Despite gaining access to and permission from several theological colleges to recruit participants, they were not forthcoming in volunteering, and my contacts at the institutions did not want to approach individuals and ask them to take part, instead opting for a general advertisement. These contacts at theological institutions, like those at churches, were made through my own networks, as well as the networks of my supervisor. Only one contact at a theological college, named Grace and Life College in this book, proved to be successful in gaining participants, though this was the smallest group, described below.

The other theologically educated participants did not come from a single institution but were recruited online using social media and relying on the extended networks of myself and my supervisor. This was in part due to the difficulty of getting participants in education to commit to volunteer but was also largely the result of the COVID-19 pandemic and having to conduct focus groups online. Two online focus groups of formal participants took place, named in this book as Wednesday Online and Thursday Online. The disadvantage of online recruitment meant that participants had a variety of

22   *Chapter 2*

experiences of theological education from different institutions. This means that insights about theological education are broad, rather than specific to a particular qualification or institutional context. The implications of this are discussed further in chapter 10.

The informal participants came from three Evangelical Anglican churches, one of which was the pilot study, named St. John's for this book, discussed below. The other two, named in this book as St. Catherine's and St. Augustus's, were recruited through my own networks.

All of the focus groups except one contained between five and ten participants, the postulated ideal size.[8] The exception contained three participants which naturally meant that the diversity of voices was decreased. However, the smaller size appeared to be predominantly advantageous as the group contained two participants with differing points of view and the small size meant they were able to engage in depth with one another's perspective, which could have been overly dominating had the group contained more participants. The overall sample consisted of thirty-four participants, nineteen informal and fifteen formal. The difference in these numbers is taken into account regarding comparative analysis.

Twelve participants were females and twenty-two males, with an imbalance occurring amongst formal participants: two females and thirteen males. Informal participants were more equally balanced with ten females and nine males. These imbalances, though not ideal, do actually reflect something of the reality of the contexts they represent. There are more women in church than men, but more men are theologically educated than women at post-graduate level and in relation to clergy training.[9] These imbalances are therefore not problematic in terms of the data being representative.

The groups in general tended to consist of participants of a similar age, though there were some mixed-age groups. There were no noticeable differences between the groups who were a similar age and those who were different. Some participants were noticeably more or less dominant, but this appeared to be personality-driven rather than because of age, with both younger and older participants exhibiting preferences to be more and less vocal.[10]

All participants were correctly assigned to their categories, as this was made a clear stipulation to participants in the information provided for their participation. They knew they were part of a comparative study (this was even occasionally referenced) and which category they belonged to.

In terms of the levels of familiarity in the groups, three groups were made up of participants that already knew one another, and two groups contained some pre-existing relationships, though not everyone knew each other. There was only one group (conducted online, discussed below) where no one knew each other prior to the focus group. Though the groups that knew each other engaged in more banter and made more jokes, the general levels of interaction did not appear to be significantly different across all three groups.

Online Groups

Two of the focus groups were conducted online as a result of the COVID-19 pandemic. This was towards the start of the pandemic, and though many people were quickly adapting to conducting all their social interaction online, the online format did have an impact upon group interaction. Participants could see and hear one another, but due to internet connections, there were occasions where a participant claimed they hadn't been able to hear another participant correctly. These instances were minimal but naturally impeded clear communication between the participants and thus had an impact upon group dynamics. Additionally, the most obvious difference in the online groups was that individuals tended to speak for much longer, as interruptions occur less naturally in the online environment. Though shorter bursts of back-and-forth dialogue did occur, these were rare, and in general participants tended to speak for several minutes at once. However, though this reduced overall interaction, participants did still reference what other participants had said, demonstrating their involvement in a conversation, rather than just putting forth their individual opinion. This accords with comparative research on in-person and online focus groups which has found that though the format of the data may differ, the content is similar across both types of group.[11] Additionally, comparative research has shown that online groups may generate a lower quantity of data, but the same quality.[12]

Focus Groups

Six focus groups were conducted in total, listed in table 2.1, where participants are listed by pseudonym.

St. John's (Informal)

St. John's (St.J's) was the pilot group which ended up being used for the research on account of the methodology being unchanged. The group consisted of seven participants who attended a large charismatic Evangelical Anglican church in a city in the south of England. All the participants were in their twenties and thirties except for Henry who was of retirement age. St.J's had a fairly relaxed atmosphere, though the conversation was initially peppered by long pauses, as participants thought through the text and warmed up to the reading environment. George was notably quieter, making fewer contributions, and

24   *Chapter 2*

Table 2.1. Group Reference Guide

		Shorthand	*Participants*
Informal	St. John's (Pilot)	St.J's	Anne, Emma, Frank, George, Harriet, Henry, Jane
	St. Catherine's	St.C's	Gavin, Michael, Neil, Pamela, Stacey, Vanessa
	St. Augustus's	St.A's	Amy, Charles, Gina, Jake, Rose, Terry
Formal	Grace and Life College	GLC	Adam, Johnny, Martin
	Wednesday Online	WO	Celia, Jessica, Nick, Sam, Winston
	Thursday Online	TO	Christopher, Dean, Jesse, Logan, Luke, Richard, Taylor

Henry was initially silent for the first half of the Genesis discussion before becoming an active participant throughout the rest of the focus group.

St. Catherine's (Informal)

St. Catherine's (St.C's) consisted of six participants all in their twenties and thirties. I only knew Stacey beforehand, and she had been the organiser of the group and gathered participants. The group was hosted at Stacey's house and all the participants knew each other from their church, a vibrant charismatic Evangelical Anglican church in a small town in the south of England. Though Anglican, St.C's is very contemporary, being a planted church, and this contemporary feel is reflected both in their service style and building. St.C's was the most jovial of the groups with lots of fast talking and banter. They seemed to enjoy the conversation and weren't afraid of dealing with the text's challenges. Neil was a dominant member of this group, whilst Michael and Gavin were much quieter. The three female participants were fairly well balanced in terms of contributions.

St. Augustus's (Informal)

St. Augustus's (St.A's) consisted of six participants. The group were all in their fifties and above, with the majority being of retired age. This group met in the side chapel of their church, an average-sized Anglican Evangelical church in a small town in the south of England. St. Augustus's has a family feel with a more typical demographic of congregants expected for an Anglican church, i.e., less of the twenties and thirties demographic. I knew none of the participants, though they all knew each other and were aware that I knew their Vicar.

St.A's was the broadest ranging in their discussion and as such were the group I had to ask the most questions to and keep on track. They often diverted onto related topics that were of more interest to them. Charles in particular evidenced atypical views of an EA, which were also mirrored somewhat by Terry. Gina and Jake were the most vocal of the group, with Rose and Terry being somewhat quieter.

Grace and Life College (Formal)

Grace and Life College (GLC) is an Anglican ordination college associated with a British University describing itself as 'openly Evangelical'. It has a robust academic reputation and offers courses for ordained and lay ministry as well as interested learners. This group was the smallest of the focus groups, with only three participants who were all male. Johnny and Adam had completed one year of their theological training, but Martin was in his second year and had also previously studied Theology. I knew Johnny prior to the focus group, but he had not been involved in organising the group and his attendance was incidental. All three participants knew each other and though the three men showed differences of opinion, the conversation had a relaxed tone and atmosphere with everyone having a lot to say.

Wednesday Online (Formal)

Wednesday Online (WO) was an online focus group made up of five participants. I did not know any of these participants and they did not know each other. All the participants except Sam were involved in a form of ministry, whereas Sam was in academia. WO was a mixed-age group. This was the only formal group to contain two women, and unfortunately Jessica had to leave the group midway due to another commitment.

Despite being online and not knowing each other, the group had a productive conversation engaging with one another's ideas. The online nature meant dialogue was less interactive, with participants speaking for several minutes at once, as has been noted.

Thursday Online (Formal)

Thursday Online (TO) consisted of seven mixed-age male participants. Logan and Taylor were largely silent only making one contribution each. Some TO participants knew each other prior to the group but not everyone knew everyone, and I didn't know any of the participants prior to the group. As with WO, the professions of the group varied. Christopher and Richard were both in

26 *Chapter 2*

academia, whilst Luke, Dean, and Jesse were in ministry. Logan and Taylor were in neither but had been theologically educated.

Though the group did have some pauses, they conversed with one another and engaged with the questions of the text from a variety of perspectives. This group more than any other, and as a result of the online environment, had a strong trend of individuals speaking for several minutes at once.

FOCUS GROUP DESIGN

As has been noted, the design for my focus groups was informed by Perrin's research. Her methodology involved groups reading three texts during a single focus group and highlights how text selection is crucial in eliciting the desired discussion content. I wanted to gather a breadth of interpretative responses which would require the reading of multiple texts and wanted these texts to implicitly challenge participants as to their beliefs about the Bible.

One of the biggest advantages of following Perrin's focus group design was that as it had been tried and tested, no practical adjustments were needed after the Pilot Study, allowing it to be included in the main body of data, discussed below. Thirty minutes proved to be adequate time for participants to discuss each text. For some text discussions, some groups seemed to be able to talk for much longer and needed to be brought to a close; for other text discussions the group didn't have as much to say. On balance therefore, thirty minutes felt an appropriate amount of time for discussion and yielded significant transcripts for analysis. Additionally, none of the focus groups significantly overran.

Some participants did bring Bibles with them and chose to consult them during the discussion even though the texts were provided on handouts with questions. This was noted at the time, but was also evident from the transcripts as participants explicitly referenced what they had looked up.

Moderator Role

I was the sole moderator, facilitating the focus groups throughout and setting the tone of the sessions. The friendliness and tone of a moderator has proven to be incredibly important in focus group discussion and can hugely affect the tone of the sessions.[13]

As focus groups offer insight into the thoughts, priorities, and choices of participants, I wanted my influence to be minimal. 'Approaches to moderating should be linked to research goals'[14] and as such, the most authentic insight into interpretive practices would be self-led studies. This would

Choice of Texts

I wanted the passages that my participants read to elicit reflections that would be insightful regarding their beliefs about the Bible. One way of doing this would be to choose texts that explicitly speak of Scripture (insofar as the Bible is able to be self-referential), such as 2 Timothy 3:16 or Psalm 119. However, this approach ran the risk of obscuring dispositional beliefs about the doctrine of Scripture. I wanted participant's beliefs about the Bible to arise naturally and not as the result of an explicit prompt which itself might affect what participants claimed or insinuated about the Bible. I therefore decided to choose passages that would indirectly challenge participant's Bible beliefs.

The main Bible beliefs I wanted to challenge in all three texts were the authority, inspiration, and divine authorship of the Bible, all of which are connected and related to one another. I therefore chose three specific challenges that would prompt such reflections, one for each text participants would read.

The first challenge I chose was a historical or factually accurate challenge. Does the divine authorship of the Bible mean its contents must be historically valid, i.e., objectively true? If a biblical text is not historical or factual, in what sense is it authoritative or inspired? How is historicity discerned, and how much of a problem does it present for readers?

The second challenge I chose was a text that presents a theological challenge. How might participants respond to a text that makes theological claims about God that are problematic? Is every single theological claim in the Bible authoritative in terms of what a Christian should believe? How might the Bible be inspired by God but make claims that are understood to be theologically problematic?

The third and final challenge related to the relevance of the text. I assumed that the text would be seen as relevant on the basis of previous research, but to what extent is relevancy determined by beliefs about the Bible? How is the Bible authoritative in terms of Christians' actions, choices, and behaviours, when the world of a contemporary reader is vastly different from the world of the text? Does the authority of the text lessen the wider cultural and historical gap between text and reader? In what sense is the text deemed to be relevant and inspired for a different context than its own?

My three texts would each reflect one of these challenges: historicity, theological legitimacy, and relevancy. Having established these were the three

28 *Chapter 2*

challenges I needed my texts to contain, I then had to choose three different genres to narrow down my text choice.

The decision to include different genres was made in order to elicit a variety of interpretive responses from my participants. As narrative is the most common genre within the Bible, I wanted to include a narrative text, which would be contrasted with something more instructional, either Law or an Epistle. As the majority of narrative occurs in the Old Testament, and I wanted to have passages from both Testaments, I decided my 'instruction' genre would be an Epistle. I wanted my third genre to be poetry, specifically a Psalm, because it provides a distinctive contrast to narrative and instruction.

In terms of matching these genres with the intended text challenges (historicity, theology legitimacy, and relevancy), the Epistle lent itself most readily to the challenge of relevancy, as specific instruction written to individuals or groups of people about correct belief and behaviour. Whilst there are plenty of theologically problematic narratives in the Old Testament where God's actions are questionable, this would mean that a Psalm was left to address the issue of historicity. Historically problematic Psalms present a much subtler challenge than a passage of narrative could, which led to the decision to include a historically challenging narrative, a theologically challenging Psalm, and a relevance-challenging Epistle. The texts I selected were Genesis 7 (chapter 3), Psalm 44 (chapter 4), and Ephesians 5:21–6:9 (chapter 5).

Text Questions

In order to give the groups a 'jumping off' point that gave their discussion some direction without interfering with their interpretative priorities, each text handout contained the same two questions at the bottom: 'What do you think is interesting/of note in this text?' 'Do you have any questions/concerns about the text?' These two questions were intended to prompt both positive and critical thoughts from participants without steering them towards a particular topic. As a result, the groups could be self-led but with enough focus to facilitate the discussion.

The final question on the handout was specific for each text, and these are discussed in their relevant chapters (3–6). These more-focused questions were deliberately placed after the two general questions to ensure that participant both discussed what was important to them but also covered the topics of my particular interests without interruption from the moderator.

As per the design, I didn't need to be overly involved in the group discussion. However, the extent to which I was involved varied across the groups depending on their dynamics. My highest levels of involvement occurred at St. Augustus's who were prone to exploring tangents unrelated to the text and therefore needed help focusing. The group appeared to quickly exhaust what they had to say about the text and were therefore asked the most specific questions of all the groups.

On two occasions (in two different groups) I asked specific participants if they had any thoughts as they were yet to contribute. This was difficult to manage, however, in the online setting and resulted in two participants from Thursday Online saying very little. On one occasion during Grace and Life College's discussion, I corrected a mistaken conjecture about the text.[15] This was the only instance where I offered specific information relevant to the texts. However, as a general tendency, the discussion was largely unled, particularly initially as participants responded to the general questions on the handout. In most groups, I drew their attention to the final question on the handout midway through the discussion. For the online groups, these questions were typed into the chat function on the online platform and were also reiterated verbally. The three questions therefore worked well in allowing space and time for participants to address their own points of interest or concern initially, but also to discuss the text in relation to the issues I was particularly interested in.

DATA COLLECTION AND ANALYSIS

I gathered data through audio recordings of the group discussion and transcribed the focus groups myself, which was an important exercise in familiarising myself with the data. Following transcription, the data was uploaded to NVivo and coded in relation to two main areas: the points that participants made about the content of the texts (interpretative conclusions) and the ways in which they engaged with the texts (engagement practices). This latter category was extremely broad, including not just specific methods or interpretive techniques, but anything that participants did with, or to, the text. In total, participants evidenced seventy-eight engagement practices, occurring 1,102 times across all three texts and all six groups. Additionally, participants made 1,444 points about the texts accounting for 279 unique interpretive points.

As my analysis continued, I also coded the transcripts for theological statements to get a sense of the theological paradigms that participants were working with. This provided a helpful background in understanding what beliefs and ideas participants were bringing to the text. Participants made a total of 108 different theological assertions occurring 394 times.

This approach allowed me to identify key points of concern for the participants, as well as group the points of concern for my own research interests.

When conducting comparative analysis of the coding, to take into account that the two categories did not contain the same number of participants and

30 *Chapter 2*

that the timings of the groups weren't strict, coding stats were constructed as percentages relative to the totals of the two categories in order for a fair comparison.

METHODOLOGICAL ANALYSIS

In general, the methodology outlined in this chapter worked well in providing me with relevant and rich data to explore my research questions.

As has been noted, issues with recruitment led to some of the flawed aspects of my focus groups, including one that was very small and two online. Though all the participants had the right credentials to be in their informal/ formal category, one of the disadvantages of this research was the lack of parameters around the formal category. Some participants were only one year into their theological training; the majority of participants trained in disparate contexts, with some having been through education many years ago. Moreover, the content of each formal participant's theological education was not recorded. As such, the formal category was diverse and the data gathered reflected this, detailed in chapter 10.[16] Further parameters upon the formal category might have produced more insightful comparative results. Given the distinction that 'ordinary theology' is non-academic and non-scholarly, having a formal category of theological academics and scholars would likely have produced a sharper contrast between the two types of participant.

In hindsight, my decision to have the groups largely self-led, whilst working well in terms of highlighting interpretative priorities, did mean that there was an imbalance of voices in the groups. Had I been slightly more active in the discussions, it would have been easier to encourage contributions from quieter members of the group without putting them on the spot. However, the resulting data is largely organic, with the directive questions being written offering a less pressurising way of steering the group.

My presence in the groups as the moderator, but with minimal input will also have affected what was said by participants. In some groups there were moments when I was consulted or participants checked if they were 'doing ok', which indicates they were mindful of the research purpose of the exercise. I was quick to reassure participants that there was no right or wrong way to be or thing to say in the focus groups, and having the trust of the participants as an 'insider researcher' will have, to some extent, helped them to feel comfortable as well.

My own perspective and biases that I bring to the research and the analysis set out in the following chapters is inevitable. Though I have tried to be as objective as possible, researchers are always coloured by their particular experiences, beliefs, and interests. Whilst this can't be mitigated, in pursuit of transparency, a reflection on my personal relationship to the matters of the project is given below. The reader can therefore know something of 'where I'm coming from' and the angle from which I approach this research, and can judge for themselves if this has detrimentally effected the conclusions I make.

Researcher Background Disclosure

I am an Anglican who has grown up in and around various Anglican Evangelical churches of a charismatic persuasion. I am also theologically educated with a BA and MSt in Theology and at the time of the research was pursuing a PhD qualification, all of which were undertaken within theological departments of secular universities in the UK. My father is also ordained in the Church of England and trained for ordination during my childhood. This means I am an inside researcher, sharing significant aspects of my identity and experience with both my formal and informal participants.

My closeness to the subject matter of this research naturally has advantages and disadvantages. Though investigating my own tradition, I am not blind to its faults, and in fact, my interest in the topic under discussion stems from an awareness of my tradition's limitations. Moreover, as will have become plain from this chapter, facilitating the research was actually possible largely through personal contacts, an advantage of being an inside researcher.

Though I knew some of my participants ahead of this study, I do not believe my relationships to them or the churches they are a part of has skewed the analysis of the data gathered. As all participants and churches are anonymous, I am not driven by a need to protect or enhance their presentation. Additionally, the subject matter of the research is not of a nature that I would be inclined to see the participants I knew in a more or less sympathetic light than the participants I didn't know. Though objectivity is impossible, I sought to hear my participants on their own terms as much as I was able to and remain detached from their contributions and subsequent analysis such that I am seeing what is really there, rather than what I was inclined to see.

Qualitative data has the advantage of providing rich and nuanced data, but it is naturally limited. The findings of the handful of participants in this study cannot be taken as representative of the whole body of Evangelical Anglicans. This book therefore doesn't make claims to sweeping statements about the doctrine of Scripture in Evangelical Anglicanism or interpretation. Yet, it offers an important window into a common practice. Though inevitably flawed in parts, the research in this book offers insight into the beliefs and practices of real Evangelical Anglicans, and seeks to understand what is happening when they read the Bible.

32   *Chapter 2*

NOTES

1. Perrin, *The Bible Reading of Young Evangelicals.*
2. Peter Bunton, '300 Years of Small Groups—The European Church from Luther to Wesley,' *Christian Education Journal* 1 (2014): 88–106.
3. Rasika Jayasekara, 'Focus Groups in Nursing Research: Methodological Perspectives,' *Nursing Outlook* 60 (2012): 412.
4. Anthony Thiselton, *The Hermeneutics of Doctrine* (Grand Rapids, MI: W. B. Eerdmans, 2007), 21.
5. Ibid., 28.
6. Alister McGrath, *The Genesis of Doctrine: A Study in the Foundations of Doctrinal Criticism* (Oxford: Basil Blackwell, Ltd., 1990), 38.
7. Jeff Astley, *Ordinary Theology: Looking, Listening and Learning in Theology* (Aldershot: Ashgate, 2002).
8. Jayasekara, 'Focus Groups in Nursing Research,' 413.
9. The 1979, 1989, and 1998 censuses, as well as the 2005 English Church Census reports higher church attendance for women than men, in: Peter Brierley, *Pulling Out of the Nosedive* (London: Christian Research, 2006), 130.
The British Academy found that more men studied Theology and Religion at post-graduate level; see: 'Theology and Religious Studies', British Academy, accessed May 31, 2020, https://www.thebritishacademy.ac.uk/documents/288/theology-religious-studies.pdf.
Additionally, men account for 71 percent of a variety of ministerial offices across the Church of England, which would involve some form of theological education. 'Ministry Statistics,' Church of England, accessed May 31, 2020, https://www.churchofengland.org/sites/default/files/2017-11/Ministry%20Statistics%202016.pdf.
10. Martha Ann Carey, 'Focus Groups—What is the same, what is new, what is next?,' *Qualitative Health Research* 26, no. 6 (2016): 731.
11. Catherine Finneran, Rob Stephenson, and Cory Woodyatt, 'In-Person Versus Online Focus Group Discussions: A Comparative Analysis of Data Quality,' *Qualitative Health Research* 26, no. 6 (2016): 741–49.
12. James Kite and Philayrath Phongsavan, 'Insights for conducting real-time focus groups online using a web conferencing service,' *F1000Research* 6 (2017): 1–6, DOI: 10.12688/f1000research.10427.1. This was evident in comparing the transcripts of my online and in-person groups. The transcript of the online groups was between 8,500 and 9,000 words, whereas the in-person transcripts were between 10,000 and 11,200 words. However, the same topics and depth of data was gathered from both.
13. Richard Krueger, *Moderating Focus Groups* (London: SAGE London, 1998), 21.
14. David Morgan, 'Focus Groups,' *Annual Review of Sociology* 22 (1996): 146.
15. I clarified that Psalm 44 was not written by David.
16. However, data gathered by Village looking at higher education showed that 'there was no evidence that the number of years on the programme influenced the changes in faith measures.' This indicates the fact that some participants having had only one year of study will not have affected the overall findings. See: Andrew

Village, "Does higher education change the faith of Anglicans and Methodists preparing for church ministries through a course validated by a UK university?" *Practical Theology* 12, no. 4 (2019) 389–401, DOI: 10.1080/1756073X.2019.1635310.

Chapter 3

The Influence of the Doctrine of Scripture

Reading Historically

In chapter 1, I outlined key aspects of an Evangelical Anglican doctrine of Scripture, namely, belief in the text as authoritative, inspired, sufficient, consistent, and clear. What do these doctrinal commitments mean about the way the Bible is to be read? In particular, do affirmations of the Bible as inspired and God's Word commit one to read the events and stories recorded as historical, real events? Before discussing the extent to which my participants read historically, I first turn to a brief overview of the debate about the Bible's historicity.

READING HISTORICALLY

Evangelicals and Anglicans affirm historicity at the heart of their faith; the person of Jesus, his teachings, miracles, death, and resurrection are historically verifiable events, recorded in Scripture. The Bible is thus vulnerable to historical investigation as its claims and stories occur within time and place, they are not abstract truths unattached to human history. Whilst Evangelicals and Anglicans are clear that Jesus was a historical figure, the historicity of other parts of Scripture, particularly the Old Testament, are often debated.

This is, in part, due to the rise of biblical criticism in the eighteenth century, which marked a significant turning point in attitudes towards the Bible, characterised by Bartholomew as 'the historical turn.'[1] Within Evangelicalism, there was an initial reluctance to engage with this approach to Scripture, but the influence of biblical scholars Brooke Westcott, Fenton Hort, and Joseph Lightfoot helped turn the tide by demonstrating that engagement with higher criticism could be compatible with traditional views of Scripture. It was with

36 *Chapter 3*

such Christian proponents that Evangelicalism in Britain took more readily to critical scholarship than in the States.[2] Nolls recounts, 'By 1900 . . . while maintaining certain features of older views on the inspiration of Scripture, churchmen and dissenters of at least relatively conservative theology still had made their peace with the new criticism.'[3]

Scholarly Approaches to the Bible and Historicity

Whilst contemporary scholars do indeed engage with historical critical research, there remain varied responses to the challenges that such research poses about the historicity or factual accuracy of the Bible, particularly the Old Testament. Bartholomew identifies two approaches: 'For some, God's revelation in Israel and Christ makes the historical accuracy of the biblical narratives vital—such scholars tend towards a maximalist view of the historical accuracy of the Bible. Minimalists, by comparison, ask what the minimum of historical truth is required for the Bible to continue to be taken seriously, as Scripture.'[4]

Maximalist approaches correspond with Sparks's identification of four 'traditional' modern evangelical responses to biblical criticism: warranted but erroneous rejections, fideistic refutations, philosophical critiques, and critical anti-criticism.[5] Proponents of these methods are seeking to uphold the factual accuracy of the text. This is mirrored in strands of popular literature. For example, Packer argues that advocating that the biblical text could attest something different to 'what really happened', 'overthrows the biblical idea of faith, which is essentially of honouring God by tenaciously trusting to what He has said.'[6] Historicity is thus a consequence of the character of God: 'The Bible must be both true and trustworthy if it is the word of the God we know as "the God of truth".'[7] The CEEC statement of faith also suggests this direction, with reference to the Bible as 'the wholly reliable revelation and record of God's grace . . . as the true word of God written.'[8]

On the other hand, and corresponding more with a minimalist view, Sparks highlights several 'progressive evangelical' scholars 'willing to reconsider how critical scholarship might be constructively integrated with an appropriately high view of Scripture's authority.'[9] For some, this includes conceding that some portions of Scripture are fictional, contradictory, or edited, amongst other views. Peter Enns offers an example of this approach.[10] For others, the Bible's historicity does not need to be upheld where it can be shown that it wasn't the intention of the author. Ward makes this distinction in relation to inerrancy: 'Inerrancy does not set down any principle that requires certain sections of Scripture be treated as intended to be largely historical or largely metaphorical. That question must be addressed through appropriate biblical interpretation and the answer is not determined in advance by the doctrine of Scripture. All inerrantists, however, do agree that whatever one decides that Scripture intends to assert, that content must be regarded as free from error.'[11] In this case, historicity is only defended where biblical scholarship affirms that the author was intending to write history.

These taxonomies refer to scholarly responses to historical criticism. To what extent is this diversity of approaches to historicity mirrored by non-scholars?

HISTORICITY AND ORDINARY READERS

Perrin's empirical research on biblical narrative identified that her millennial readers tended to assume the historicity of the narrative texts they read in 1 Samuel, 2 Kings, and Acts. Contrastingly, Village found that his participants' belief in the historical factuality of texts was based more on the doctrinal weight of the text than the feasibility of the events. He found 'there was a distinction between events associated with the life of Jesus and those from the Old Testament.'[12] In particular, on Village's 'literalism scale', Noah, Adam and Eve, and Jonah 'scored significantly lower, with only around half the participants answering "definitely" or "probably" happened.'[13] This suggests that Evangelical Anglican readers do not approach the question of historicity monolithically but assess this on a case by case basis, weighing up the doctrinal significance of the events, the plausibility of their occurring, and the nature of the text in question.

In a now somewhat dated quantitative study, Fisher, Astley, and Wilcox found that amongst the Anglicans they surveyed there was much confusion around the subject of historicity.[14] In response to the statement 'The Bible is not always accurate when it describes history', 32.8 percent didn't know/ respond and 55.3 percent agreed, suggesting a turn towards less 'literal' understandings of Scripture, though it's notable that the respondents weren't specifically Evangelicals. Only 11.9 percent disagreed, thus affirming the historical accuracy of Scripture.

HERMENEUTIC: HISTORICAL-CRITICAL EXEGESIS

Regardless of a determination of historicity, biblical criticism is valued amongst Evangelical Anglicans in aid of the task of exegesis. This is the exercise of trying to understand texts in their original context, including what the original author might have meant by exploring the historical, cultural, geographical, linguistic, and literary background. On the more conservative end of the spectrum, this is couched as ultimately discerning God's intention in communication. What the original author meant is what God meant.

Another approach frames this process of exegesis as 'distancing'. This is a slightly more dynamic way of construing the historical exploration of the text. Rather than collecting and applying relevant knowledge, the process of 'distancing' places an emphasis on the personal involvement of the individual in respecting a text's historicity. According to Stott, 'this means we have to acknowledge "the pastness of the past", disengage ourselves from the text, and allow it its own historical integrity. We must avoid letting ourselves intrude into it or deciding prematurely how it applies to us. Careful exegesis of the text necessitates studying it on its own cultural and linguistic terms.'[15]

Putting these two perspectives of exegesis together paints a task that involves both acquiring and employing relevant knowledge to illuminate the world of the author and their purposes and intentions and remaining self-aware of one's own agenda and cultural conditionings in order to do justice and effectively engage with the historical knowledge acquired. This is done in service of answering the question 'what did the author mean?'

The task of exegesis is to be conducted within a commitment to the fundamental nature of Scripture which, for those at one end of the spectrum, limits the scope of the conclusions that can be drawn. Packer would not have readers follow what he sees as the mistakes of critical scholarship which 'committed itself to a method of study which assumed that Scripture might err anywhere. It told the Church that the Bible could never be rightly understood till belief in its inerrancy was given up.'[16] The doctrine of Scripture dictates the exegetical conclusions that are reached. At the other end of the spectrum, however, is the opposite approach where exegetical conclusions inform the doctrine of Scripture. Enns writes, 'the Bible is ultimately from God and . . . is God's gift to the church. Any theories concerning Scripture that do not arise from these fundamental instincts are unacceptable. On the other hand, how the evangelical church *fleshes* out its doctrine of Scripture will always have a provisional quality to it . . . when new evidence comes to light, or old evidence is seen in a new light, we must be willing to engage that evidence and adjust our doctrine accordingly.'[17]

GENESIS 7

To assess how my participants handle the question of historicity, they were given Genesis chapter 7 to read and discuss. Genesis 7 is the middle section of the account of Noah, the ark and the flood which begins in 6:9 and ends in 9:17.

The Influence of the Doctrine of Scripture: Reading Historically 39

Chapter 7 begins with the ark having been built and God instructing Noah to go inside with his family and seven pairs of clean animals and birds and a single pair of unclean animals, because in seven days God will send forty days of continuous rain. Noah does what God asks and he enters into the ark with male and female pairs of animals and birds. After seven days the flood arrives. The story then recounts the specific time and age of Noah when he entered the ark and the floods came, and Noah enters the ark again, this time, shut in by God. The flood continues for forty days and the waters rise so that they cover the tops of the highest mountains. Everything that had life left on the earth is destroyed and the chapter ends with Noah and the animals left in the ark as the waters increase.

RATIONALE FOR SELECTION

Given Perrin's empirical research demonstrated that millennial readers tended to assume the historicity of narratives,[18] I wanted to choose a text likely to raise scepticism as to its historicity. The story of Noah is just such a text; one does not have to be highly educated to recognise the seemingly impossible 'miracle' of a worldwide flood and the collection of all the world's species on a man-made vessel. Additionally, the story has gained some notoriety beyond Christian spheres with atheists, especially given the advancement of scientific and geographical knowledge that indicates a worldwide flood did not occur. Indeed, scientific advancement has meant that Genesis as a whole has been called into question as a text of history. Is Noah and the flood an event that is meant to be understood as factual history, something that actually happened to a person called Noah and his family? Or is it intended as a type of myth or legend? For Evangelicals, the designation of the Bible as the Word of God means that it must be truthful, but how is this expectation dealt with when a story presents events that contradict scientific evidence? Can the text be truthful but non-historical? What does this mean for the text's authority and inspired nature? Additionally, the actions of God in the text are seemingly inconsistent with a creator God of love. Does what the text recounts of God's action affect readers' assessment of its historicity?

To read the entirety of the Noah narrative would take too long and give too much for participants to discuss in the allotted time. The central chapter was therefore chosen, which includes the two most 'unbelievable' elements of the narrative: the animals boarding the ark and the worldwide flood.

In order to illicit discussion of the historicity of the narrative, the third question on the participants' handout (following two general questions to stimulate conversation) asked, 'Do you think this text is historically accurate?'

40   *Chapter 3*

SCHOLARSHIP OVERVIEW

Before discussing how the participants handled the text, it is worth giving a brief summary of the issues identified by scholars. There are five predominant issues that scholars, commentators, and writers frequently address in relation to Genesis 7: (1) genre, (2) how to handle extrabiblical knowledge, (3) repetition and contradiction in the text, (4) the morality of God, and (5) how Noah is read in relation to the rest of the canon.

First, the genre of Genesis: What is the purpose of this book and what is it intending to do? Answers to these questions are by no means monolithic, particularly within Evangelicalism, and are connected to broader issues relating to the authority and inspiration of Scripture. Some determine the text's genre according to what it claims or indicates about itself.[19] Others distinguish Genesis 1–11 as a 'primeval narrative' which is fundamentally different from the narrative of Genesis 12 onwards.[20] Moreover, the category of 'history' has been questioned as to its appropriateness for texts of Genesis's cultural origins, leading some to see the text as primarily theological[21] or mythological[22] or both. This is discussed in more detail in chapter 8.

Second, evaluations of the historicity of Genesis 7 may be determined by approaches to extrabiblical information. Archaeological, geographical, and scientific evidence suggests that the account of Noah and the flood did not take place. The existence of numerous other ancient Near Eastern (ANE) flood narratives complicate this. There are a variety of ways readers and scholars might handle this: ignoring the evidence, appealing to miracles, accepting the evidence, or harmonising evidence and the text.[23] The latter often takes the form of claiming the flood was local rather than universal, and/or the flood appeared to be universal to the writer based on their knowledge and experience of the world.

Third, scholars highlight the repetitions and contradictions of the narrative. Whilst many attribute this to multiple sources being editing together,[24] some opt for a chiastic structure to explain this feature of the texts.[25] Others have gone further to claim the repetitions and contradictions of the text are purposeful as a literary technique.[26]

Fourth, whilst Psalm 44, below, is the main measure of readers' response to the theological challenge of God's 'immorality', Genesis 7 also prompts reflections on the moral character of God. The majority of Christian scholars actually focus on the positive qualities of God the story highlights: God's intimate involvement in the world that causes him to grieve in chapter 6 and God's heart to save and rebuild.[27] Moreover, the narrative suggests God is both sovereign over the world yet intimate with it.[28]

The Influence of the Doctrine of Scripture: Reading Historically   41

Finally, commentators note recurring references to Noah throughout the rest of the biblical canon, in the gospels and 1 Peter. They also highlight the flood's similarity with the creation narrative, with some scholars finding parallels in prophetic literature.[29]

DISCUSSION SUMMARIES

History and Truth

I assumed when writing the handout question, 'do you think this text is historically accurate?' that participants would understand 'historically accurate' to equate to events that actually happened, as opposed to fictional events that did not happen. In this sense, 'historically accurate' equates to 'factual'.[30] The conversations that took place reflected this understanding of history, such that participants could have equally been discussing the question 'did the events in this text happen in reality?'

However, it was not always the case that 'historically accurate' was synonymous with 'truthful' for participants; the text's truthfulness was not measured solely on the basis of whether the events of the text took place. Instead, participants seemed to be working with two understandings of truth. First, truth in the sense of factual and accurate information. Second, truth which was something more like 'revelation', akin to spiritual insight.[31] For example, at St.J's, several members referred to the Noah narrative as 'true myth', which was initially Henry's designation, quoting C. S. Lewis.[32] This designation was used by Henry to suggest that whilst the details of the text might not be completely historically accurate, the text was not devoid of historical content. In other words, the narrative was partially factually accurate. Henry also asserted that, 'when I don't know the answer to these things, my response is—this is a mystery, so I'm not going to understand, but it's true.' Here, he evidences a baseline belief in the truth of the text which, if using 'true' in the factual sense would contradict his earlier declaration that the narrative was true myth. This therefore suggests that Henry is using 'true' in the second understanding described above—a truth of a deeper kind which is compatible with details of the story being inaccurate.

This view also seemed to be affirmed by St.C's, such as Stacey's response when presented by another group member with the options of Genesis 7 being either a metaphor or historical: 'But they're not the only two options is what I mean. So, you can have stories that are, that have truths in them that are not, they're not completely metaphorical but they're also not . . . it's also about the language . . .' This was an unfinished thought as Stacey then went on to discuss the difficulties of language and reading from another culture, but

42 *Chapter 3*

her assertion that stories can have 'truths in them' seems to affirm Henry's view that the Genesis account contains truth in a deeper sense than historical reality.

A similar distinction could also be found at St.A's where truth was also a contested issue. After a lengthy speech raising some of the difficulties of defining what is historical and what is not, Jake finished with the statement, 'it's alright as long as you don't want to interpret every single detail as being literally true.' The term 'literally true' would seem to correspond to truth as factually accurate. This seemed to be the 'truth' in Amy's mind when she stated, 'even if I don't really understand whether it's true or what . . . it's in the Bible because God wanted it there, that's what I think.' Amy affirms the divine purpose of the text, despite uncertainty about its factual truth. Gina made a similar statement but explicitly differentiated between the two truths, saying, 'but I think it is truth but it's a different truth.' This statement was in conversation with Charles who was concerned that the literal reading of the creation narrative does not give a factual account of the creation of the world. Gina, in response, affirms the Bible's truth but relegates it to the second type of 'truth' described above, which is compatible with details not being factual.

Similarly, Christopher from TO asserted his belief that the narrative was true but clarified that 'I don't know if that means it's not mythology.' In other words, he felt committed to the truth of the narrative, but this wasn't necessarily connected with the historical reality of the text; that the story was 'true' didn't mean that it was factual. Equally, Nick from WO made a more assertive statement in the same vein; 'I can't take these stories literally. And that doesn't mean I don't think they're true. It means that I don't think they're meant literally.' Whilst Christopher wasn't sure if the narrative was mythology, Nick was confident that the stories weren't intended to be literal but that they were true, presumably in a deeper spiritual sense.

These varied uses of 'truth' demonstrate the influence of a commitment to Scripture's truthfulness that leaves room to question the historical accuracy or factuality of the texts. But in what sense can the text be understood to be 'true' but not factual? No one addressed this explicitly but Amy's quote above suggests that for her, the truth of Scripture is the divine intention behind it. This was explicated more fully when she said, 'But I think to myself that it's in there because God wanted it in there and I might not understand, but I try and draw from it what God is wanting me to learn from that.' The deeper truth for Amy was about learning and communication; God has something to say to her through the narrative. Similarly, Gina also stressed learning as a crucial aspect of the narrative: 'Actually that's the most important thing, whether we individually believe bits of it and not other bits is irrelevant if we're taking on board the reflection of God.' In other words, the question of historicity is not important in light of the theological lessons that can be learnt from the text.

The Influence of the Doctrine of Scripture: Reading Historically 43

This view was shared by various other participants; for example, Jane (St.J's) commented that her main concern with the narrative was to understand 'how can I apply it to my life and live now?'

Similarly the TO group stressed that the issue of historicity was not central to reading and interpreting the narrative. For example, Dean chose to sidestep the historicity question saying, 'I suppose as a preacher and pastor, I would try to stay away from the academics of the question and see how this can be pastorally presented to my flock . . . I would look at it as a story, a warning, but a story of redemption.' Equally, Jesse stated, 'God has a plan and a purpose, there is a rainbow, there is a promise . . . whether it was a worldwide flood or not, I've never really invested a massive amount of time into . . . I just kind of focus in on some of the key aspects of the narrative.' Johnny made the same point at GLC: 'I guess like theologically, regardless you know, of whether global or local . . . I would look at the theology of it being . . . God having a fresh start in creation.' Similarly, Nick's indirect application about whether the reader is like Noah or everyone else when the final judgement occurs, reflects his understanding of non-literal truth: 'I think that's a really powerful lean in to the story; when you're reading the story, and some of us take this as a literal history, some of us take it as a kind of poetic parable maybe, or something similar, some of us take it as a reinterpretation of pagan stories to tell us something about the real God, but it's also telling us about the world we live in.' These quotes suggest that any non-historical 'truth' relates to a theological reading which is largely unattached from whether the event actually happened. This reflects Andrew Todd's findings from his participants who 'at more than one point . . . discussed the secondary nature of the historical perspective.'[33] The text was taken to be true theologically, in that what it reveals about the nature of God or humanity is a factually true insight, regardless of whether the text was taken to be factually true. Two participants with opposing views on historicity demonstrate this. Martin (GLC) spoke of the text as a myth, which he defined as 'a foundational principle surrounded by a narrative.' The foundational principle he identified in Genesis was 'the sovereignty of God in all creation.' Conversely, Jessica (WO) stated her belief that the text was 'literal', but like Martin, highlighted that a key point of the text was that 'God is sovereign.' Whilst not all participants believed in the factual truth of the text then, they did believe in the non-historical truth of the text, and this related to its theological insight.

Ultimately, this focus upon theological learning and application for contemporary life suggests that the sense in which participants understood the text to be true, yet not historical, was in the text's portrayal of God and its ability to be a vehicle to receive communication from God. This is how participants who opted for a non-historical reading continued to uphold the truth of the text as God's Word.

44   *Chapter 3*

The Bible's Function

What does this emphasis upon theological insight and application suggest about participant's doctrine of Scripture? Though a variety of comments were made, all such statements about the non-historical truth of the text articulate that the Bible is a resource through which the reader learns both about God and how to live in the light of God. In other words, the text is perceived as containing teaching, which prescribes that the reader's engagement with the text is for the purpose of learning. This can be seen more explicitly in Johnny's (GLC) comment about historicity: 'I wonder if sometimes whether questions about historical accuracy, do you think they . . . distract us from what . . . God's saying through the text?' Johnny evidences a view of the Bible as being a source of divine communication and elsewhere in the discussion, as noted above, focused on the purpose of the Genesis text as 'God's fresh start.' His job as the reader therefore, was to seek divine communication in the text, which took the form of teaching, and what was taught was theological insight.

What this suggests is that participants' doctrine of Scripture was conceived less in terms of the Bible's inherent characteristics and more in terms of how the Bible functions in the life of the believer. What the Bible *is*, is construed in terms of what the Bible *does*, and what the Bible does is teach the reader what God wants them to know, believe, and do.

Partial Historicity

Having established that participants distinguished between two understandings of truth, it is unsurprising that none of the groups asserted a purely historical or fictional understanding of the story. This was the conclusion from the general thrust of the conversation, so it should be noted that this does not mean that some participants personally held to a fictional or historical interpretation. However, based on the discussion, all groups proposed and vocalised a hybrid understanding of the text that took the narrative to have historical components but also metaphorical, fictional, or embellished elements.

Reading Historically on the Basis of the Doctrine of Scripture

Though perhaps implicit at points in some groups, only two participants explicitly stated that the nature of Scripture was a reason to take the text as historically accurate. Neil articulated that his understanding of Scripture sets the expectation that the story should be historical: 'Because I think with

The Influence of the Doctrine of Scripture: Reading Historically   45

Scripture, if we believe Scripture is God-breathed, that's the word, the phrase in the New Testament: God-breathed. In some translations it says "God-inspired" but the most accurate is God-breathed. That is, we as Christians believe this is the Word of God, so how do we reconcile that with potential hyperbole or embellishment or whatever?' Neil's statement implies that the text as 'the Word of God' or 'God-breathed' (which he uses synonymously) is at odds with hyperbole or embellishment. He does not expressly state that the nature of the Bible as God's Word indicates it must be read historically, but this is a fairly safe assumption based on his point that the nature of Scripture as God's speech or God's utterance sits in tension with literary conventions that obscure a plain reading. In other words, the doctrine of Scripture (the Bible as God's Word) sets an expectation that the text is truthful in a literal, objective sense which is incompatible with hyperbole/embellishment.

Similarly, for Adam (GLC), the historicity of the narrative and his belief in the Bible were directly related. Though willing to accept the flood may have been local, he expressed concern at the idea that the narrative was one particular interpretation amongst many of a large flood which occurred naturally. Instead, he wanted the thrust of the story to be historically reliable; i.e., God caused the flood to occur. Adam's belief in the narrative hinged upon the events having taken place: 'The second you do remove all of the history, you're basically detaching it from reality, as such, and you're like saying, "well the guy who wrote this . . . why should I believe him? Why should I believe this interpretation of reality rather than the Gilgamesh epic?"' Additionally, 'Why should I believe Scripture if it's not attached to this world which I can test?'

Belief in the Bible was therefore connected with a degree of historical veracity. This is particularly interesting given that many participants demonstrated a belief in the Bible despite a lack of historical underpinnings, as has been noted in usages of the term 'truth'. For Adam, the text's historicity was an important facet of its being Scripture.

These two instances demonstrate that the doctrine of Scripture certainly has a role to play in participants' determination of the historicity of the narrative. Interestingly, however, these were the only times a participant referenced the doctrine of Scripture as motivation to read the text historically. On the whole, other reasons were offered including extrabiblical evidence and the omnipotence of God. This latter point is worth exploring more fully.

Reading Historically on the Basis of the Doctrine of God

On several occasions, participants' concern for the historicity of the text did not stem from the doctrine of Scripture but from the nature of God. This was articulated by Neil from St.C's: 'if you say it's a metaphor, the subtext is you're belittling what God could do and God is by nature, omnipotent. Like, you have to . . . he is otherwise he's not God. But then, if you say it is not a metaphor, you're left with all these conundrums.' Neil's concern at this point is not that the text might be unhistorical and therefore questionably the 'Word of God' or truthful (though this was also expressed by him, as noted above), but that suggestions of 'metaphor' were being made on the grounds that the account of Noah was materially impossible, which was to question the nature of God.

Similarly, in response to group reflections on the scientific plausibility of the flood, Jane from St.J's was concerned to protect the character of God when discussing the historicity of the account: 'I believe God can do whatever he wants to do. So, he could have done it, I'm not gonna say he can't have done it because of the way we understand science or whatever now, but also, maybe he didn't and maybe it's just a story for us to learn from.' As with Neil, Jane's concern about the scientific plausibility of the account wasn't in relation to the accuracy or reliability of the Bible but what this says about the capacity of God to orchestrate a worldwide flood. This was also reflected at St.A's where Gina makes the same connection but positively: 'I don't have a problem with thinking that this happened. I know that there's evidence that seashells and things have been found right on the top of mountains and stuff . . . that would show there is a flood. But it's like [Jake] said, what is the point of it? And the point of it to me is that God is all powerful, and that he does . . . even though you can think about everybody being wiped out bar this family and these particular creatures, he does care.' Gina affirms that she does not have difficulty believing the account really happened because of her understanding that God is powerful, a view she both brings to the text and reads from the text.

A further example comes from Jessica (WO), whose doctrine of God explicitly determined her stance on the historicity of the narrative. She stated, first, that she believed God was capable of the seemingly impossible worldwide flood and, second, that God's faithfulness in keeping his promises meant that the flood had to be universal. If it had been local, then God has not kept his promise that such a flood would not occur again. Jessica's belief in God's power and faithfulness were reasons for her to take the narrative as historical.

These assertions of historical accuracy were not motivated by the doctrine of Scripture or the reliability of the Bible, but by a concern that God is understood to be powerful and able to do anything. It is significant that concern to protect the character of God was more frequently articulated than concern for the doctrine of Scripture.[34]

Reading Historically on the Basis of the Text

Some participants read the text historically because they believed the text indicated that it was historical. Winston (WO) suggested that the narrative itself gives the reader clues that it is to be read literally because of the phrase 'as it were in the days of Noah.' Claiming that parables or symbolic stories were clearly differentiated from history in the oral tradition, Winston gave the example of the story of Lazarus, which he contrasted with the other parables and noted 'how it is written, how it is referred to, and how it is referenced . . . they are different.' Believing there to be no internal suggestion within the Noah narrative that the story is not historical, Winston assumed it was.

Adam (GLC) also pointed to the detail within the text to argue that the story was historical: 'It seems to me that there is a real retelling of something that . . . there's details that are just . . . you don't need them!' In opposition to Martin's claim that the story was monotheistic propaganda, Adam pointed to the detail of the narrative as evidence that there was more to the story than this agenda—why include details superfluous to the main point?

Reading Historically on the Basis of a Secular Scientific Context

Though participants offered other factors than the doctrine of Scripture in their assessment of the text's historicity, it is difficult to discern whether these were suggested in the context of a commitment to Scripture's truthfulness. In other words, did participants believe the narrative to be historical solely on the grounds of physical evidence or their beliefs about the omnipotence of God, or the style of the text, or were these factors simply bolstering a precommitment to a historical reading determined by the doctrine of Scripture? If the latter, why was the nature of the Bible only mentioned twice as the grounds for belief in a historical reading, if this was indeed an influential factor?

The broader context of participants' comments could provide an answer. Several participants approached the narrative as those belonging to a secular scientific world. At St.C's, despite appreciating that God is omnipotent and can do anything, participants were not content with this as an explanation of the story, instead wanting to understand pragmatically how the events could occur, leading to a lengthy discussion of the science behind the story. This concern for a rational explanation stemmed from an anticipated backlash from atheists, as Neil later stated, 'cynically, sceptically, this is what atheists will come to you and say, "how is that possible?" And frankly, I don't have the answer.' This statement suggests Neil is perhaps imagining either an antagonistic or evangelistic exchange whereby he would be required to offer a rational or convincing explanation for how a worldwide flood could occur

48   *Chapter 3*

to someone who believed Christianity was delusional. Additionally, Henry from St.J's mirrored Neil's consideration of how 'non-Christians' would receive the text:

> Henry: What do you do when non-Christians ask you 'do you believe in x, y and z?'
>
> Anne: I've never had somebody question me about a passage like this actually. I mean, I'm sure other people have, but I've never had someone actually ask me that.
>
> Henry: It's probably because I grew up when a lot of people went to Sunday school and heard all these stories and as they got older, they thought 'that was a load of rubbish' and started to challenge the Christians about it, you see. Maybe people don't do that so much these days, I don't know.

Henry was considerably older than the other members of his group, who were in their twenties and thirties, hence his reference to having grown up in a context where Sunday school attendance was much more common. His reading of the text was affected by his experience of his peers losing their faith and coming to question the narratives they had been taught, including Noah, concluding that the whole thing was made up. Considerations of the text's historicity therefore seemed to incorporate an 'atheist' mind-set, which meant that recourse to the inherent truth of the Bible won't be a sufficient explanation. In other words, claiming the text is historical (at least in part) 'because it's in the Bible' could have been understood as being an inappropriate response, which might be why participants offered other reasons for their historical reading.

What is interesting to note about all these affirmations of the historicity of the narrative is that, with the exception of two participants, the doctrine of Scripture is not offered as a reason to believe the story actually happened. It could be fairly safely conjectured that commitment to the doctrine of Scripture did play a part in participants' understanding that the narrative was historical, but crucially, this was not what was suggested. It would seem that belief in historicity was therefore more nuanced than simply asserting 'it's in the Bible, so it happened.' Even in Adam's case, though he demonstrated significant concern that the Bible have a historical component to it, he was open to the flood being local and did not simply take the story exactly as it is written on account of it being 'in the Bible'. What these other grounds for reading historically indicate is that a determination of historicity, whilst not unconnected from the doctrine of Scripture, might be text-based, rather than Bible-based.

Non-Historical Readings

In the case of non-historical readings, the grounds on which this was argued differed amongst the groups, with various factors holding more weight for particular individuals.

Participants' discussion and ultimate conclusion lived in the tension of these factors, seen most starkly at St.C's. The participants struggled to hold together different pieces in their understanding of the text: their scientific understanding of the world demanded a rationalistic explanation of events which undermined the ability of God to do anything; their understanding that God can do anything left them vulnerable to accusations of ignoring science; their belief in the truth of Scripture made them want to accept the events reported, but their respect for scientific plausibility made them believe that the author exaggerated Noah's age from 60 to 600, etc. The weight placed on these factors differed across the groups and individuals.

At GLC, TO, and WO, a mythical or non-historical reading of the text was influenced by their knowledge of the Gilgamesh epic and other ancient flood stories. The existence of these similar narratives led participants to conclude that the Genesis account had a particular agenda in the face of other similar stories promoting different worldviews. For some, all such stories did refer to a large-scale flood that took place, and represented different understandings of this phenomenon. For others, the Genesis text was reactionary in response to other accounts of the flood. Nick took the latter view, whilst Martin took the former:

> It makes more sense to say we're hearing these stories from the Babylonians or whatever and saying, 'well that's a story about what gods are like, I'm going to rewrite it to say what the real God is like'. (Nick)

> The closeness of the narrative seems to suggest to me that there was something that occurred within the geographical area which was of such great significance that it was written and accounted for in many different cultures and many different religious interpretations of that event. (Martin)

However, Martin also went on to concede that the narrative could have also been reactionary to other narratives: 'Unless he's doing here what some interpreters say is happening in Genesis 1, which is he's creating a monotheistic interpretation of something which is known broadly and well . . . there is one God who is responsible for the flood rather than many.'

Luke also referenced extrabiblical writings but didn't indicate either way how he interpreted the relationship between them and Genesis, but his designation that the passage is 'in the language of myth' indicates that the existence of other stories contributes to this understanding.

50   Chapter 3

The resultant emerging partial historicity (designated 'true myth' and 'origin story' at St.J's and St.C's, respectively) understood that the flood was probably local, rather than global. Only one explicit affirmation of 'accommodation' was suggested by Henry, who claimed that to the author, it would have seemed like the whole earth was flooded and they therefore were not being deceptive in claiming that the waters covered the earth. Other participants did not indicate whether they understood the author to have been deliberately exaggerating, using a turn of phrase and therefore never intending to suggest the flood was global, or simply writing from an uninformed point of view and genuinely believing the flood to be global.

However, whilst half of the groups seemed to conclude the narrative was partially historical, the other half did not demonstrate a strong consensus as to the historicity of the narrative. This diversity of opinion demonstrates that a commitment to the truthfulness of Scripture does not prescribe a stance on the historicity of the text. Though a commitment to the historical truth of the text does not preclude the non-historical truth of the text, for some participants such non-historical truth was the only way in which the text could be understood to be truthful. In this they demonstrated a commitment to the truth of the text where 'truth' meant theological insight.

HISTORICITY AND THE DOCTRINE OF SCRIPTURE

Doctrine of Scripture ≠ Historical

It is clear from the discussions that participants were committed to the truth of the narrative, but that this did not necessarily mean that the narrative was to be taken as historical. The doctrine of Scripture was only given as a reason to read historically on two occasions and though it cannot be dismissed as an influential factor, it is of note that such articulations were rare. This suggests that whilst the nature of the Bible indicates participants read historically, their decision to do so is also informed by other considerations both internal and external to the text. Though Perrin's research found that her participants accepted textual authority unless there was anxiety surrounding the text's theological or ethical message,[35] the discussion of Genesis demonstrated that textual authority (in terms of facticity) was questioned on broader grounds, including scientific and authorial. The doctrine of Scripture alone did not govern participants' determination of the factual truth of the text.

However, as has been noted, the doctrine of Scripture cannot be dismissed as unrelated to the choice to read historically. Few participants advocated for a purely fictional understanding of the text, demonstrating a concern that the text have some elements of historical veracity. This concern could relate to

The Influence of the Doctrine of Scripture: Reading Historically 51

another issue that some participants raised, which was the implications of a non-historical reading for the rest of the Bible. Underscoring a belief in the unity of the text, some participants questioned what a non-historical reading would imply for other biblical content, or how one might make clear distinctions between which elements of the Bible are historical and which aren't. Two participants explicitly linked this concern with the New Testament, recognising that the stakes are much higher concerning the historicity of the life of Jesus, his crucifixion, and resurrection, than the existence of Noah and the flood. This demonstrates two points of note.

First, participants prioritise biblical texts with regard to historicity; it is more important that some are historical than others. This prioritisation of historicity related to the content of the text rather than the doctrine of Scripture. The concern wasn't whether the text was reliable, but whether the central elements of their faith (the life of Jesus) were reliable. This point is supported by Village's research, outlined above.[36] This underscores what was noted above, that participants' determination of the text's historicity was not based on beliefs about the nature of the text, but on other factors.

Second, such comments may also reveal that despite text prioritisation and differing genres, participants' conception of Scripture as a unit led them to want to have a consistent approach across the entirety of the Bible, which didn't leave room for shifting concepts of truth according to the text at hand. Participants' comments about historical consistency could therefore be reflective of the struggle inherent in handling texts differently according to genre despite them being designated as the same according to doctrine.

Doctrine of Scripture and Reading Agenda

If the doctrine of Scripture didn't primarily have an impact on how participants read the text, how did it appear to influence interpretation?

Both advocates and sceptics of the text's historicity ultimately placed greater emphasis on the text's non-historical truth, which took the form of theological insight and guidance for behaviour. This non-historical truth might be more fruitfully referred to as the text's ultimate meaning. Rather than the doctrine of Scripture dictate that participants read in a particular way, it appeared to dictate where the ultimate meaning of the text was found. This is demonstrated by the way in which participants spoke of the Bible as God's resource for communication and teaching. Rather than traditional doctrinal articulations about Scripture (some of which have been mentioned and others of which are discussed in chapter 6) participants' conception of the text seemed to be related to its teaching function. What the Bible is, is construed in terms of what the Bible does, and what the Bible does is teach the reader what God wants them to know, believe, and do. As a result of this conception of the Bible, participants sought the ultimate meaning of the Genesis text in its non-historical truth: theological insight and life guidance.

It wasn't therefore that participants' belief in the Bible as the Word of God meant Genesis had to be read in a particular way (historical), but rather that participants' belief in the function of the Bible as God's resource meant Genesis had to be read for this particular purpose. The doctrine of Scripture thus set the reading agenda by locating the text's meaning in its teaching.

This suggests that the role of the doctrine of Scripture in the process of interpretation is related to reading purpose rather than method: beliefs about the Bible (in this case the belief that the Bible teaches) determine the overall agenda for reading (to learn and be taught) and thus establishes where the ultimate meaning of the text is to be found (information about God and how to live accordingly). Yet, does this role of the doctrine of Scripture continue when it comes to a text that poses a theological challenge? This is the subject of the next chapter.

NOTES

1. Craig Bartholomew, 'Introduction' in Craig Bartholomew, C. Stephen Evans, Mary Healy, and Murray Rae, *'Behind the Text': History and Biblical Interpretation, Vol. 4* (Cumbria: Paternoster Press, 2003), 3.

2. Mark Noll, *Between Faith and Criticism: Evangelicals, Scholarship and the Bible* (Leicester: Apollos, 1991), 72.

3. Ibid., 74.

4. Bartholomew, 'Introduction', 7.

5. Kenton L. Sparks, *God's Word in Human Words: An Evangelical Appropriation of Critical Biblical Scholarship* (Grand Rapids, MI: Baker Academic, 2008), ch. 4.

6. Packer, *God Has Spoken*, 74.

7. Thompson, *The Doctrine of Scripture*, 148.

8. "Basis of Faith," Church of England Evangelical Council.

9. Sparks, *God's Word in Human Words*, 169.

10. Enns, *Inspiration and Incarnation.*

11. Ward, *Words of Life*, 134.

12. Village, *The Bible and Lay People*, 66.

13. Ibid., 65.

14. Jeff Astley, Elizabeth Fisher, and Carolyn Wilcox, 'A Survey of Bible Reading Practices and Attitudes to the Bible among Anglican Congregations', in Jeff Astley and David Day (eds.), *The Contours of Christian Education* (Great Wakering: McCrimmons, 1992), 382–95.

15. Stott, *The Bible*, 37–38.

16. Packer, *God Has Spoken*, 27.

17. Enns, *Inspiration and Incarnation*, 14.

18. Perrin, *Bible Reading*, 59.

The Influence of the Doctrine of Scripture: Reading Historically   53

19. For example: Vern Poythress, 'Dealing with the Genre of Genesis and its Opening Chapters,' *Westminster Theological Journal* 78, no. 2 (2016): 217–30.

20. For example: Lloyd Bailey, *Noah: The Person and the Story in History and Tradition* (Columbia: University of South Carolina Press, 1989).

21. For example: Walter Brueggemann, *Genesis* (Atlanta: John Knox Press, 1982).

22. For example: David Pleins, *When the Great Abyss Opened: Classic and Contemporary Readings of Noah's Flood* (Oxford: Oxford University Press, 2010), 17, Oxford Scholarship Online.

23. For a summary of such approaches see: Paul Seely, 'Noah's Flood: It's Date, Extent, and Divine Accommodation,' *Westminster Theological Journal* 66 (2004): 291–311.

24. For example: Claus Westermann, *Genesis 1–11: A Continental Commentary* (Minneapolis, MN: Fortress Press, 1994).

25. Gordon J. Wenham, *Genesis 1–15* (Waco, TX: Word Books, 1987).

26. For example: Victor Hamilton, *The Book of Genesis Chapters 1–17* (Grands Rapids, MI: W. B. Eerdmans, 1990); Thomas Brodie, *Genesis as Dialogue: A Literary, Historical, & Theological Commentary* (Oxford: Oxford University Press, 2001), 168, Oxford Scholarship Online.

27. For example: Terrence Fretheim, 'The God for the Flood Story and Natural Disasters,' *Calvin Theological Journal* 45 (2008): 21–34.

28. David Atkinson, *The Message of Genesis 1–11: The Dawn of Creation* (Leicester: Inter-Varsity, 1990), 136.

29. For example: Robert Alter, *Genesis* (London: Norton, 1996), 32–33; Richard Belcher, *Genesis: The Beginning of God's Plan of Salvation* (Fearn: Christian Focus, 2012), 95; Brodie, *Genesis as Dialogue*, 172; Brueggemann, *Genesis*, 79; Pleins, *When the Great Abyss Opened*, 141.

30. Debates about the existence of 'objective history' given the subjectivity of any human record, though valid, are not of concern here, but rather how participants understand history in relation to the question and the text.

31. This is my interpretation of this second usage of 'truth' and it should be noted that no participants used these terms to describe truth in this way. This description stems from my understanding of what participants meant in their usage of 'truth' when the context implied that they were not referring to the text's factuality.

32. The usage of the term by Henry does not actually fit C. S. Lewis' use of the term, which he applied to the Gospel and used to indicate that the events of Christ had actually happened. In his letters to his friend Arthur Greeves, he explained: 'Now what Dyson and Tolkien showed me was this: that if I met the idea of sacrifice in a Pagan story I didn't mind it at all: again, that if I met the idea of a god sacrificing himself to himself . . . I liked it very much and was mysteriously moved by it: again, that the idea of the dying and reviving god (Balder, Adonis, Bacchus) similarly moved me provided I met it anywhere except in the Gospels. The reason was that in Pagan stories I was prepared to feel the myth as profound and suggestive of meanings beyond my grasp even tho' I could not say in cold prose "what it meant". Now the story of Christ is simply a true myth: a myth working on us in the same way as the others, but with this tremendous difference that it really happened.' (C. S. Lewis, Arthur Greeves,

54 *Chapter 3*

Walter Hooper, *They Stand Together: The Letters of C. S. Lewis to Arthur Greeves [1914–1963]* [New York: Collier Books, 1979], 427–28.)

33. Todd, 'The Talk,' 240.

34. This reflects Perrin's participants, who also believed in the supernatural events in the texts they read on account of God's ability to do anything. See: Perrin, *Bible Reading*, 193.

35. Ibid., 237.

36. Village, *The Bible and Lay People*, 66.

Chapter 4

The Influence of the Doctrine of Scripture

Reading Theologically

The previous chapter explored the influence that the doctrine of Scripture had upon participants' choice whether or not to read the text historically. Whilst beliefs about Scripture did play a part in participants' consideration of the text's historicity, this was found to be largely determined by a number of other factors. Instead, the doctrine of Scripture had more of a role in determining that the text had valuable content to learn from and that this was to be found in a theological reading, rather than the text's facticity.

The question this chapter then asks is whether the doctrine of Scripture influences participants' choice to read the text theologically, when the theology the text poses is problematic. First, I consider of Evangelical Anglican approaches to theological readings of Scripture.

READING THEOLOGICALLY

The Bible has always been inextricably linked with theology. It is the source and norm of theology. Yet, this relationship is somewhat reciprocal. Whilst theology is based upon the Bible, it is also the lens through which the Bible is read—this is the rule of faith. Common in patristic interpretations of Scripture, the rule of faith is a reading of the Bible according to and in line with the creed and orthodox faith. The circularity of this comes from the recognition that the rule of faith is itself derived from the Bible. The Bible and theology have therefore always existed in a dialectical relationship. Typically Evangelicalism has tended to emphasise the Bible as a source of theology, though a resurgence of the rule of faith has emerged in recent years amongst some Evangelical scholars, discussed below.[1]

56 *Chapter 4*

Theological interpretation of Scripture is also a practice originating in the patristic era, but with roots in earlier Jewish interpretative practices. The four senses of Scripture offer four interpretative approaches to the text: literal, moral, allegorical, and anagogical. Though intended to be utilised together, these four senses highlight something of a distinction between reading historically and theologically. This became all the more disparate with the division of the disciplines 'biblical studies' and 'systematic theology' in the modern academy.[2] The problem can often be referred to using the shorthand of Lessing's 'ugly broad ditch' which pitched an unbreachable chasm between faith and history, revelation and reason.[3] In reality and with regard to biblical interpretation, this is a false dichotomy, as Sarisky writes, 'the grave problem that results from differentiating two approaches absolutely is that it suggests that theological reading, as the alternative to historical reading, is itself a historical, that it is not based on a construal of the text of the Bible that is in any sense rooted in the past. This is misleading.'[4] However, the prominent emphasis upon history that the rise of historical criticism brought, discussed in chapter 3, led to responses which prompted a renewed focus on the theological interpretation of Scripture, a brief overview of which I now turn to.

Scholarly Approaches to the Bible and Theology

Though a theological reading of Scripture is by no means new, there have been various modern movements within biblical studies that have emphasised the theological nature of Scripture, in response to historical criticism. Sparks sees the majority of these constructive approaches to higher criticism having their root in 'neo-orthodoxy's dual commitment to biblical authority and to the essential validity of biblical criticism.'[5] It was Karl Barth who insisted in response to historical exegesis that 'the proper focus of Christian exegesis was not history but theology, and the proper starting place for theological exegesis was the final canonical form of the Bible.'[6]

Subsequent movements with this primary contention include kerygmatic exegesis, which interpreted the Bible according to 'salvation history' or *Heilgeschichte*.[7] In this movement, whether or not an episode in the Bible actually happened was irrelevant to accessing a given passage's theology which could be situated within the overarching story of Scripture—redemptive history.

Though similar in some respects, the biblical theology movement, albeit something of a slippery term amongst scholars,[8] emphasised God's revelation in history. 'The emphasis on history as a vehicle for revelation was set over against seeing the Bible as a reflection of eternal truths, or a deposit of right doctrine, or particularly a process of evolving religious discovery.'[9] However, in contrast to kerymatic exegesis, the movement sought to utilise the insights

The Influence of the Doctrine of Scripture: Reading Theologically   57

of historical criticism to understand the events and acts in which God has revealed himself.

One of the problems with this method was the theological diversity that resulted. In response, Brevard Childs spearheaded the canonical interpretation movement.[10] In this view, the proper context within which to understand diverse biblical texts is the biblical canon and the final shape of Scripture. Though historical-critical approaches may yield interesting results, they do not provide insight into the theological interpretation of Scripture which is properly accessed in a text's canonical context.

More recently, the 'Theological Interpretation of Scripture' movement has gained ground amongst Evangelical scholars in America.[11] This approach to the Bible embraces doctrinal presuppositions as a proper starting point for interpretation, but equally claims to not undermine historical enquiry of the Bible. In the words of Vanhoozer and Treier, 'Theological exegesis does not automatically reject author-centred hermeneutics or historical concerns, but rather addresses the frequent tendency of so-called historical criticism to go beyond offering helpful tools and to function as an antitheological research program.'[12] How it is distinguished from the biblical theology movement, if at all, is debated amongst scholars.[13]

How might these different movements be reflected amongst non-scholars? Chapter 3 has already highlighted how in the face of uncertainty about historicity, participants turned to a theological reading. What does other relevant fieldwork suggest about theological readings and ordinary readers?

Theology and Ordinary Readers

An important dynamic that some of the studies described in chapter 1 have highlighted at various points is the relationship between theology and Scripture.

Malley's research suggested his participants' beliefs and biblical interpretations often have separate origins, rather than the former being based on the latter. He posits that the goal of Evangelical hermeneutics is what he terms 'transitivity', the activity of validating beliefs by making a connection between them and Scripture.[14] Malley claims that Evangelicals seek to corroborate their beliefs in the biblical text so that traditional doctrines become traditional interpretations. However, there is not one set way in which beliefs and the biblical text are connected; rather a variety of such connections can be made. This connection between text and belief does not take a particular form as long as some connection exists, thus Malley claims that whilst an interpretative tradition exists (connecting beliefs with the biblical text), Evangelicals 'are not inheritors of a hermeneutical tradition, a socially transmitted set of methods for reading the Bible'[15] (the form of connection between belief and the Bible). This raises a host of questions concerning what theological frameworks are in place prior to the interpretive task and how these are formed. What is the relationship between pre-existing beliefs and the Bible? If beliefs were solely biblical then the Bible would never conflict with these beliefs. Yet, Perrin's research demonstrated instances where this wasn't the case.

Perrin's participants showed an array of responses to the violence of God in the texts that they read. It was here that the groups' unspoken doctrine(s) of Scripture came into contention with their doctrine of God. Perrin organises these responses into five categories: (1) unquestioning acceptance, (2) reader limitation, (3) uncomfortable resignation, (4) explicable misrepresentation, (5) partial resistance.[16] Partial resistance came the closest to breaching unspoken doctrinal boundaries within the group. Perrin notes, 'for a majority of the time, participants were prepared to accept the text as authoritative and truthful, it was only when anxieties emerged about the theological or ethical message of the narrative that participants engaged these negotiations, demonstrating varying levels of willingness to challenge it or strategies to engage it.'[17] This suggests readers approach Scripture through a theological or ethical framework. The relationship this framework has to Scripture, is unclear. If Evangelicals profess that their beliefs and doctrine are biblically based, what is the exact nature of this basis?

In terms of theological interpretation, Bielo identified what he terms a 'textual ideology' amongst his participants, which he terms 'biblical textuality,' which aligns somewhat with canonical interpretation. He found his participants read texts as being part of the biblical canon and practiced intertextual linking and resolving tensions between texts as a way to protect this ideology (discussed further below).[18]

Finally, the survey data of Anglicans by Fisher, Astley, and Wilcox, whilst finding just over 10 percent belief in the historical accuracy of the Bible, found a greater agreement about the accuracy of the Bible's theological content. The statement 'The Bible is not always accurate when it talks about God, God's acts and God's will for humans' had a 43.5 percent disagreement response, indicating a much higher belief in the Bible's theological accuracy than historical accuracy.[19] This concurs with the responses of my participants detailed in chapter 3 where the historicity of Genesis was questioned, but not its ability to teach theological truths about God.

Hermeneutic: Canonical Reading and Harmonisation

One of the hermeneutics to arise out of theological readings of Scripture is that of canonical context. Each passage has to be read in light of its context in the Bible, not simply its historical context. This is emphasised amongst popular Evangelical literature. Beynon and Sach recommend that Bible readers

The Influence of the Doctrine of Scripture: Reading Theologically   59

ask the following questions: '1) Where is this passage on the Bible timeline? 2) Where am I on the Bible timeline? 3) How do I read this in light of things that have happened in between?'[20]

The canonical task thus goes beyond exegesis, outlined in the previous chapter. In exegesis, the answer to the questions posed by the interpreter could be provided by the author in question, but a canonical reading goes beyond what the original author knows and places their writing in the context of the rest of the Bible.

It is important to note that this hermeneutical practice is determined by the divine nature of the text and a belief in its sole author God and resultant unity and consistency. It is also worth recognising that this hermeneutic is not a specific method. It is not clear whether one is to generally understand a passage in the light of the Bible's overarching narrative and themes (and what exactly those are), or whether it should also be specifically compared with similar texts in theology, content, or style.

Finally, canonical reading is not necessarily espoused by all Evangelical Anglicans. Thiselton explicitly calls for interpretation that does not read concerns or theological themes from other parts of the Bible back into particular texts, arguing, 'the distinctive message of each particular text should be accorded its proper rights.'[21] This is not to say that Thiselton pays no heed to the canon of Scripture and treats texts as purely isolated, but rather that a canonical context should not be practiced too quickly without hearing the text on its own terms first.

Connected to the practice of reading texts within the context of the canon, is the hermeneutical practice of harmonisation. As a consequence of God being the author of all Scripture, and particularly as a result of a commitment to inerrancy, the Bible is understood to be non-contradictory. If canonical context brings texts into conversation with another, then hermeneutics therefore involves harmonisation, 'not setting text against text or supposing apparent contradictions to be real ones but seeking rather to let one passage throw light on another in the certainty that there is in Scripture a perfect agreement between part and part, which careful study will be able to bring out.'[22]

Though many Evangelical Anglican writers agree that Scripture is not contradictory and are committed to canonical reading and the truth of Scripture, some express a reluctance to insist on the principle of harmonisation if this results in manufactured interpretations or a failure to appreciate the diverse perspectives the Bible offers.[23]

On the other hand are the arguments that see the contradictions in the Bible as a key to understanding its nature. To read canonically, is to read with an appreciation that the Bible witnesses to the developing theology and practice of a worshipping community, which results in contradictions as views change over time.[24]

60 *Chapter 4*

Generally speaking, however, it would be expected that Evangelical Anglican readers would tend to deny contradictions in the Bible or accept that discrepancies might not be easily explained, whilst understanding passages in the light of the canon, particularly its broader themes and insight gained from the unity of the testaments. In the words of Thompson, 'Though study and the exercise of a faithful teaching ministry are both enjoined in Scripture itself, and though the Spirit attends the word to bring about conviction in the human heart, Scripture is its own interpreter. Careful attention to what is written, its context—most particularly in the biblical canon—and the comparison of one biblical text with other guards against misunderstanding.'[25] To what extent did these hermeneutical practices appear amongst my participants?

PSALM 44

To assess participants' theological readings of Scripture, they were given Psalm 44 to read, the first of eleven communal laments Psalms. It is attributed to the Korahites and described as a maskil. The Psalm alternates in voice throughout, transitioning between the first-person plural and the first-person singular, suggesting the context of a community 'gathered together in a sanctuary or in the Temple in Jerusalem to cry out to God about a situation of grave danger.'[26] This situation is one of military defeat with significant losses of both people and possessions.

The first section of the Psalm recalls what God has done for his people in the past, and how it was only through God's power that their armies were successful and that they secured land. This recollection goes beyond the living memory of those in the community and recalls the events of their ancestors that have been passed down through the generations. A striking turn occurs in the Psalm at verse 9 introducing an accusation that brings the situation of the present day into sharp contrast with that of the past—'yet you have rejected and abased us.' This sentence begins a string of accusations that all start with an emphatic 'you', building up the sense and weight of the current injustice. God has not done what he did in the past and secured success in battle for the present community. God is the reason that people are being killed, exploited, and shamed by those around them. The Psalmist then goes on to protest that this is unjustified, that the community has been faithful in following God's ways and has not committed idolatry or failed its covenantal obligations. God is acknowledged as knowing all and his omniscience is appealed to as validation of the community's innocence—the cry is that God knows they have done all that is required of them and yet still, he has rejected them. The final section of the Psalm turns to appeal and implores God to wake up and come to

The Influence of the Doctrine of Scripture: Reading Theologically   61

their aid in action. As they 'sink down' God is called upon to 'rise up', to not forget his people and to bring redemption 'for the sake of your steadfast love.'

Rationale for Selection

Psalm 44 was chosen for discussion and interpretation by focus groups predominantly because of the theological dilemma it poses regarding God. To what extent does the doctrine of Scripture prescribe that the Psalm must be theologically accurate?

Whilst there are several theologically challenging psalms, Psalm 44 provides an adept challenge because not only are claims made about God that Christians would usually reject (God abandons people), but these claims are justified on the grounds of the community's innocence. Readers can't therefore understand God's actions as warranted as a result of the people's disobedience or sin, as could be claimed in the case of Noah. In the Psalm, it appears that completely unwarrantedly, God has abandoned his people. Will readers accept what the Psalm claims about God because of the authoritative and inspired nature of the Bible? If they do, how will readers understand the problem of theodicy, the suffering of the innocent? Will interpreting through the rule of faith or canonical context ensure that a doctrine of God as loving, faithful, and loyal to his people triumph over the picture given in Psalm 44?

Moreover, genre plays into this central challenge. The Psalms are a form of poetry or creative expression which offers a certain degree of flexibility when it comes to interpretation. The unique nature of the Psalms for believers who hold to an Evangelical doctrine of Scripture is found in their dual nature of being human utterances to God, i.e., prayers, that due to their incorporation into Scripture, are equally considered to be God's utterances to humanity. This creates an interesting dynamic for application and interpretation—are all psalmic utterances to be taken as theological truth given they're God's Word? Or can and should some be dismissed on the grounds that they represent the view of the psalter and do not represent reality?

Psalm 44 offers a particularly interesting test case on another front: the first half of the Psalm declares typically accepted truths about God before turning to more questionable claims. If readers are inclined to dismiss the theological claims of the Psalm about God, will they also dismiss the more orthodox claims at the start of the Psalm?

To prompt participants to discuss these issues, the third question on the handout under the two general questions was 'Does this text provide an accurate depiction of God?' The use of the term 'accurate' is consistent with the Genesis question and as was the case there, indicates that I am referring to the text's relation to the reality of the nature and character of God. Before turning

62   *Chapter 4*

to participants' discussion, I'll briefly consider how some of these challenges are responded to amongst scholarship.

Scholarship Overview

The key issues discussed by scholarship in relation to Psalm 44 are: (1) genre and structure, (2) theodicy, (3) historical context, and (4) Psalm 44 in relation to the rest of the Bible.

First, whilst the psalmic genre is taken as a given, scholars note the distinctive turn in the Psalm at verse 9[27] and reflect on whether the first section is best understood as praise or invocation.[28] This determines how the Psalm fits together as a whole. This is discussed further in chapter 8.

Second, the issue of innocent suffering in the Psalm is pointed out in relation to covenantal expectation.[29] Commentators highlight the paradox of the Psalm affirming God's loyalty and faithfulness in the act of addressing and calling upon Him, whilst discrediting God's loyalty and faithfulness in content.[30] This leads some Christian commentators to centre on the issue of petitionary prayer.[31] Others, however, make Christological comparisons, making sense of the Psalm's tension in light of the suffering of Christ.[32]

A third issue that scholars address is the lack of historical moorings that anchor the Psalm to a specific event in the life of Israel.[33] Most commentators agree that there is not enough evidence to historically locate the Psalm. Contextual suggestions that have been made include the Babylonian captivity[34] (though this is unlikely given the Psalm's claims to innocence), the persecution of Greek Emperor Antiochus IV Ephiphanes in 163–164BCE or the capturing of the ark by the Philistines recounted in 1 Samuel 4.[35] Such suggestions are in the minority with most concluding that the Psalm cannot be historically located.

Finally, as with Genesis, this Psalm is discussed in relation to the rest of the Bible. Specifically, scholars have noted thematic similarities with the book of Job[36] and textual similarities with Psalm 37.[37] The Psalm is also quoted in Romans, where a subtle change is made from being made sheep for slaughter by God, to having chosen to be sheep for slaughter for God. This usage of the Psalm further opens up christological readings for some commentators, described above.

DISCUSSION SUMMARIES

Character of God

Despite the Psalm's claims to the contrary, participants demonstrated a fundamental belief in, and commitment to, God as loving and good, though this was expressed using a variety of language. This preconceived understanding of the nature and character of God as good was a significant factor in participants' assessment of the truth of the psalmist's claims. They understood the text in light of their previously held understanding of God which led to their denial of the psalmist's portrayal of God. For example, Emma's (St.J's) comment about the repeated accusatory refrain 'you have . . .': 'And I think that the statements "you have made us", I think they're the psalmist's felt sense, not necessarily an inerrant fact. Because they don't necessarily fit, if that like, you could make them fit, but I think they are a statement of that crying out and hurt.' Emma does not clarify what the statements don't 'fit' with, but it could be fairly safely conjectured that she denies the truth of these claims because they don't fit her understanding of the character and actions of God. Similarly, at St.C's, Neil expressly stated his understanding of God to be different to that of the text: 'But it seems to imply that God is, in this case, lazy or lethargic or unresponsive. And although, there's perhaps . . . I don't think he is but that's certainly what the text or the writer seems to imply in that moment.' Neil claims that he does not believe God to be lazy or unresponsive despite the text indicating that he is. In other words, his understanding of God was a dominating factor in how he interpreted the text.

The emotional state of the psalmist was also a factor in participant's consideration of whether the text spoke rightfully of God (below), but it's highly probable this was largely only considered because of participants' pre-existing understanding of God. If participants had been presented with an exultant, praising Psalm declaring God's goodness and love, it is unlikely that they would have questioned whether the psalmist was too 'excited' or 'passionate' to be taken seriously. Or conversely, if participants had been presented with an equally melancholy psalm written from a similar place of despair but which spoke of God as faithful and sovereign, it is doubtful that the psalmist's desperate situation and emotional state would have led to them questioning the truth claims about God. What actually led to participants' consideration of the psalmist's emotional state and situation was that the psalmist professed beliefs about God that were not in keeping with participants' own doctrine of God. For example, Jesse (TO) commented that the psalmist's emotions leads to 'a bad way to . . . express who God is as a result', which relies on a preconceived understanding of the nature of God, which Jesse believes the psalmist to not be doing justice to.

64   *Chapter 4*

Conversely, participants treated the final verse, which speaks of God's steadfast love, differently and did not dismiss this claim like they did for the others, such as Martin (GLC) who said, 'what they're saying is "this is happening but we know you're good, we know you're loving" hence "rise up, come to our help, redeem us for the sake of your steadfast love".' In this statement, Martin acknowledges that the psalmist does know who God is and speaks rightfully of him.

Johnny (GLC) provides a further example of interpreting the text in light of his understanding of the nature of God. Bringing to the text his belief that God is faithful to the covenant, he interpreted that the psalmist can't be correct in what they assert: 'If you accept God's covenant promise, you know, God is definitely holding up his side of the bargain as it were, so if there's going to be a fault somewhere it's going to be on the human side with us, with the author.' Johnny's prior understanding of the character of God as faithful thus shaped his understanding of the truthfulness of the psalmist's claims about God. Though the psalmist presents God as not upholding his covenant promise, Johnny believes that God does uphold his covenant promise and therefore the psalmist's perception/account of the events they have experienced must be incorrect. Johnny placed emphasis on what he knows to be true about God's character and thus determined the reliability of the psalmist's claims according to this knowledge.

There was only one participant, Nick (WO), who affirmed that the text did give an accurate depiction of God on account of the doctrine of Scripture. In response to the denial of this by his fellow participants on account of the emotional nature of the Psalm, he claimed: 'I take [Celia] and [Jessica's] point that this is the honest outpouring of someone's thoughts and feelings to God, but it's also God's Word to us. In the end of Luke, it says that Jesus explained to his disciples what was said about him in the Psalms . . . so as Christians I think we have to take this as the Word of God, as much as any Scripture.' Nick does not state explicitly that he understands God to be culpable for the psalmist's situation, but his understanding that the Psalms are the Word of God suggests that he believes the Psalmist is right in what they're asserting. This was an anomaly, however. All other participants believed the Psalm wasn't giving an accurate picture of God and this was justified on the basis of the character of God.

Causes of Suffering

A corollary of participants' belief that God is good was their understanding that God is not responsible for evil and suffering. As such, various participants put forward alternative explanations for what has caused the suffering of the psalmist (or suffering in general) as further proof that the psalmist's

The Influence of the Doctrine of Scripture: Reading Theologically   65

claims about what God has caused are unfounded. The examples below also highlight the role of the reader's Christian context and tradition which underscores the importance of individual context in reading, explored further in chapter 9.

Gina (St.A's) was the only participant to attribute evil and suffering to Satan. As a result of being in a fallen world she understood that 'Satan is allowed power here as well'. When pushed by Charles as to why God would create Satan, Gina explained that Satan was a fallen angel who fell because of free will. She ultimately therefore attributes evil and suffering to the consequences of free will, thus absolving God. The belief that God does not cause suffering was seen most clearly in Amy's amendment of Charles' comment that 'you're believing that God is doing it' to which she responded, 'no he's allowing it.'

Vanessa and Pamela from St.C's both reflected on human nature and the tendency to blame or attribute causation incorrectly to God. Pamela reflected on this in terms of the Psalm: 'Was God associated with those things happening or was that just part of what was happening, and God was lumped in . . . just because the psalmist was writing to the leader saying "this is what God did"—is it? Or is that just life? And God's getting the blame for it?' This is a further articulation of the argument that evil and suffering are a product of a fallen world, but with the focus instead on how humans can believe God to be the cause of their suffering by associating their experience of a fallen world with the action of God. This view was shared by Jane from St.J's who couched it in theological terms, claiming that the psalmist's perspective is a consequence of their theological understanding of God's sovereignty: 'I think they're also acknowledging God's sovereignty and especially for them . . . everything is related to what God was doing, it was very much like "he's in control of everything so if this is what's happening to us, this is what he's doing to us" . . . God was their world, when they were succeeding it was because of God, when they were failing, it was because of God . . . so in a sense I think it just speaks of their understanding of his sovereignty over every situation.' Jane suggests that the theological understanding prevalent at the time of the psalmist is to attribute everything to God. Rather than this being a human tendency, as suggested by Vanessa and Pamela, Jane claims it as a theological stance; everything that happens is an act of God's sovereignty. This understanding further underscores the interpretation that the psalmist's claims are not to be taken literally.

It must be noted, however, that Jake did show some uncertainty about God's causation in relation to natural disasters and that Jane was more open to the idea that God might sometimes act or cause things to happen that result in suffering. However, she does not go as far as claiming God causes evil and modifies her claim:

66   *Chapter 4*

> Unless God tells me, there's no way I can know whether something bad has happened because he willed it or it's just happened because we live in a fallen world, or it was something we did that caused it, but I do know that there are all those possibilities, that sometimes, he's actually willing something quite, that we would perceive as negative, to happen to us. Sometimes it's something we've done ourselves, sometimes it's just like, life. So, you know, sometimes it is him. Sometimes it is his fault.

An openness to God willing something bad to happen was not expressed by any other participant and is therefore something of an anomaly, but Jane does modify her claim to say that God causes what we might 'perceive as negative'. Suffering is therefore relative to perspective, which bolstered the interpretation that the psalmist is blaming God who has not caused their suffering.

Human Perspective

In addition to the causes of suffering, participants also reflected on the limited perspective of the psalmist as a human, in contrast to God. Taylor (TO) framed this as 'tunnel vision' and commented how humans often want God to work according to their timescale when in Taylor's words, 'God can see far more.' Adam (GLC) also made a very similar comment: 'in the Psalmist's point of view, he's right, because in his limited lifespan, that's what it seems like. In God's point of view when you've got eternity, well actually salvation is just around the corner but you're not going to see it. So, I think there is that tension of our view versus the grand narrative.' Here, Adam contrasts the limited perspective of humans and the eternal perspective of God, highlighting that humanity's temporality can lead to incorrect depictions of the character of God.

Richard (TO) also reflected on the limited human understanding of God but specifically in relation to a progressive view of the Bible, stating 'as far as the perception of God is concerned of the people in the time when the Psalm was written, it does represent how they thought about God and the world.' Richard didn't elaborate on his understanding of the biblical development of perceptions of God, but he is making a similar point about the limited understanding of the psalmist.

In these types of reflections, the psalmist's limited understanding was not a characteristic particular to them but a condition of the human experience. As such, participants drew upon their own experiences to see themselves in the psalmist, fostering greater connection with the psalmist's experience, as they too are humans with limited perspective. The role of experience was thus important in their engagement with the text, explored more in chapter 9.

The Influence of the Doctrine of Scripture: Reading Theologically   67

Additionally, participants were sceptical about the psalmist's claims to innocence on the basis of their understanding of human nature/perspective and the tendencies of the Israelite people. As Stacey (St.C's) says, 'Like, I dunno, that's unbelievable . . . I mean nobody lives that way.' It was deemed to be highly unlikely that the psalmist and the community as a whole were entirely righteous, which perhaps played into participants' distrust of the psalmist's claims about God.

In addition to participants' beliefs about God, the causes of suffering, and the nature of human perspective, the genre of the Psalm played a significant role in participants' determination of its theological accuracy.

Genre

Though St.A's were the only group to explicitly state that the Psalm was a form of poetry, and the sub-genre of lament was only noted at TO, all groups understood the Psalm as a form of worship or prayer. This understanding of the genre of the Psalm meant that participants treated the text in a particular way. The Psalm was seen as an expression of feelings and emotions and not to be read for information or instruction. The clearest articulation of this came from Neil at St.C's addressing the third question on the handout sheet: '"Does this text provide an accurate depiction of God?" I think the answer to that is probably no. But I think it provides an accurate depiction of how people perceive God when they are in distress. . . .' The Psalm was understood to not speak truthfully of God because of the emotional state and nature of the psalmist's address. This was reflected at TO where Logan stated, 'I don't think we can make an overriding claim to say that God does abandon people like that but it's obviously what he was feeling at that moment.' Similarly, Jesse commented, 'for me, it isn't a reflection of God but it's certainly an image of this interaction . . . it's almost "poor me" in some senses and I think that's a bad way to kind of express who God is as a result.' For these participants, the psalmist was truthfully expressing how they felt about God, but because they were so 'caught up' in their situation and the emotion it triggered, this did not reflect who God actually is. Whereas the narrator or author of the Noah narrative is understood to be recounting an episode in the life of God and God's people, the psalmist was understood to be emotionally charged and reflecting on and responding to their current experience; as Henry (St.J's) said, 'There's real pain in there.' As such, what was significant for many participants was not the claims made but how the psalmist addresses God and responds to their experience.

As a result of the personal nature of the Psalm, participants saw the form and address of the Psalm as a paradigm for personal prayer. At GLC, the first comment of the discussion by Johnny centred on this: 'I just have real

68   *Chapter 4*

admiration for this as a way of prayer.' Similarly at WO, Celia commented, 'I think it's a wonderful example of somebody being totally honest before God and just opening up their heart and pouring out what they're actually feeling with no pretence.' The genre of the text as personal expression thus led participants to dismiss the psalmist's claims but not to dismiss the Psalm, which was seen as a valuable example of prayer.[38]

THEOLOGY AND THE DOCTRINE OF SCRIPTURE

Rather than the doctrine of Scripture determining that the text makes theological claims, participants demonstrated in their response to Psalm 44 that their doctrine of God had a significant role in their interpretation. As a result, participants nearly unanimously claimed that the Psalm did not provide theological truths about God. What does this reveal about their doctrine of Scripture?

Doctrine of God > Doctrine of Scripture

One of the first things participants' responses to the Psalm indicates about their doctrine of Scripture is how central and clear it is as a belief in readers' minds. When contrasting the way participants interpreted in light of their beliefs about God and their beliefs about Scripture, it appears that the doctrine of Scripture is not a clear and unyielding commitment in the minds of participants. Whereas the majority of participants were extremely clear about God's actions and character, and these were actively employed to guide interpretation, the doctrine of Scripture was not clearly articulated or considered as a reason to believe the psalmist to be speaking rightly of God (with the exception of Nick). The doctrine of God therefore has a significant role in interpretation and this will be explored further in chapter 7.

Doctrine of Scripture and Reading Agenda

The second issue the Psalm discussion highlights about participants' doctrine of Scripture builds on what was established in the Genesis discussion: the text was conceived in terms of its purpose to teach. Participants thus read for the purpose of learning. This is illustrated by the fact that participants' dismissal of the psalmist's claims did not lead them to the conclusion that the Psalm was a bad example of how to speak to/about God, or had no relevance to them. Participants' conception of Scripture's teaching function meant the text had a pedagogical purpose, but unlike Genesis, the Psalm didn't teach theological truths, but instead taught readers how to pray through the text's format, rather than content.

The Influence of the Doctrine of Scripture: Reading Theologically   69

What this says about the doctrine of Scripture accords with what was found in Genesis—participants' doctrine of Scripture located the meaning of the text in its teaching, and thus set the reading agenda: participants read for the purpose of learning and saw the Psalm as a paradigm for prayer.

Genre and the Doctrine of Scripture

The third and final insight the Psalm discussion highlights about the doctrine of Scripture, is that beliefs about the Bible are manifested differently according to genre. On account of the 'personal' and 'emotional' genre and the Psalm's claims about God, the Psalm was not inspired as a source of factual information or of theological insight but as an example of how to pray and live; its authority and inspiration was thus limited. By contrast, Genesis was inspired in relation to its theological insight about God. This shows that participants' beliefs about the Bible manifest themselves differently, according to the content and nature of the text at hand. The potential inconsistency of this was not raised by participants as it was for Genesis where participants were concerned what a non-historical reading of Genesis might infer for the New Testament. This could be because Genesis as a narrative drew out interpretive parallels with the Gospel narratives, whereas the Psalms are predominantly contained to one book. The role of genre is thus an important factor in considering the role of the doctrine of Scripture, and this will be explored in chapter 7.

NOTES

1. Daniel J. Treier, *Introducing Theological Interpretation of Scripture: Recovering a Christian Practice* (Grand Rapids, MI: Baker Academic, 2008).

2. This is exemplified by the twin books: Scot McKnight, *Five Things Biblical Scholars Wish Theologians Knew* (Downers Grove, IL: IVP, 2021); Hans Boersma, *Five Things Theologians Wish Biblical Scholars Knew* (Downers Grove, IL: IVP, 2021).

3. Gordon E. Michalson, Jr., *Lessing's "Ugly Ditch": A Study of Theology and History* (University Park and London: Pennsylvania State University Press, 1985), 2.

4. Darren Sarisky, 'Introduction,' in Darren Sarisky, ed., *Theology, History and Biblical Interpretation: Modern Readings,* 1st ed. (London: Bloomsbury T&T Clark, 2020). This reader offers a comprehensive overview of modern influential writings on the relationship between theology and history.

5. Sparks, *God's Word in Human Words,* 172.

6. Ibid., 174.

70 *Chapter 4*

7. For example: Walter Brueggemann, 'The Kerygma of the Deuteronomistic History: Gospel for Exiles,' *Int* 22 (1968): 387–402; Hans Walter Wolff, "The Kerygma of the Yahwist" (trans. Wilbur A. Benware), *Int* 20 (1966): 131–58.

8. Edward Klink and Darian Lockett, *Understanding Biblical Theology* (Grand Rapids, MI: Zondervan, 2012).

9. Brevard Childs, *Biblical Theology in Crisis* (Philadelphia: Westminster, 1970), 39.

10. Ibid.

11. Treier, *Introducing Theological Interpretation of Scripture.*

12. Kevin Vanhoozer and Daniel J. Treier, *Theology and the Mirror of Scripture: A Mere Evangelical Account* (London: Apollos, 2016), 175.

13. Daniel J. Treier, 'Biblical Theology and/or Theological Interpretation of Scripture?: Defining the Relationship.' *Scottish Journal of Theology* 61, no. 1 (2008): 16–31, DOI:10.1017/S0036930607003808.

14. Malley, *How the Bible Works*, 83–85.

15. Ibid., 119.

16. Perrin, *Bible Reading*, 234–37.

17. Ibid., 237.

18. Bielo, *Words Upon the Word*, 63–67.

19. Astley, Fisher, and Wilcox, 'A Survey of Bible Reading Practices and Attitudes to the Bible among Anglican Congregations', 382–95.

20. Beynon and Sach, *Dig Deeper*, 126.

21. Thiselton, 'Understanding God's Word', 98.

22. Packer, *God Has Spoken*, 98.

23. Ward, *Words of Life*, 139–40.

24. Enns, *Inspiration and Incarnation.*

25. Thompson, *Doctrine of Scripture*, 163.

26. Nancy deClaissé-Walford, Rolf Jacobson, and Beth Tanner, *The Book of Psalms* (Grand Rapids, MI: W. B. Eerdmans, 2014), 408.

27. For example: William Bellinger and Walter Brueggemann, *Psalms* (New York: Cambridge University Press, 2013), 209; Loren Crow, 'The Rhetoric of Psalm 44,' *Zeitschrift für die Alttestamentliche Wissenschaft* 103, no. 3 (1992).

28. For 'praise' see: Dalit Rom-Shiloni, 'Psalm 44: The Powers of Protest,' *The Catholic Biblical Quarterly* 70, no. 4 (2008): 686. For 'invocation' see: James Mays, *Psalms* (Louisville, KY: John Knox Press, 1994), 177.

29. For example: Peter Craigie, *Psalms 1–50*, 2nd ed. (Nashville, TN: Nelson, 2004), 333.

30. Ibid., 335.

31. For example: Nancy deClaissé-Walford, 'Psalm 44: O God, Why Do You Hide Your Face?,' *Review and Expositor* 104 (2007): 757; Eric Lane, *Psalms 1–89* (Fearn: Christian Focus, 2006), 204.

32. Lane, *Psalms 1–89*, 204.

33. Robert Alter, *The Book of Psalms: A Translation with Commentary* (New York: Norton, 2007), 156.

34. For example: Lane, *Psalms 1–89*, 201.

The Influence of the Doctrine of Scripture: Reading Theologically   71

35. Rabinnic tradition placed the Psalm under Greek persecution and the Catholic Lectionary connects the Psalm with the capturing of the ark, described by Nancy deClaissé-Walford, 'Psalm 44,' 755–56.

36. For example: deClaissé-Walford et al., *The Book of Psalms*, 408.

37. For example: Rom-Shiloni, 'Psalm 44,' 694.

38. Rogers refers to instances where readers take something in the text as a behaviour/belief to be emulated as an 'examplar hermeneutic' which renders the text and congregational horizon as proximate. He notes the presence of this hermeneutical practice both in public and small group settings. See: Rogers, *Congregational Hermeneutics*, 104.

Chapter 5

The Influence of the Doctrine of Scripture

Reading for Today

Chapter 3 highlighted how the doctrine of Scripture had a minimal role in determining whether Genesis was historically accurate and chapter 4 established that the doctrine of Scripture had an almost non-existent role in determining whether the Psalm was theologically sound. This chapter explores the doctrine of Scripture's influence on the relevance of texts for readers today. Relevance is a given for all Christian readers, but *how* a text is understood to be relevant and the way in which relevancy functions is debated. The following overview gives a brief history of approaches to the Bible's relevancy, before turning to contemporary scholarship and fieldwork to get a sense of different approaches to reading the Bible for today.

READING FOR TODAY

Ever since there have been readers of the Bible, there have been assertions that the Bible is relevant for such readers. What it means for the Bible to be relevant is for it to in some way effect or shape the life of the reader, but this can happen in a number of ways.

At a basic level the Bible is relevant because, as Article 6 of the Church of England states, 'Scripture containeth all things necessary for salvation.'[1] The Bible is the only record of the life, death, and resurrection of Jesus Christ through whom salvation comes. In addition to this, the Bible is relevant as a source and norm of theology, as God's Word.

Yet more commonly, the relevance of Scripture refers to the individual, and the impact of the text upon their life and experience. Evangelicalism's forebearers, the Puritans of sixteenth- and seventeenth-century England, held

74   *Chapter 5*

to 'two levels of meaning in the text: "the grammatical construction" and "the spiritual and divine sense."'[2] It was the latter that made the Bible relevant for today. The Pietist movement of the eighteenth century developed the Puritan two levels of meaning in Scripture by arguing that the internal testimony of the Spirit was necessary to properly understand—in other words, to interpret the Bible properly readers must be guided by the indwelling Holy Spirit. Grenz summarises the influence of these two traditions for Evangelicalism: 'As Puritan concerns and Pietist renewal converged in the eighteenth century, they gave birth to an Evangelicalism that looked to Scripture as the vehicle through which the Spirit accomplishes the miracles of salvation and sanctification.'[3] This was the way in which Scripture was relevant, as a source of spiritual sustenance and a vehicle through which to meet God.

However, the Bible's relevance takes another form, namely, application, which has become predominant within Evangelicalism. The Bible's relevance is found in its ability to be applied to the life of the individual. In the introduction to the Tyndale NIV Life Application Bible, application is defined as 'knowing and understanding God's Word and its timeless truths. . . . A good application brings the truth of God's Word into focus, shows the reader what to do about what God is teaching, and motivates him or her to respond with action and appropriate change.'[4] The relevance of the Bible in this form is the truths that it teaches and the resultant behaviour or action this requires.

This focus upon application dovetails with another movement that has influenced Evangelical approaches to the Bible—protestant scholasticism. Whilst the Puritan and Pietist influences developed the sense of Scripture as a source of spiritual sustenance, emerging Protestant Scholasticism of the same time developed the sense of Scripture as a source of propositional truths. In the course of establishing itself against the authority of tradition and the Church in Roman Catholicism, Protestant Lutheran theology in the seventeenth century became concerned with the authority and inspiration of Scripture. Grenz notes that 'as a result, many came to treat Scripture as accurate in every detail and as a storehouse of revealed propositions.'[5] This approach to Scripture paved the way for the dominance of application. Texts are mined for their truths which will have a specific export in the life of the reader. Thus Evangelicalism has been influenced by the convergence of two seemingly disparate conceptions of the Bible's relevance. On the one hand, it is a medium of God's presence, and on the other, it is a depository of life lessons. Noll highlights the unity and diversity of Evangelicalism's dual inheritance: 'The Bible come alive for personal spiritual renewal was always foundational. But almost as prevalent were differences of opinion over how Scripture should be used to shape Christian thinking and guide the Christian life.'[6]

Scholarly Approaches to the Bible and Relevancy

As was discussed in the previous chapter, the supposed distinction between reading historically and reading theologically has had a widespread impact across theological scholarship, including implications for biblical relevance. With an increasing awareness and appreciation for the historical contingency of biblical texts, came an increasing sense of the difficulty of relating such culturally and historically distinct texts to a contemporary readership. Lessing's 'gap' within biblical scholarship became that of the chronological gap, the problem of overcoming the distance between the text and the reader such that the text can have meaning in the present. Kristen Stendahl developed categories to speak of this distinction that have become commonplace, distinguishing between what the text meant and what it means.[7] This has developed into a two-step hermeneutic, advocated in much popular evangelical literature, such as Beynon and Sach: 'We need to take care to understand before we apply. But we must get to application in the end . . . Stage 1 is to work out what response the author was looking for . . . Stage 2 is to work that out in the nitty-gritty of our lives.'[8] A further example of this hermeneutical method is below.

Within the field of hermeneutics the distinction is often referred to in terms of the author's and reader's 'horizon.' Drawing upon Gadamer, to speak of one's horizon is to refer to their context, culture, knowledge, and perspective. When it comes to interpreting texts, 'working out the hermeneutical situation means acquiring the right horizon of inquiry for the questions evoked by the encounter with tradition.'[9] The reader needs to recognise the horizonal difference between themselves and the other, and let their interpretation unfold from an appreciation of the author's horizon, rather than their own. If this is something of the discussion within scholarship, how does this compare to the way relevance functions amongst ordinary Bible readers?

Relevancy and Ordinary Readers

All empirical research on Evangelicals has found that relevance is a key expectation that readers bring to the biblical text.

Astley, Fisher, and Wilcox's Anglican survey data showed a strong consensus regarding the relevance of the Bible. In response to the statement 'The Bible is not very relevant to us today', 70.8 percent disagreed, showing a belief in the relevance of the text.[10]

Malley's interpretation of the centrality of relevance amongst his participants was that the understanding of God as author of Scripture heightened what is a common human instinct to search for relevance in a way that made Bible reading amongst Christians a unique activity.[11] Whilst Malley identifies

76   *Chapter 5*

relevance as a result of belief in the Bible's nature, his links between the doctrine of Scripture and interpretation could be illuminated. His insights prompt the question, what does it mean for the text to be 'relevant'? Might interpretive practices for establishing relevance vary according to a text's content?

Bielo identifies relevance as a key 'textual ideology' that governs Bible reading, as Malley does, which he claims guarantees fresh readings regardless of the number of times a text is read, as well as precise application to specific situations. Relevance is consequential to biblical authority 'because only the "Word of God" possesses this inherent assurance to forever be directly, personally applicable.'[12] Relevance would appear to be a specific reading habit derived from the doctrine of Scripture.

Utilising the language of horizons, Village also found that relevance proved to be an essential feature of horizon separation and preference (between the authorial and reader horizon), with a tendency for those he surveyed to avoid the author horizon for the sake of making meaning in the present.[13]

Finally, Todd suggests that interpretation is a dynamic process centred around three poles. Biblical authority is one of these, but it is held in tension with close study of the text and individual personal experience. These three poles are brought together in the interest of the sought-after outcome: learning, not in the sense of necessarily gaining knowledge, but 'gaining insight'.[14] This goal of reading is approximate to relevance—'insight' is what makes Bible study worthwhile, because it makes a difference to the reader.

It seems clear from this research that relevance is connected to the doctrinal belief that the Bible is God's Word and thus speaks to its readers. But what form does such 'relevance' take and how does it relate to the location of meaning? How is relevance discerned?

Hermeneutic: The Holy Spirit and Application

One of the keys to the relevance of the text is the work of the Holy Spirit who ensures right understanding and enables fresh insight and revelation. This is a prominent feature of both Anglican and Evangelical interpretation. To underscore this biblically, texts such as John 14:26 and 16:13 are often cited, which is Jesus' speech to the disciples that the Holy Spirit will teach and guide them in truth.

How exactly the Holy Spirit works is difficult to describe and pin down, so theologians and biblical scholars tend to focus on its effects both in terms of the historical text and the contemporary reader. In relation to the former, the Holy Spirit enables the ability to make connection with the Bible's authors: 'But the capacity to put oneself in the shoes of Isaiah, or Paul, or John, and see with his eyes and feel with his heart is the gift, not of academic training, but of the Holy Spirit through the new birth.'[15] For Thiselton, the

The Influence of the Doctrine of Scripture: Reading for Today 77

work of the Spirit in accessing the past is not independent of exegesis: 'Once again, the Spirit is not a shortcut to by-pass the need for reflection and study. The Spirit of God works through human means, and not normally independent of them.'[16]

On the other hand, the work of the Holy Spirit is also crucial in hearing God's voice through the text as a contemporary reader. As Ward puts it, 'it is only by the Holy Spirit opening our hearts and minds to his words in Scripture that we come to accept Scripture as the Word of God, to understand it and trust it.'[17] It is the work of the Holy Spirit that thus provides insight into how the text is relevant for the reader.

As has been noted, however, relevance is frequently construed in terms of application and this is often posited as found through a two-step hermeneutic. Stott refers to this as cultural transposition, which distinguishes between a text's meaning (the revelation) and its medium (its communication). Cultural transposition involves recognising the eternal revelation amidst the cultural communication of the message. 'The procedure now is to identify the essential revelation in the text (what God is saying here), to separate this from the cultural form in which he chose to give it, and then to re-clothe it in appropriate modern cultural terms.'[18] This is deemed to be only necessary and appropriate when the text in question contains 'two levels of discourse'—doctrinal and ethical teaching on the one hand, and its cultural and social expression on the other. This is therefore an adept method for the New Testament epistles and Jesus' teaching, but not for the majority of Old Testament narrative, poetry, or prophecy.

How is one to apply texts which are not ethical or doctrinal teachings? Stott draws upon Stendhal's distinction above, between a text's meaning (what the author meant), which is fixed, and its significance (how it affects different people and has an impact in different contexts), which is variable. The process of application thus involves the work of exegesis to identify authorial intent and then assess what this means in today's contemporary culture. Quite how this leap is made is not specified, but this is 'fusion', the counterpart and next step after 'distancing' (chapter 3).

This view of application understands the Bible to be prescribing propositional truth either for knowledge or obedience, in line with the influence of protestant scholasticism outlined above. As Ward puts it, 'Scripture, like all spoken or written language, is made up of propositional content and authorial purpose, and the two ought never to be separated if we wish to hear what God is saying in Scripture.'[19] The consequence of this is that the application is obedience; 'the privilege of knowing God's truth with certainty and precision carries with it the responsibility of obeying that truth with equal precision.'[20]

However, an alternative understanding of application questions the idea that the Bible can be reduced to instruction and conceives of Bible reading as a transformational process in and of itself, not just through the process of obeying instruction. Indeed, Ward also affirms this: 'When we read the Bible, we must be ready, in the first instance, for God to *act* on us and in us. For, as we encounter his words, and as we encounter the actions he performs by means of them, we are encountering God himself.'[21] Yet for Ward, this manifests itself in asking the questions 'what is the Lord teaching me here? . . . and what . . . is the Lord wanting to *do* with that teaching, to me and in me?'[22] For others, application doesn't come about through asking lessons of applied learning, but is rather something that happens in and through the process of reading, rather than afterwards. It focuses on the experiential quality of Bible reading rather than specific concrete calls to action. Brigg's summarises this well; 'The "application" of the story comes through the wholesale effect of being transformed by watching/hearing it properly, as a word about who this God is that we are trying to know and love in our Christian lives.'[23] In addition, then, this view does not suppose that application involves reading the Bible for answers about specific life situations: 'The Bible is not a textbook guide to modern situations, but is what makes the Christian the person he is. Because the Bible makes him into a person of Christian mind and Christian judgement, the Christian may reflect responsibly and rationally about God's will in and for the present. The Bible makes the Christian; the Christian responds to the situation.'[24] This view is not at odds with application in the form of applied learning but demonstrates a different emphasis with regard to the nature of application. In the first view, the Bible is understood as a book of propositional truths to be learnt and obeyed in specific choices and behaviours. In the second view, the Bible is understood as a transformational text that changes character through the virtue of reading, which then informs specific choices and behaviours.

EPHESIANS 5:21–6:9

The test case for how participants made the Bible relevant was their reading of Ephesians 5:21–6:9, given the subtitle 'The Christian Household' in many modern Bible translations. This passage sets out the nature and conduct of three different relationships: wives and husbands, children and parents, and slaves and masters. This comes in the context of a larger discussion about the new life 'in Christ' and what that means for everyday behaviour and living.

The first relationship, wives and husbands, begins the household instructions and is given more explication than the other relationships. Wives are told to submit to their husbands on the grounds that the husband is head of the wife, analogous to Christ being head of the church. Husbands are then told to love their wives analogous to Christ's love for the church, which is described

The Influence of the Doctrine of Scripture: Reading for Today   79

as having a sanctifying quality. Christ loves the church as his own body and so husbands should do the same to their wives. Genesis 2:24 is drawn upon to validate that a husband and wife are one flesh, and therefore to love one's wife is to love oneself.

Children are addressed next and told to obey their parents according to the commandments in order to receive the promise of inheriting the earth. Fathers are then instructed not to provoke their children but to raise them in the discipline and instruction of the Lord.

Finally, slaves are told to obey their masters as they would obey Christ and to do this with integrity and willingness as if to God, because good will be rewarded regardless of position. The masters are then addressed and told to do the same, to refrain from threats and are reminded that all serve the same God who is impartial.

Rationale for Selection

The challenge of relevancy in Ephesians is twofold: first, how the text is understood to be relevant, and second, to what extent relevancy is related to the doctrine of Scripture.

There are several instructional sections from the epistles that I could have chosen, but Ephesians has clear overlaps with contemporary life in speaking of family relationships yet also areas of difference in speaking of slaves. Moreover, the topic of relationships not only is something Christians care about and seek to conduct in accordance with God's will, but is also culturally bound, making it a fruitful issue for exploring relevance.

As Evangelical Anglicans are concerned to follow the Bible's ordinances considering they are from God, the question becomes how to do this given the cultural distance between the time of writing and the reader. In the case of Ephesians, how is relevance navigated across three different relationships, one of which (slaves and masters) simply does not apply to modern-day readers? The key point to observe is not that the text is deemed relevant but both how it's understood as relevant across the 'gap' and also how consistent approaches to relevancy are.

A specific component of this challenge will be the text's acceptance and upholding of the institution of slavery. Considering Christian leaders were a significant driving force behind the abolition of the slave trade, it is troubling for some readers that the Ephesians passage condones slavery and does not question its practice. If slavery is inherently wrong and against the principles of Christian faith, then how can support for it be in God's own word?

In order to prompt participants to discuss issues of relevance, the third question on the handout asked, 'Do you think this text has any relevance for life today?' It was anticipated that participants would likely discuss these issues

80   *Chapter 5*

without the need for a prompt question, but the inclusion of the question would sharpen these reflections as to what specifically is relevant and why.

Scholarship Overview

The main topics discussed by commentators in relation to Ephesians 5:21–6:9 are: (1) the cultural gap between the time of the writer and the modern reader, (2) understanding the concepts of submission and headship, (3) the practice of slavery, (4) the author and audience of Ephesians, and (5) the text in relation to the rest of the Bible.

Interpreters of Ephesians tend to fall into two categories regarding the cultural gap between the text and reader: direct application[25] or application of underlying principles.[26] The latter has a tendency to consider more aspects of the text's culture and context to ascertain what the key 'principle' is that can be enacted today.[27] The former tends to focus on the text and take it as it stands for contemporary life. This approach provides various rationale for the consistency of direct application, with claims being made as to how to draw the lines between what is directly applicable (marriage and family advice) and what is cultural (owning slaves).[28]

A topic of discussion amongst scholarship concerns how to understand submission and headship. Whilst many commentators acknowledge the dignity of submission and differentiate it from 'obedience', others conflate the two terms.[29] Much debate also occurs around verse 21 inciting all to submit to one another, and how this relates to understanding wifely submission.[30] Approaches to headship tend to form two camps with one side arguing the term is authoritative and reflects hierarchy[31] and the other claiming the term means 'source' or origin.[32]

Slavery is also given much attention and Christian scholars in particular are keen to stress that slavery was such a part of life at the time of Ephesians that it's unreasonable to expect the author to condemn it. Commentators also stress that slaves are treated as equal members of the Christian community by being addressed in the letter and the instructions promote fair treatment.[33]

Moving away from the cultural issues surrounding the Ephesians text is the issue of the authorship and audience of Ephesians. Whether the text was written by Paul or not becomes an issue of immense importance when apostolic authorship is connected to biblical authority.[34] Arguments for and against Pauline authorship are complex and no general view emerges. Some scholars choose to believe the text was written by Paul because this is what the text claims for itself,[35] but others reflect that pseudepigraphy is common and does not necessarily imply the text was intended to be deceptive.[36]

The final topics discussed by commentators is how Ephesians compares with other passages such as Galatians 3:28, which declares the eradication of

The Influence of the Doctrine of Scripture: Reading for Today 81

gender and position in light of Christ.[37] Scholars also point out Ephesians's similarity with Colossians,[38] as well as the references it makes to Genesis and the commandments.

DISCUSSION SUMMARIES

Application

As was expected, participants sought to apply the text, which in corroboration with McClintock Fulkerson's American empirical research, highlights how readers 'understand the nature of Scripture as a text that makes claims upon their lives.'[39] On the whole, my participants wanted to take the underlying principles of the text and apply them to their own lives, rather than take the instructions straight off the page. Jake (St.A's) articulated this most clearly: 'Once you've understood the historical context, you don't I think in my view, you don't map across from that to the present day literally in every respect, you would look for the underlying principles and you see which ones you would apply to the present day.' Jake articulates the need to understand historical context and specifies that it is the underlying principles of the text that are applicatory. At St.C's and St.A's, where this view was most strongly espoused, the resulting applications were fairly broad and general. Both discussions concluded that the application for them as modern individuals is to love, accept, and serve whoever they come into contact with. This application goes far beyond the content of the text, which only addresses three specific relationships. This is not to say that participants at St.C's and St.A's didn't believe the text to have an applicatory force for the specific relationships mentioned, but rather that the underlying principles could be more broadly applied.

Such broad applications were closely connected with considerations of the historical societal context of the text. This allowed participants to reflect on how the first recipients would have heard the letter's instructions and the extent to which they would have been surprising or subversive, establishing the revolutionary nature of the instructions. The link between historical context and modern-day application was therefore something akin to the 'spirit' of the instructions. The author was proposing something radical and progressive for the time. This knowledge was then utilised not only to emphasise that the instructions are positive and not oppressive, but also to underscore that modern application should encapsulate the same 'spirit' of the original instructions, leading to applications focusing on the instruction's 'underlying principles,' which took the form of a general attitude or ethic,

82 *Chapter 5*

rather than specific behaviours and actions. An example of this comes from Vanessa (St.C's):

> I think because it addresses quite specific relational situations, sometimes we look at this kind of passage like an instruction manual. And try and then cookie-cutter apply it to our own lives but I think that there is a huge amount of relevance in the principles behind it, the principles that, where you have power, you have it to serve the person that you have power over, the principle that we should submit to one another, that we should prefer one another, the principle that we should serve those who are in power over us as if they were Christ. Those kind of principles are really applicable in any relationship, in any walk of life, you know any one of us will have power dynamics in a lot of our relationships and this speaks quite heavily into how we handle those power dynamics.

Vanessa offers broad applicatory lessons to relationships of power and rejects that the text should function as an 'instruction manual' but rather offers principles to follow. This comment was made towards the end of the group's discussion, which was largely focused on the historical societal context of the text.

A further example comes from TO who reflected on cultural context, and several participants made the point that the instructions were 'ground-breaking' and 'radical' for their time. This led Luke to make the following reflection: 'I just wonder when people look back on the postmodern turn, how they're going to look at what we did with the Gospel and what we did with Paul's teaching and how we applied it today—how much of it would seem really weird to them? Anyway, just reckoning with that point of: are we as radical as Paul is being, in our day?' Recognition that the text was radical for its historical context led Luke to reflect on whether contemporary application was as equally radical.

However, in addition to such broader applications related to attitude and ethics, it should be noted that specific applications were also considered, particularly at St.J's, where the conversation was slightly more personal than the other two groups. St.J's extensive discussion concerning the contractual nature of the instructions demonstrates a close reading of the text and a tendency to apply the instructions directly, seen in Frank's question: 'Do you think it's ok, if you're in one of these scenarios, to say "this is what I'm doing, this is how you're making me feel?" is that allowed in this passage, to confront, not confront, to challenge or to explain how one's feeling, if you know what I mean? Is that allowed?' Frank is looking to the passage to understand specifically what actions and behaviours are 'allowed'. This reading takes the passage as instructional, determining what can and can't be said to the other relational party. This demonstrates the converse of the positive correlation

The Influence of the Doctrine of Scripture: Reading for Today 83

between historical context and general applications—St.J's reflected on the context of the text much less and therefore focused on more specific behavioural applications. As participants at St.J's didn't explore the historical context with regard to marriage, they did not reflect upon the 'spirit' of the instructions and therefore didn't apply the text through the identification of underlying principles.

In some groups, applications were more equally split between the two forms: specific behaviours or actions, or broader attitudes or ethics, and these weren't always mutually exclusive. For example, Martin from GLC offered his specific application that when he and his wife can't reach a mutual decision, he has the final say as the head of the household. This was a specific outworking of their understanding of the text. However, Adam, also from GLC and who was unmarried, offered an application that encapsulated a general attitude, which was that you love and serve others. The specifics of what this actually means in terms of behaviour or action was not explored but is an example of taking the 'underling principle' or 'meaning' of the text.

Some participants recognised that the application of the 'underlying principle' or 'meaning' of the text would look different depending upon context, such as Luke (TO) who said:

> It might look different in the way that we work it out and we apply it but you know, it's a question of, wherever you are in life, whatever our station is, so to speak, if we can talk in those terms, if we're serving Christ then we're serving other people and we do that to the best of our ability in the midst of our circumstances and the Kingdom of God transcends our current culture, it calls us to a different culture, the culture of the Kingdom, the culture of heaven, whatever you want to call it. And that might look different to different cultural contexts in different times and societies in the world, but I think that point still stands.

Luke explicitly states that the 'principle' of the text, which for him is serving Christ by serving others and living according to the Kingdom of God, manifests itself differently according to context.

Reasons for Relevance

Though participants clearly subscribed to the text's relevance in seeking to apply it to their lives, this was rarely articulated as a consequence of the doctrine of Scripture. Just because this was not articulated does not mean it was not a considerable factor, but it is worth considering what reasons participants did provide for their belief in the text's relevancy.

In general, relevancy was simply assumed. For example, Amy began the discussion at St.A's exclaiming that she'd always found the passage difficult

84   *Chapter 5*

because her husband wasn't a Christian, so she didn't know how to apply it. This reveals that Amy believes in the text's relevancy as she sought to apply it, but she gave no discernible reason as to why she would seek to apply it.

Content

The majority of rationales provided for the text's relevancy related to the content of the text itself—it was relevant because of its subject matter, which still made sense for contemporary society. For example, Neil from St.C's commented on the similarity between the text's context and his own, 'I think ancient Rome, we are like a modern Rome in the sense of immorality, inequality, infidelity, you know, all those things make it startlingly relevant.' The text was relevant on account of it addressing a similar context. Similarly, Henry (St.J's) articulated that the instructions to husbands and wives reflect contemporary gender differences:

> It is actually, natural in a sense for a woman to love a man, much more so for a man to love a woman, and a man that's been married often has to work how he can make that real and how it can actually demonstrate that and he can reflect that so that the wife can actually feel like that. But the woman, as I say, loving is so natural that women will support their husbands even if they're murderers and everything else or rapists and all that sort of stuff, because that's part of how women are. But what a man needs is not that his wife should love him but that the wife should respect him, value him, affirm him, bless him, encourage him.

Henry believes the instructions given to reflect how men and women function in relationships today, which affirms their relevancy. In both these examples, the context of the reader plays a part in establishing the text's relevance. A strikingly similar comment to Henry's was made by Adam (GLC) who stated:

> It really stands up because I think some psychologists did the languages men and women speak and women have this language of love and men have this language of respect. And you know, it's here, two thousand years ago. So, a man should love his wife 'I should learn that means something to her that it doesn't quite mean for me', and a wife should respect her husband. I think women do tend to tell people that they love them more, but as a man I don't always hear that but if she says 'hey, I respect you man!' it's like 'ah cool!' and it kind of goes through to a man in a way in which the word 'love' might not and vice versa.

Here Adam demonstrates belief in the relevancy of the text because its emphasis upon a man's need for respect and a woman's need for love is mirrored in Adam's personal experience and by psychological research. Similarly, Luke

The Influence of the Doctrine of Scripture: Reading for Today 85

(TO) also demonstrated the text's relevance according to its content: 'that point that we've all got a boss, we've all got a Lord, is still true today isn't it really?' The text is relevant because contemporary readers still exist within the matrices of relationships that the text speaks of. Though the practice of slavery no longer exists in Western culture, Luke equates the slave master of the text with the bosses of today and therefore sees the content of the text as still relevant because it reflects the human experience. The reader's context is a crucial factor in this determination of relevancy, discussed in chapter 9.

Authorship

There were two occasions upon which relevancy was predicated on the author of the text. In response to the third question on the handout asking whether the text was relevant, Neil (St.C's) stated: 'Course it has relevance. I think Paul, you know, Paul's work, his letters work, God-breathed, look at the book of Romans, look at Corinthians . . . he clearly had the Holy Spirit in him and anyone who says otherwise does not know what they're talking about so, and we have to apply, we have to assume it's the same in Ephesians.' For Neil, the relevance of the text was a corollary of the spirit-filled nature of the author that produced 'God-breathed' works. This is also an indirect affirmation of the doctrine of Scripture but couched in terms of the author's sensibilities rather than the text's nature as a whole. Implied in Neil's comment is the idea that as the text is 'God-breathed' it is also divine communication, which is understood to be intrinsically relevant.

Sam (WO) also suggested that the authority or relevancy of the text for readers often derives from its author: 'I think that this text causes so much debate and discussion among Evangelicals in particular from my experience because we start with the presumption that Paul must have been right, whatever he was saying.' Sam observes that Evangelical understandings of Pauline authorship lead readers to an unquestioning acceptance of Paul's writings simply because of who he is. As such, Sam maintained that many readers believe 'submitting to Paul's authority is more important' than any other source of authority. In other words, Sam believes that for many, the text is relevant to life today because its author is believed to have the authority to speak into how life should be lived. Interestingly, Sam didn't equate Pauline authorship with divine authorship as Neil did, though this could be implied. The implications of what this reveals about Sam's approach to authority is discussed in chapter 6.

86   *Chapter 5*

Doctrine of Scripture

A more specific articulation of the relevancy of the text based on its being biblical came from Jane (St.J's) who, addressing the issue of a modern reader's ability to understand, said,

> I take the stance that we should be able to understand it because it's what we have to understand how God wants us to live our lives and He knows that and also we have the Holy Spirit who guides us in all the truth and hopefully helps us to interpret what's going on, and then we also have people who know loads of stuff and can give us context but if we can't understand this text because it's not culturally relevant then how can we use the Bible to live our lives?

Jane understands that in addition to the work of the Holy Spirit and contextual information, the text was relevant by virtue of the fact that it's a biblical text, given by God who is concerned to communicate through the Bible how contemporary life should be lived.

Nick also claimed the text was relevant because of its biblical nature. Nick actually didn't use the term 'relevant' but referred to the text's authority. However, these are closely connected concepts; a text can't be actively authoritative but irrelevant. Nick stated, 'for me, it's in the Bible, so there is no higher authority. I believe in Scripture, tradition and reason as an Anglican, but I believe that you can't just say "but I think the Bible's wrong".' Nick offers the traditional Anglican triad of 'Scripture, tradition and reason' as authoritative sources but stresses this does not allow readers the freedom of contradiction, because of Scripture's status as the ultimate authority. This comment was made in response to Sam who questioned the relevancy of the text for contemporary life based on moral and ethical principles. Nick reasserts that the text is relevant, or authoritative, because of its biblical nature. This was the only articulation of the text's authority and relevance based directly from the doctrine of Scripture.

It should also be clarified, however, that various participants did articulate points at which they felt the text was not relevant or didn't relate to contemporary society. However, this did not detract from an overall thrust that understood the text to be relevant to life.

RELEVANCY AND THE DOCTRINE OF SCRIPTURE

What do these insights about the relevancy of the text indicate about participants' doctrine of Scripture? Participants showed that they believed the text to be relevant to contemporary life by seeking to apply the text. Relevancy is thus closely connected with authority because participants demonstrated the text's authority in looking to it to inform their attitudes and behaviours. However, subscription to the relevancy of the text was rarely accounted for as a consequence of the doctrine of Scripture. Instead, it was predominantly validated in terms of the text's content. Though it could be that participants based their belief in the relevancy of the text solely on the text's context, I think it is more likely that their appreciation of the relevancy of the text's content is offered as additional support for a pre-existing belief in the relevancy of the text on account of the doctrine of Scripture. I would suggest this is the case on several grounds.

First, the relevancy of the text as a biblical text was evident in the Genesis and Psalm discussion. Participants sought meaning in the text's teaching about belief and/or behaviour as a result of a conception of Scripture in terms of its function: teaching. What the text taught was theological insight about God and how to live—meanings that related to the life of the reader.

Second, it is likely that the ubiquity of the text as relevant as a result of its teaching function meant that participants didn't need to account for it on biblical grounds. This can be seen by the fact that the assumption of relevancy, which was rarely defended or explained, sits in contrast with how participants handled the question of the text's historicity in relation to Genesis. Relevancy was assumed, but historicity was certainly not a given. This suggests that relevancy is a significant component of participants' working doctrine of Scripture.

Third, that participants spoke more of the text's relevancy on the grounds of its content could also perhaps be seen in light of the secular cultural context of participants that proved to be influential for the reading of Genesis. Participants were keenly aware that the Bible is problematic for contemporary culture and therefore their demonstration of its relevance on the basis of its content could be seen as the influence of such a culture, where the Bible's assumed relevance because of its divine origins would hold no weight.

On account of these reasons, it could be said that relevancy was a significant component of participants' doctrine of Scripture as a result of their perception of the text's teaching function. The doctrine of Scripture's role was thus the same as it was for Genesis and the Psalm: it determined the purpose of reading for learning and thus the location of meaning in the text's teaching with regards to theological insight and life guidance.

Having analysed participant's responses from the final text challenge, it is worth putting the insights from the three texts together to begin to form a picture of the influence of the Doctrine of Scripture upon interpretation. This is the task of the next chapter.

88   *Chapter 5*

NOTES

1. 'Themes and Principles', https://www.anglicancommunion.org/media/254164/2
-Themes-Principles.pdf.

2. Stanley Grenz, 'Nurturing the Soul, Informing the Mind,' in *Evangelicals &
Scripture: Tradition, Authority and Hermeneutics*, eds. Vincent Bacote, Laura Miguélez, and Dennis Okholm (Downers Grove, IL: Inter-Varsity Press, 2004), 26.

3. Ibid., 27.

4. NIV Life Application Study Bible, 3rd ed, A20.

5. Grenz, 'Nurturing the Soul,' 28.

6. Mark A. Noll, 'Evangelicals and the Bible', in ed. Andrew Atherstone and David
Ceri Jones, *The Routledge Research Companion to the History of Evangelicalism*
(Abingdon: Routledge, 2019).

7. Kristen Stendahl, "Biblical Theology, Contemporary", in *Interpreter's Dictionary of the Bible* (Nashville: Abingdon Press, 1962), A–D: 418–32.

8. Beynon and Sach, *Dig Deeper*, 139–40.

9. Hans-Georg Gadamer, *Truth and Method*, 2nd ed., trans. Joel Weinsheimer and
Donald G. Marshall (New York: Crossroad, 1991), 302–3.

10. Astley, Fisher, and Wilcox, 'A Survey of Bible Reading Practices and Attitudes
to the Bible among Anglican Congregations', 382–95.

11. Malley, *How the Bible Works*, 105–8.

12. Bielo, *Words Upon the Word*, 59.

13. Village, *The Bible and Lay People*, 84.

14. Todd, 'The Talk,' 245.

15. Packer, *God has Spoken*, 98.

16. Thiselton, 'Understanding God's Word,' 119.

17. Ward, *Words of Life*, 92.

18. Stott, *The Bible*, 47.

19. Ward, *Words of Life*, 174.

20. Packer, *Truth and Power,* 29.

21. Ward, *Words of Life*, 175.

22. Ibid.

23. Briggs, *Reading the Bible Wisely*, 94–95.

24. Thiselton, 'Understanding God's Word,' 118.

25. For example: Robert Sproul, *Ephesians* (Fearn: Christian Focus, 1994).

26. For example: Lisa Baumert, 'Biblical Interpretation and the Epistle to the Ephesians,' *Priscilla Papers* 31, no. 4 (2017): 28–32.

27. For example: Gordon D. Fee, 'The Cultural Context of Ephesians 5:18–6:9,'
Priscilla Papers 31, no. 4 (2017): 4–8.

28. For example: John Stott, *The Message of Ephesians: God's New Society* (Nottingham: Inter-Varsity Press, 1979), 220–21.

29. For example: Ralph Martin, *Ephesians, Colossians and Philemon* (Atlanta,
GA: John Knox Press, 1991), 70; Stott, *The Message of Ephesians*, 232–33.

The Influence of the Doctrine of Scripture: Reading for Today   89

30. Both sides of this debate are summarised by Benjamin L. Merkle, 'The Start of Instruction to Wives and Husbands—Ephesians 5:21 or 5:22?,' *Bibliotheca Sacra* 174 (2017): 179–92.

31. For example: David M. Park, 'The Structure of Authority in Marriage: An Examination of Hupotasso and Kephale in Ephesians 5:21–33,' *Evangelical Quarterly* 59, no. 2 (1987): 117–24.

32. For example: Baumert, 'Biblical Interpretation,' 31.

33. For example: Benjamin L. Merkle, *Ephesians* (Nashville, TN: B&H Academic, 2016); Stott, *Ephesians*, 252.

34. Stephen E. Fowl, *Ephesians: Being a Christian, at Home and in the Cosmos* (Sheffield: Sheffield Phoenix Press, 2014), 10.

35. For example: Stott, *Ephesians*, 21.

36. Fowl, *Ephesians*, 10.

37. For example: Sproul, *Ephesians*, 137–38; Stott, *Ephesians*, 216.

38. Frederick Bruce, *The Epistles to the Colossians, to Philemon, and to the Ephesians* (Grand Rapids, MI: Eerdmans, 1984), 401.

39. Mary McClintock Fulkerson, *Places of Redemption: Theology for a Worldly Church* (Oxford: Oxford University Press, 2007), ch. 6, https://hdl-handle-net.ezproxyd.bham.ac.uk/2027/heb.30685, EPUB.

Chapter 6

The Influence of the Doctrine of Scripture

Some Conclusions

What has been established so far from the text challenges in chapters 3–5 is that participants conceived of the Bible in terms of its function as God's resource and this function related to divine communication and teaching. This indicates the role of the doctrine of Scripture is in setting the reading agenda—reading for the purpose of learning theological insight and life guidance. Take the following quotes, for example:

'it's for us to use, to learn'

'it's a story to learn from'

'the most important thing . . . is taking on board the reflection of God'

'my main learning from this text . . .'

'teaching for the future'

'we can learn a lot from'

'it's another part of God we're learning about'

'the Bible teaches'

These quotes are not exhaustive but evidence participants' emphasis on learning and information.

92   *Chapter 6*

Learning and Teaching

A dominant emphasis on learning and teaching resonates with Smith's 'hand-book model' of the Bible: 'The Bible teaches doctrine and morals with every affirmation that it makes, so that together those affirmations comprise something like a handbook or textbook for Christian belief and living.'[1] Smith identifies this as his tenth feature of 'Biblicism', a theory of Bible-use popular in America, which he acknowledges is difficult to pin down. My participants certainly showed aspects of these ten features, but whether or not they can be fairly classed as 'Biblicists' is questionable, particularly given the differences between Evangelicalism in America and Britain. One of the significant differences, stemming back to the 1960s and 1970s, was that whilst in America the 'battle for the Bible'[2] raged with subscription to 'inerrancy' becoming, for some, a hallmark of true Evangelicalism, the situation in the UK was somewhat different. Bebbington has noted that it is remarkable that assertions of inerrancy were minimal in England.[3] This is not to say that the UK was completely impervious to the discussion, as can be seen in the Churchman/Anvil split,[4] but rather that inerrancy didn't hold as much sway for Evangelical belief to be considered authentic. This is one of the factors that has played into several differences between British and American Evangelicals, and their approaches to the Bible.[5] To outline these differences in any more detail is beyond the scope of this book, but it is important to note regarding American Evangelical research, which should be understood as contextually distinctive from the British context.

What is clear from the British context, is that an emphasis on learning and thus the Bible as a teaching resource was not unique to my participants. Perrin found that her millennial participants 'considered that there would be something of relevance in any given passage, a lesson or principle to learn.'[6] Equally Rogers' participants at one of the churches he researched demonstrated the same emphasis: 'personal Bible reading (PBR) was described by interviewees using educative language such as teaching, training, instructing, informing and learning, although the language of rebuke and challenge was also common.'[7] Rogers describes this as rationalist emphasis, which cohered with a 'tendency to treat the Bible propositionally.'[8] A similar finding comes from Todd whose research participants, when asked what they hoped to get out of reading the Bible, 'spoke of relationship with God, and about learning. The subject of learning was expressed theologically . . . learning was seen as always providing something new, even if that was about re-appropriating the familiar.'[9] Todd nuances the learning in questions, however: 'Although all three groups identified what they did as about learning, and two groups had a tutorial-like structure, yet their kind of learning was not so much about increased knowledge and understanding of the text, as

The Influence of the Doctrine of Scripture: Some Conclusions   93

about the search for "insight". In this context insight appears to be about personal and/or shared identity being enhanced or affirmed by talking about the Bible.'[10] This demonstrates that though learning is central, there is a personal and engaged component to it, that an overemphasis on propositional content can be easily missed.[11]

Indeed even in non-Christian contexts in the UK, a perception of the Bible related to learning prevails. Recent research by Theos found that 24 percent of their survey respondents, inclusive of Christians and non-Christians, believed the Bible to be 'a useful book of guidance and advice for our lives but not the Word of God.'[12] Moreover, David Ford's research involving non-Christian male participants read the Bible primarily as a textbook; 'no matter the genre nearly all the passages were handled as if they were guidebooks of didactic texts (of questionable quality).'[13] Conceptions of the function of the Bible as about learning and therefore its nature as a teaching resource are common.

However, my participants also used more traditional doctrinal language to speak of the Bible, some of which has been mentioned already. To continue to build an understanding of participant's doctrine of Scripture, I will now turn to a consideration of what participants said/implied about the authority, sufficiency, inspiration, unity, and clarity of the Bible. How did these statements relate to a conception of the Bible in terms of its teaching function?

REFERENCES TO THE BIBLE'S NATURE

Authoritative (Sufficient)

As was noted in the Ephesians discussion, Nick (WO) gave the most explicit defence of the Bible's authority, claiming there was no higher authority, though he recognised the role of tradition and reason. As a result of the Bible's authority, Nick claimed, 'you can't just say "but I think the Bible's wrong."' Nick thus affirms the sufficiency of the Bible as source of information and the authority of the Bible in submitting to what the text asserts. However, interestingly, Nick was not a proponent of Genesis's historicity. This suggests that Nick's submission to what the text asserts is actually in relation to its teachings in the form of theological insight and life guidance, rather than information. This is further demonstrated by what Nick stated after affirming the authority of the text: 'my main learning from this text, is that . . . when we find ourselves with power over someone legally as all these three relationships involve, we should hold that lightly, again because it's provisional, it's relative to our relationship to Jesus.' What is authoritative for Nick is the underlying principle of what the text teaches about relationships of power.

94 *Chapter 6*

The same approach to authority appeared to be true for Martin (GLC) who made an implicit affirmation of the Bible's authority after Johnny repeated an interpretation he'd read that the Noah flood prefigured baptism. Johnny couldn't remember if this was an interpretation of the early church, or in the New Testament. Martin responded:

> My immediate mind with that . . . wants to argue that it's an early church inter-pretation reading a little bit too much into the text. But the problem is, if it's scriptural then I have to approach it in a different way. If it's scriptural without the faith, you just look at it academically you could just say this was their attempt to bring Jesus into the Old Testament at the very beginning of biblical theology . . . and it was wrong. But the faith element makes me not want to do that. The faith element wants me to go 'if it is in Scripture, then I need to re-examine what I think about that'.

Here, Martin evidences a clear distinction between what is biblical and what is not, demonstrating that the authority of the text, as for Nick, requires sub-mission. Like Nick, Martin also did not believe the Noah story to be histori-cal. What is authoritative is thus the Bible's theological teaching, which in this instance was the New Testament's interpretation of the meaning of the Noah narrative.

This also seemed to be the sense of Gina's (St.A's) assertion of the Bible's authority. In response to Charles' claim that he does not believe in Satan, Gina replied, 'I only go by what my Bible tells me Charles and I do believe most of it, maybe not always literally but if I don't believe it then . . . what am I trusting in if I don't trust, to me, what is a basic thing?' Gina affirms the Bible as a foundational authority in terms of its teaching about faith and thus its sufficiency; her understanding of the Christian faith comes from what the Bible says. Curiously, however, Gina also states that she does not always take the Bible literally. Like Nick and Martin therefore, this suggests that Gina's understanding of the Bible's authority relates to its teaching, which is sometimes literal—informing the reader of the state of things (such as the existence of Satan), and sometimes not literal, such as in Ephesians where Gina affirmed the text shouldn't be taken literally but its 'guidelines' were authoritative.

One participant, Sam (WO), demonstrated his resistance to the authorita-tive sufficiency of Scripture. Sam stated that one of the problems he perceives with the way the Ephesians text has been handled has been the assumption that 'submitting to Paul's authority is more important than submitting to moral law.' Two points are of note here: first, Sam refers to Paul's authority, rather than the Bible's authority. Second, it's unclear what Sam means by 'moral law.' Is this moral law related to God? The second half of his comment

The Influence of the Doctrine of Scripture: Some Conclusions   95

provides some insight: 'OK I can take this text and that's fine but it comes with a history of interpretation that's led to so much immorality . . . that if Paul did have in his mind the things that people have said historically . . . then I'm more than happy to kind of say I'm moving away from Paul because it's led to so much un-Christly action.' Sam's willingness to submit to the authority of the text's teaching is not based on the nature of the text but on its content and how in keeping with the teachings and person of Christ it is. For Sam therefore, the person of Jesus appears to be what is authoritative and the Bible is authoritative insofar as it reflects Jesus' person and teachings. Sam does not claim that the Ephesians text is not authoritative, but rather that if the author's meaning was to defend and promote slavery, as has been claimed in the past, then he could not accept the text's authority. Sam therefore demonstrates a more stringent approach to authority. In the comments noted above from other participants, the authority of the text was related to its theological teaching and insight. It appears that Sam would agree with this but with the added caveat that this had to be consistent with the person and teachings of Jesus. This was a unique approach to the authority of the text amongst participants.

In sum, participants affirmed their belief in the sufficiency of the text in their statements about the Bible's authority, which were also in keeping with a conception of the Bible related to function in the form of teaching. What was authoritative for participants was what the Bible taught, and this took a variety of forms. Consideration of how participants discerned what the Bible taught is discussed in chapter 8.

Inspired (Word of God)

Two participants explicitly referenced the inspiration of the Bible and three references were made to the Bible as the Word of God. Though both terms seemingly confirm the divine authorship of the text, curiously they appeared to have a different force in participants' usage.

Neil (St.C's) referenced that the Bible was 'God-breathed' on two occasions, the first of which was in relation to Genesis and included a mention of the Bible as the 'Word of God.' Neil was concerned how the Bible could be God's Word if it included hyperbole or embellishment. In other words, he felt the text should be read in a certain way as a result of its divine authorship and this was at odds with stylistic devices associated with human authorship. The Bible as the Word of God implied it should be read in a particular way. Similarly, Nick (WO) affirmed that the psalmist's claims must be taken as true on account of the Psalm being God's Word. The nature of the Bible as the 'Word of God' was reason to take the claims of the psalmist at face value, i.e., inform the way in which the text is read.

96 *Chapter 6*

Finally, Adam (GLC) referenced the Bible as the 'Word of God' in opposition to Martin, who suggested that the psalmist was arrogant. In response, Adam claimed this wasn't appropriate because one can't judge the Bible as it is the 'Word of God.' The nature of the Bible as God's Word thus informed what Adam could say about the text.

In all these three instances, reference to the Bible as the Word of God impacted the way in which the text was read and the conclusions that participants made about the text.

By contrast, references to the Bible's inspiration reflected participants' perception of the Bible as being predominantly functional.

Neil's second affirmation of the Bible as God-breathed in the Ephesians discussion included an affirmation that the Holy Spirit was at work in Paul,[14] which confirmed the text's relevance. The text was relevant to the reader, by virtue of its inspired nature. The inspiration of the text underscored its function to be relevant. Similarly, Martin (GLC) stated, 'I'd say that the spirit allows . . . works within and through the writer, to put forward what God desires the individual and the people of God to know. I'd say the root of all Scripture comes through the inspiration of the Spirit.' The focus of this statement of inspiration was to confirm that the final text is divinely ordained by God and carries God's intended communication. As with Neil, inspiration underscored the text's function as a medium of divine communication.

In sum, these comments confirm belief in the inspiration of the Bible and its being God's Word. References to the Bible being the Word of God functioned as justification for reading the text in a particular way, as a result of its nature. References to inspiration functioned as a validation for the Bible's nature—its relevance and ability to communicate God's meaning.

Unit/Consistent

Though some participants did affirm their belief in the consistency of God across the testaments, affirmations of the Bible's unity were instead implied, through interpretive practices where participants linked or connected disparate biblical texts, demonstrating their belief in the unity of the texts.

Gina (St.A's) implicitly affirmed her belief that the Bible was consistent in highlighting that the verse in the Psalm which speaks of God sleeping is 'controversial' because the Bible elsewhere states that God does not sleep. This is an acknowledgment that the Bible does not contradict itself and led to an interpretation of the verse in Psalm 44 as metaphorical. This instance demonstrates an expectation that the Bible was to be consistent. This is corroborated by the concern raised by some participants in the Genesis discussion about the consistency of interpretation regarding historicity and what a non-historical interpretation of Noah implies about other biblical texts.

The Influence of the Doctrine of Scripture: Some Conclusions 97

However, participants' expectation that the Bible should be consistent did not blind them to instances where it was not. On several occasions, participants contrasted the text they were reading with other biblical texts, either to identify what was unique about the text at hand, or to raise the question of why their text was different. For example, Anne (St.J's) compared the judgement of God in Noah with other occasions in the Old Testament: 'with other times when God's been angry at people or the world for not being Godly, there's usually a warning? Or like, a prophet will come and be like "repent!" But this is very much "this is going to happen" and I can see the mercy in saving a portion of mankind, but it feels quite different from a lot of the other Old Testament narratives.' By comparing God's actions in Noah with other occasions in the Old Testament, Anne highlighted the uniqueness of a lack of warning or opportunity to repent that occurs. However, neither this example nor any of the other instances where differences were noted led to claims that the Bible was inconsistent. Some participants accounted for differences on the basis of a developmental or trajectorial understanding of the Bible that witnesses to the growth of human thinking, which would explain some of these variances. On other occasions, solutions or explanations were offered as to the differences. This suggests that participants were actively committed to the consistency of Scripture and operated under this principle.

Though no explicit link was made, this commitment to the consistency of the text can be seen in the context of participants' conception of the Bible as having a teaching function. If the purpose of the Bible is to teach, then it can't be contradictory, because then it is failing to fulfil its teaching function. It could be that rather than conceive of the Bible's consistency as a result of the character of God and the nature of the Bible as God's Word, the Bible was seen as consistent because of its teaching function.

Clear

Very few participants made claims about the clarity of Scripture. The most affirmative comment came from Jane (St.J's) who stated in the Ephesians discussion that readers have to be able to understand the text as a result of the Bible being God's chosen method of communication with his people. God wouldn't provide something that people couldn't understand.

Two participants explicitly stated their inability to understand the Bible but didn't see this as an obstacle to engaging with Scripture. Rose (St.A's) affirmed that sufficient prior knowledge for reading is impossible, so she has to embrace learning as she goes: 'you just follow what you can and learn as you go. So for me, I don't expect to have a full understanding, but I just learn as I go.' Similarly, Amy (St.A's) was encouraged by Psalm 131, which she described as promoting an attitude of trust in God despite not understanding:

98   *Chapter 6*

'I get a bit of comfort from, I think it's Psalm 131, it's a short Psalm that says you know, "perhaps I'm not understanding everything but I'm just leaning on God, trusting" . . . there's probably more than 50 percent of the Bible that I just don't understand but . . . we learn a bit more as we go along.'

These quotes demonstrate that the Bible was clear enough that both Amy and Rose believe and trust it, but not enough so that they understood everything. In these comments the Bible's clarity was an issue relating to the reader and their ability to understand, rather than the text.

It appeared that the majority of participants adopted the approach of Amy and Rose without explicitly claiming so. Participants had questions and discussed and debated various aspects of the texts, which shows that they were not entirely perspicuous, but no one articulated this as egregious, instead seeing it as part of the process of engaging with the Bible, rather than an inherent flaw of the Bible itself.

The Role of References to the Bible's Nature

Analysis of why and when the above articulations about Scripture were made highlights an important further aspect of the role of the doctrine of Scripture.

In several instances, the nature of Scripture was referenced in order to validate or to argue against another participant's interpretation. This was seen in participants' references to the Bible being the Word of God in particular. The doctrine of Scripture therefore acted as a form of interpretive validation to bolster the case for a particular understanding of the text and was called upon to set interpretive boundaries, what can or can't be said of the text. This reinforces a link between doctrinal affirmation and interpretive conclusions; the former has a role in prescribing or setting limits on the latter.

However, this wasn't always the case as has been seen in the preceding chapters. Participants did not frequently defend the text's relevancy or historicity on account of the text being biblical, instead offering other reasoning. In both these instances, contemporary culture was speculated to play a role in this behaviour. This shows that whilst the doctrine of Scripture does have a role in shaping the outcomes of interpretation, it is not the only significant influence. The role of contemporary culture is explored in chapter 9.

On other occasions, the Bible's nature was referenced by participants in order to validate the divine origins of the text, particularly in light of the human elements of the text which might challenge this. These references to the doctrine of Scripture were therefore for the purpose of reassurance that the text is from or of God and underscored and validated its teaching function. Rather than validate a particular interpretation, the doctrine of Scripture was called upon to validate that the text was capable of divine communication despite the complications associated with human authorship.

The final reason that participants referenced the doctrine of Scripture was to validate the overall purpose or agenda of their interpretation. This has already been noted in the text challenges. By calling upon what they perceived to be the ultimate end of Scripture, its function to teach, participants could set the ground for their interpretive goals. The doctrine of Scripture was called upon to determine overall interpretive direction.

In summary, the doctrine of Scripture articulations functioned in the course of the discussion as a validation for interpretive conclusions, the divine origins of the text, and interpretive goals.

ENGAGEMENT PRACTICES

Having considered what participants explicitly said about the Bible, it is also worth summarising the extent to which participants' doctrine of Scripture influenced hermeneutical activity.

The focus group transcripts were coded for anything participants did with the text, distinguished from what participants said about the text. These practices were broad. For example, an engagement practice might be quoting the text, or reflecting on the author's meaning, or comparing the text to another. The following overview draws on this coding to make some statistical reflections of the doctrinally derived hermeneutical activity of participants.

Historical Practices

Participants engaged in a number of practices that related to the historical, human nature of the text, accounting for 24 percent of their overall hermeneutical activity. These included reflecting on the author's identity, intention, thinking, or worldview; the circumstantial context of the text; the theological context of the text; the text's original recipients; and the specifics of the text's language and translation.[15] Though participants often lacked relevant knowledge for proper 'historical-grammatical' exegesis, the fact that just under a quarter of their engagement practices were aimed at elucidating the text's historical context reflects participants' appreciation of the human and historically embedded nature of the Bible and exegetical approach.

However, as has been seen, the conclusions of such exegesis were not always concurrent with a commitment to a doctrine of Scripture that would insist on the historicity and factual truth of the biblical material.

Doctrine of Scripture Practices

Whilst historical engagement practices might be employed by any reader of the biblical text, participants demonstrated a number of practices that were underpinned by their belief in the text as Scripture, accounting for 26 percent of their hermeneutical activity. Much of this activity was underlined by a belief in the unity of the biblical canon. Participants contextualised the texts they were reading within a canonical trajectory, as well as compared and contrasted the texts with other biblical material. Canonical practices accounted for just under half of the total 26 percent of doctrinally derived practices. The majority of the rest of doctrinally derived practices related to the practice of application—seeking guidance from the text as to belief and behaviour for the contemporary reader. Participants offered specific applications, and discussed application possibilities and the text's relevant underlying principles.

Belief Practices

In addition to canonical readings and application, participants also engaged in practices that put the text in conversation with their broader beliefs and doctrines, accounting for 10 percent of their engagement practices. Although these ways of engaging with the text didn't specifically reference the Bible, they drew on Bible-related content, such as salvation history or the person of Jesus, and were thus an extension of a canonical approach.

Personal Practices

Moreover, 9 percent of engagement practices drew upon the reader's personal context. These were not instances of application, but various ways in which participants brought the text in dialogue with themselves, such as responding to Ephesians 'as a wife' or empathising with the character of Noah. Whilst application as a practice is more closely tied with the doctrine of Scripture as a result of the text's relevance, these personal practices reveal a willingness to personally engage with the text, and this can be seen as a consequence of a belief in the relevancy of the text.

Taking biblical, doctrinal, and personal engagement practices together then, 45 percent of participants' engagement practices appeared to be the result of their belief in God and the text as Scripture.

It was previously outlined that an Evangelical Anglican doctrine of Scripture is ultimately a belief in the Bible as both God's Words and human's words and as a result hermeneutics must encompass practices that reflect both these aspects of the text. This did appear to be the case for my participants,

The Influence of the Doctrine of Scripture: Some Conclusions   101

given that historical and doctrinal practices together accounted for 69 percent of engagement practices, reflecting participants' belief in the dual authorship of the text. In particular, by engaging more with practices that derived from belief in the text as Scripture, participants demonstrated that their doctrine of Scripture did dictate a lot of what participants did with the text. However, the text challenges discussed in the previous chapters have demonstrated how this was not always reflected in participant's interpretative conclusions. In other words, the practices participants used to explore the text were reflective of a commitment to the doctrine of Scripture, but the conclusions they came to seemed to prioritise different commitments. This suggests there are other key factors at work that affect the interpretative process.

THE DOCTRINE OF SCRIPTURE AS A LENS

What is the overall emerging picture of participants' doctrine of Scripture given their response to the text's challenges, references to the nature of the Bible, and their engagement practices?

Participants subscribed to the inspiration, authority, truth, and especially the relevance of the text as closely related concepts. The relevance of the text appeared to be particularly dominating in participants' perception of the Bible, resulting in a conception of Scripture that was predominantly concerned with its teaching function in the readers' lives. As a result, the role of the doctrine of Scripture was to set the reading agenda. Participants' belief in the Bible as a teaching resource determined where the meaning of the text was to be found. However, participants also demonstrated diversity in both how they read the text and what conclusions they came to. A commitment to the text's truth did not ipso facto lead to a belief that the text was historically or even theologically accurate. Participants' determination of such issues was influenced by a number of factors both external and internal to the text, including the doctrine of God, the genre of the text, and aspects of their individual context, issues which the following three chapters will explore.

In the field of hermeneutics, these influential factors, inclusive of the doctrine of Scripture, are known as the reader's 'horizon.' Thiselton describes the reader's horizon as follows,

> The horizon or pre-intentional background is thus a network of revisable expectations and assumptions which a reader brings to the text, together with the shared patterns of behaviour and belief with reference to which processes of interpretation and understanding become operative. The term 'horizon' calls attention to the fact that our situatedness in time, history and culture defines the present (though always expanding) limits of our 'world', or more strictly the

102   *Chapter 6*

limits of what we can 'see'. The term 'background' calls attention to the fact that these boundaries embrace not only what we can draw on in conscious reflection, but also the pre-cognitive dispositions or competences which are made possible by our participation in the shared practices of a social and historical world.[16]

The language of horizon has been advocated for by Thiselton, who was himself influenced largely by Gadamer,[17] because it incorporates the idea that one's horizons can expand and move. This is often the result of engaging with the horizon of another, and in the case of reading, the reader's horizon is confronted by the horizon of the text and the text's author.

It has long been acknowledged in the field of hermeneutics that what the reader brings to the text, in terms of their horizon, affects what is read, understood, and interpreted. However, when considering the doctrine of Scripture and other specific factors that make up a reader's horizon, the metaphor becomes less adept. Though a horizon can change and expand, only one horizon can exist at any one time; the metaphor breaks down if one starts to speak of multiple horizons. Yet a reader's horizon contains multitudes, as Thiselton draws attention to above. How do particular features of a reader's horizon affect their engagement with the text?

In order to explore the dynamics of the reader's horizon in more detail, the language of horizons will not suffice. Instead, I will be using the metaphor of reading the text through multiple lenses. This does not preclude the concept of a reader's 'horizon.' Indeed, the combination and totality of a reader's lenses equates to their horizon. What the metaphor of lenses allows for is nuance as to the specifics of the 'expectations and assumptions' and 'patterns of behaviour and belief' that readers bring to texts, how these relate to one another in the forming of a horizon, and what impact they have on interpretation. The metaphor of lenses appreciates the complexity of what a reader brings to the text.

In physical optometry, a person can look through a number of lenses at any given time. One might wear glasses or contact lenses, or both, and be looking through binoculars, a telescope, a microscope, or a camera. The same is true for reading but to a much greater extent. Readers view the text through a large number of lenses at any given moment, and these can vary in combination and strength, affecting what it is 'seen'.

What has been explored in this chapter is how the doctrine of Scripture functions as a lens through which the text is viewed. But what the preceding chapters have also identified is that this wasn't the only lens through which participants read the Bible. The other dominant reading lenses participants demonstrated will be explored in the following three chapters but are depicted in figure 6.1. I am indebted to Andrew Todd for this diagram structure that depicts the use of lenses, following his portrayal of the interaction of prominent opposing 'voices' identified from his empirical research.[18]

Todd's analysis of 'voices' in the Bible study process places focus on the social dynamics of interpretation, or 'interpretation-in-interaction' and views the Bible as one voice amongst those of the group.[19] As my research is doctrinally and hermeneutically oriented, the framework of 'lenses' centralises the role of the Bible and reflects on interpretive activity from an ideological angle, rather than a relational one. It also recognises the interplay of dynamics between all four lenses (explored in chapter 11), as opposed to two binary dynamics. Indeed, it should be noted that Figure 6.1 depicts the dominant lenses that appeared to be at work amongst my participants in relation to the doctrine of Scripture, but countless other lenses could be included, such as culture, education, race, and gender, as either additions or sub-lenses.

Initial Conclusions

With this metaphor as a controlling framework, the role of the doctrine of Scripture in interpretation can be articulated on three levels, based on what has been established in this chapter.

First and primarily, reading the text through the lens of the doctrine of Scripture sets the agenda for reading. Participants read with the goal of learning theological insight (belief) or guidance for life (behaviour) as a consequence of their belief that the Bible was God's teaching resource. This was the predominant influence of the doctrine of Scripture lens across all three texts. The doctrine of Scripture lens determined the reading agenda and located where the text's ultimate meaning was found—in God's communication,

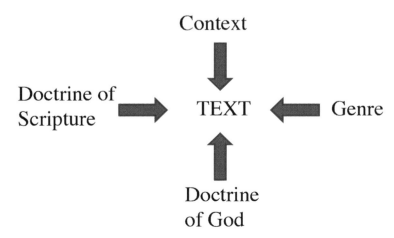

Figure 6.1. Reading Lenses.

104 *Chapter 6*

which participants had to learn in the form of belief or behaviour. This insight accords with Perrin's research, which equally identified amongst her millennial participants that they prioritised theological questions and personal reflection when reading and were motivated to read for the purpose of establishing and justifying doctrine and making contemporary applications.[20]

Secondarily, reading the text through the lens of the doctrine of Scripture had a role in determining the engagement practices with which participants handled the text. This is demonstrated in that 26 percent of participants, overall engagement practices with the text were specifically related to their beliefs about Scripture's divine association. Some of these practices were directly related to agenda, above, such as the practice of application. But many of these practices simply underscored belief in the unity of the Bible and stemmed from a belief in the canon of Scripture.

A final and tertiary role of the doctrine of Scripture lens related to the interpretive conclusions that participants made. This role was minimal and largely the responsibility of the other active lenses, as will be seen in the next chapter. However, as was noted, participants did call upon their Bible beliefs to support, validate, or justify their interpretative conclusions about the text, or question, criticise, and reject other participants' interpretative conclusions. The doctrine of Scripture therefore did seem to have a role to play in the outcomes of interpretation, but this largely seemed to emerge in relation to other participants and as a result of the dynamic of group discussion.

If determining the location of meaning and thus setting the interpretive agenda is the primary role of the doctrine of Scripture lens, how did the other prominent lenses at play influence this role? Additionally, what role did these lenses have to play in participants' interpretive practices and conclusions, if these weren't determined by the doctrine of Scripture? I now turn to a deeper analysis of these other lenses to provide further insight into the role of the doctrine of Scripture in interpretation.

NOTES

1. Christian Smith, *The Bible Made Impossible* (Grand Rapids, MI: Brazos Press, 2012), 5.

2. Harold Lindsell, *The Battle for the Bible* (Grand Rapids, MI: Zondervan, 1976).

3. Bebbington, *Evangelicalism in Modern Britain*, 189.

4. Andrew Atherstone, *An Anglican Evangelical Identity Crisis: The Churchman–Anvil Affair of 1981–1984* (London: Latimer Trust, 2008).

5. Whilst inerrancy is a theological difference, the majority of these differences are cultural, with 'evangelical' functioning as less of an identity 'label' in the UK. Imogen

The Influence of the Doctrine of Scripture: Some Conclusions   105

Ball outlines: 'the primary identification of British Evangelicals with "Christian" rather than "Evangelical" distinguishes them from Evangelicals in America. The "us and them" mentality, so prevalent in U.S. Evangelicalism and fuelling ongoing culture wars, is not present in Britain.' See: Imogen Ball, 'Political and Religious Identities of British Evangelicals,' Theos Thinktank, August 15, 2017, https://www.theosthinktank .co.uk/comment/2017/08/15/political-and-religious-identities-of-british-evangelicals.

6. Perrin, *Bible Reading*, 100.

7. Rogers, *Congregational Hermeneutics*, 132.

8. Ibid., 133.

9. Todd, *The Talk*, 132.

10. Ibid., 237.

11. For the Bible as propositional revelation, see: Normal L. Geisler and William C. Roach, *Defending Inerrancy: Affirming the Accuracy of Scripture for a New Generation* (Grand Rapids, MI: Baker Books, 2011).

12. Hannah Waite, 'The Nones: Who Are They and What Do They Believe?' *Theos* (2022): 29.

13. David Ford, Reading the Bible Outside the Church: A Case Study (Eugene, OR: Pickwick, 2018), 150.

14. Paul was the presumed author of Ephesians.

15. The extent to which these practices constituted 'distancing' is discussed in chapter 11.

16. Thiselton, *New Horizons*, 46.

17. Gadamer, *Truth and Method*.

18. Todd, 'The Talk', 275.

19. Ibid.

20. Perrin, *Bible Reading*, 49.

Chapter 7

The Influence of Belief

Reading through Doctrine

The previous chapter demonstrated how reading the text through the lens of the doctrine of Scripture had the effect of directing participants to read with the goal of learning theological insight (belief) or guidance for life (behaviour) as a consequence of their belief that the Bible was God's teaching resource. Yet, chapters 3–5 also noted alternative lenses through which the text can be read which affected the reading and interpreting process.

This chapter, therefore, explores the first of these lenses in more detail: the doctrine of God, asking first, what participants did when they were engaging with the text through this lens, second, how the overall force of the lens shaped interpretation, and third, how this relates to the doctrine of Scripture lens.

THE DOCTRINE OF GOD

When participants read the text through the doctrine of God lens, they were letting their beliefs and assertions about God colour their understanding of the text. Though reading the text through the lens of the doctrine of God naturally resulted in a focus upon the character of God in the text, it should be noted that this is also the result of the doctrine of Scripture. The doctrine of Scripture lens meant participants sought to gain insight into belief about God as one of their goals of reading, as was noted in the previous chapter. Additionally, such theocentric reading was enhanced by the content of the text in question: the presence of God in the text and the level of difficulty associated with God's portrayal. In other words, reading through the doctrine of God lens is not the same as a theocentric reading which focuses upon the portrayal of God. Instead, it is a reading that puts the text's portrayal of God in conversation with the reader's own understanding of the character of God. Before looking at such practices in more detail, however, it is worth

107

108   *Chapter 7*

considering what participants believed about God in order to have a sense of what the doctrine of God lens actually consists of.

The Content of the Doctrine of God Lens

The data gathered was not geared towards discerning participants' doctrine of God. However, it is worth briefly summarising what participants did say about God in order to ascertain something of the 'norm' and establish a basic framework of beliefs participants had about God.

Participants had a varied doctrine of God. A total of forty different statements were made about the character/nature/actions/intentions of God. Interestingly, not one statement occurred in all six groups. However, the statements that achieved the most consensus (five out of six groups) were affirmations that God is loving, powerful, and sovereign. Additionally, four out of six groups made declarations that God is creator and God is good. These higher consensus statements across the groups were reflected in overall frequency. The most frequently made statements about the nature of God overall were that God is loving, good, powerful, relational, creator, and sovereign.

This demonstrates a central cluster of ideas around the nature of God that proved to be pre-eminent in participants' reading of the Bible. The emphasis on God's goodness, love, and relationality resonates with Todd's identification in his dialogical analysis that the 'voice of God' is conceived as a concern or care for people. A such, 'people's voices and the Bible's voices may be criticised for their inhumanity, but if that is the case they are both perceived as being of human origin. God is never, within this data, criticised for being uncaring.'[1] It should be noted, however, that the subject matter of the texts themselves will have strongly influenced what participants stated about God, so different texts may have prompted different reflections.

With this overview of what participants believed about God in mind, we can examine the consequences of reading the text through this understanding of the character of God.

Extrapolating from the Character of God

As was noted in the previous chapters, participants extrapolated from the character of God to discern what actually happened in the text. For example, in Genesis, several participants called upon the omnipotence of God to affirm the historicity of the text. If God can do anything, then what is scientifically impossible is actually possible and not grounds upon which to dismiss the historicity of the story. Additionally, Jessica also pointed to the faithfulness of God who keeps his promises to dismiss a local flood interpretation. Similarly, in the Psalm, participants denied that God abandons his people as

The Influence of Belief   109

the psalmist professes because of their belief that God is omnipresent and faithful. Beginning with their knowledge of the character of God, participants discerned what 'really happened'. The character of God was taken as a primary foundational basis upon which to explore their understanding of the narrative. This suggests that participants have a clear and defined doctrine of God that they were confident in asserting. By employing deductive reasoning that extrapolated from the doctrine of God rather than the doctrine of Scripture, participants were articulating that they had more faith in the character of God than the character of the text. This implies, first, that God is a primary and core element of a Christian reader's faith, more so than the Bible, and second, that as a primary core element of faith, readers are much more confident about the nature of God than the nature of the Bible.

Tensions Relating to the Character of God

Participants' reading through the lens of their doctrine of God also involved identifying tensions. As noted in the previous chapter, Genesis and the Psalm were challenging for some readers because the actions of God in the text did not fit with their understanding of how God operates. If a participant had no prior expectation or beliefs about who God is or how God operates, then whilst they might find the texts disturbing or upsetting, they would not produce tension or feelings of confliction. It is a commitment to the belief in the character of God as good and loving that ultimately leads to tension regarding the actions of God in the text. This is confirmed in Anna Strhan's empirical research where her evangelical participants 'experience the personality of God as coherent', which underscores why emerging tensions from reading the Bible were experienced as problematic for my participants.[2] Indeed, the presence of tension would seem to prove Malley's contention that the goal of hermeneutic activity is to establish transitivity between the text and beliefs.[3]

Participants did not always identify a resolution to their felt tension but addressing the tension and trying to understand it was a focus of the discussion. An example of such tension is the following comment made by Neil (St.C's) in discussion of Psalm 44: 'one concern is the extent to which, certainly the first half, God seems to be partisan. He sides with one army and then helps them destroy the other . . . I almost never got my head around that because the other army were slaughtered and surely God made the "amekalites", and the "hittites" and "hashites" and whomever. . . .' Neil's concern about God being partisan stems from his understanding that God is the creator of all humanity—why would God create portions of humanity he intends to destroy? Neil brings to the Psalm his understanding of God as creator and benevolent and this sits in tension with the Psalm's declaration that God actively defeats other armies.

110 *Chapter 7*

Such instances of tension are a result of reading the text through the doctrine of God lens, i.e., bringing to the text certain expectations and assumptions about who God is and how God acts. This tendency was also identified by Andrew Todd but in a more active fashion, who noted that for his research participants, 'a "voice" of God . . . is recruited to critique the Bible.'[4] This reinforces the notion that participants had a strong concept of God that they brought to bear upon the text, causing tensions to emerge.

Contextualisation of the Character of God

Whilst reading through the doctrine of God lens produced tension, it also provoked attempts to solve, or at least ease, such tension. This took the form of contextualisation, the practice of participants employing their pre-existing doctrine of God in order to address this tension rather than state it. Participants used their broader knowledge of who they understood God to be in order to balance the picture provided in the text. Different types of contextualisation occurred but predominantly participants read the God of the text in the light of other facets of God's character.

The 'judgement' of God in Genesis provides the best example of this. The following five participants all placed God's 'judgement' in the context of their broader understanding of God, though interestingly, the precise context adopted differed for different participants.

Martin's (GLC) understanding of God as a saviour, who fights for light against darkness and good against evil, led him to believe the flood was a required judgement of God, on account of God's love and salvific purposes. Johnny (GLC) brought to the text the understanding that God is creator and perfectly good and loving. He understood that the extremity of sin caused the flood but leaned on God's characteristics of being creator, good, and loving to suggest that God was thus qualified to judge humanity and act as he sees fit. Dean's (TO) understanding of God that he brought to the narrative was derived from the New Testament which he quoted (2 Peter 3:9)[5] to establish that God is patient and does not want humanity to perish. It was against this backdrop that he framed the narrative of Noah as a warning story of God's judgement that demonstrated an atypical side to God's character. Winston (WO) understood God's judgement in the context of God's sovereignty and salvific purposes. His understanding that God's sovereignty leaves room for human free will and that God judges in response to human choice, framed the flood as God being obligated to respond to sin.

In all these instances, participants were reading through the lens of the doctrine of God in bringing to the text their broader understanding of the character of God that helps them to contextualise the actions of God in the text.

The Influence of Belief 111

This highlights an interesting consideration about the relationship between the doctrine of God and the doctrine of Scripture, or more broadly speaking, between theology and the Bible. Participants had a clear working understanding of who God is and though this was likely derived from the Bible, it also seemed to conflict with the Bible. This suggests beliefs about God do not originate solely from Scripture and therefore have a complex origin, which is worth exploring next.

Origins of the Doctrine of God Brought to the Text

The fieldwork data was not designed to determine where participants' ideas about God came from. Insight into this can only be gleaned from occasions where participants stated the basis for their belief. This did not often occur, as most frequently participants presented their theological claims about the nature of God as being self-evident, with no justification or explanation made either explicitly or implicitly from context.

On some occasions, participants' conception of God drew directly upon their personal experience, such as Emma (St.J's) who said, 'I do not think of God as someone whose name is used as a way to tread down other people, like that is the exact opposite of the God that I experience who is about, not oppressing, and freedom, and you know, the reunification of all things.' The experience Emma is referring to is unclear, but by referencing 'experience' she implies that she is drawing upon her own personal understanding of God which centres on freedom and reconciliation. It could be that this experience is shaped by the Bible or tradition, but this does not reduce the personal element of her understanding of God.[6]

More rarely, participants' claims about God were made on the basis of biblical material, such as Dean (TO) who quoted 2 Peter to claim that God is patient. Only a couple of participants drew directly upon biblical material to make claims about God, though it could be argued to be implied in other claims that participants made.

Some claims were based on tradition, such as Henry's (St.J's) references to 'practicing the presence of God'. Though not explicitly stated, this phrase comes from the writings of Brother Lawrence.[7] For Henry, this statement meant that God is always present despite how it feels. This is not to say that this understanding about the nature of God is not also an experiential, biblical, or self-evident reality, but rather that it was presented by Henry in terms of a tradition associated with Brother Lawrence.

Though not a dominant approach, Sam and Winston, both from WO, explicitly demonstrated a Christocentric doctrine of God. This emerged in relation to the issue of divine violence which was a topic of discussion prompted by Psalm 44. Sam's understanding of God through the revelation

112   *Chapter 7*

of Jesus led him to question whether the violence involved in the taking of the promised land was what God really instructed. His perspective is worth quoting at length:

> If you really want to take the Christocentric lens to its fullest extreme, Jesus is the full revelation of God, which means that it's not simply that the Old Testament or the Hebrew Bible shows us what Jesus is like, but Jesus shows us some of the problematic elements of the Hebrew Bible that make us wonder 'did God really command Joshua to do those things?' . . . 'Was Jesus with the Israelites slaughtering the Canaanites and the other nations in that sense?' and I think for me, Jesus Christocentric hermeneutic leads me to say no, I don't think that's what was going on.

Reading the Psalm with the person of Jesus in mind was problematic for Sam because it highlighted what, for him, was an inconsistency in the Bible's depiction of God. This inconsistency was accounted for by Sam's understanding that the Bible witnesses to a progressive development of people's understanding of the nature of God culminating in the revelation through Jesus.

Winston also allowed for a sense of development within the biblical canon which he referred to as 'progressive revelation'. Rather than this be humanity coming to an increasingly accurate understanding of God, Winston understood God to be accommodating according to the needs of the people in the historical time in which they occupied.

> Revelation is progressive in that God also worked with these people with revelation levels that were different, in kind of getting to where we are today and understanding Christ, his character, his nature and just his fullness, the whole Godhead embodied in Christ himself. But in the olden days . . . wars were part of their culture, were part of their tradition, were part of their lifestyle, and so for them to see the victor of God they had to see their God defeating their enemy physically.

Winston acknowledges that his understanding of God is shaped by the person of Jesus, 'the whole Godhead embodied in Christ' but that this wasn't how those in the Old Testament understood God and so God acted in accordance with their expectations. In both these cases, Sam and Winston pointed to the character and person of Jesus as a dominating force in their understanding of the character of God and God's behaviour.

Though by no means conclusive, this brief overview identifies enough evidence to suggest that the doctrine of God is built upon and from a variety of sources. As such, when participants read through the doctrine of God lens, they're reading through a lens that has a potentially complex multi-origin, specific to the reader's context, making each reader's doctrine of God

The Influence of Belief 113

lens unique.[8] The particulars of the doctrine of God lens in operation will impact the tensions identified and the contextualisation employed to solve such tensions.

Unique Doctrine of God Lenses

A clearer insight into individual participant's doctrine of God can be seen on occasions where participants demonstrated beliefs about God that were against the general thrust of the discussion and the central cluster of views presented above.

On the occasions where most participants identified a tension between the text's portrayal of God and their own conception of God, some found agreement between the two. These participants' conception of God seemed to more readily incorporate facets of God that other participants articulated tension about.

Jesse (TO) provides a particularly striking example of this in relation to the Genesis narrative. This was first articulated in terms of the text's portrayal of 'judgement': 'I don't have a problem with the judgement aspect of it! I mean, I don't see a need for us to explain why God does what he does.' This statement demonstrates comfortability with the idea of God as judge and an open doctrine of God such that God's actions don't need explaining. Jesse later went on to expand his view in more detail:

> I don't think we ever just read the text from the perspective of 'God is a God of love and therefore everything goes', I think that would be a very shallow reading of any text and I certainly think it would be a shallow understanding theologically of who God is, so I don't have a problem counterbalancing a God of love with a God of justice, I don't have a problem with understanding grace and mercy as kind of aspects that go together in some senses.

Here, Jesse demonstrates a complex doctrine of God that holds within it characteristics that are seemingly in tension. Because of Jesse's ability to hold conflicting ideas within his dominant conception of God, he didn't find tension in the text because his understanding of God already encompassed the portrayal of God found in the Genesis narrative. In contrast, he spoke against what other participants seemed to demonstrate, which was that the concept of God as love or loving was so dominant that it didn't allow room for ideas such as judgement, which were pushed to the periphery and therefore caused tension when the text was read.

Another example, not so strongly stated, was Jane's (St.J's) openness to the psalmists claims about God being true. Unlike many participants who denied the psalmist's claims, Jane's doctrine of God included the idea that God does sometimes cause events that may seem negative and therefore she does not find as much of a tension between the psalmist's claims and her understanding of God. Both Jesse and Jane's doctrine of God included aspects that were more challenging for other participants. What does this suggest about participant's doctrine of God lens, given its multi-origin and the different dynamics this produces?

MAPPING THE DOCTRINE OF GOD

Given what has been noted so far, Figure 7.1 below offers a helpful depiction of the emerging understanding of the doctrine of God lens. The circle in the centre at the heart of the doctrine of God consists of participants' most dominant and secure conceptions of God's character, which I've named 'core comfortable'. As the circles widen moving outwards, they contain increasingly uncertain, insecure, or tentative conceptions of God, such that the outer layers could be considered conceptions that are 'periphery uncomfortable'. These are ideas about God that are accepted, but not with ease. Beyond the circle are conceptions of God that are firmly denied, the 'extrinsic intolerable'. Though not included in a participants' doctrine of God, these 'extrinsic intolerable' conceptions of God have a crucial role to play in the formation of the doctrine of God. God is defined just as much by what God is not as by what God is.

What this chapter has demonstrated is how participants see the text through their 'core comfortable' conceptions of God. This core comfortable conception of God at times became the foundation from which the reality of the text was explored, and at other times provided the cause and resolution of the text's central tension. In these practices, participants demonstrated that they had a clear and confident core understanding of the nature and character of God. This might be classified as a form of epistemological foundationalism wherein 'the foundations of our belief system are a set of basic beliefs which

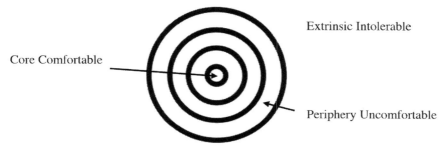

Figure 7.1. Doctrine of God Lens.

The Influence of Belief 115

in themselves require no justification. These basic beliefs provide support to all of our other non-basic beliefs of 'noetic structure' and offer a sure foundation for knowledge.'[9] This functions similarly to Rappaport's 'ultimate sacred postulates'[10] which Malley claims is the case for biblical inspiration for his research participants.[11] I contend that conceptions of God are much more deeply rooted and embedded in the Christian belief framework than those of the doctrine of Scripture.

If the doctrine of Scripture lens determined the reading agenda of finding the text's meaning in its divine teaching about right belief and behaviour, then the function of the doctrine of God lens was in regulating what these meanings could be. The doctrine of God lens therefore set parameters in relation to the interpretative conclusions that participants made: they couldn't just dismiss the flood on scientific grounds, because God's omnipotence goes beyond science; Psalm 44 couldn't be affirming the theological truth that God abandons as this is 'extrinsic intolerable'; and where Genesis insinuates that the flood is God's judgement upon a sinful humanity, this was understood in the context of love, sovereignty, and goodness.

Reading through the lens of the doctrine of God therefore primarily affected the interpretative conclusions that were made. These had to accord with the particulars of the reader's pre-existing beliefs about God.

THE DOCTRINE OF SCRIPTURE THROUGH
THE LENS OF THE DOCTRINE OF GOD

So far, this chapter has examined instances where participant's read the text through their doctrine of God lens and has suggested what the results of such readings were and how the lens ultimately functioned in the process of reading.

However, participants not only viewed the text through the lens of the doctrine of God but also evidenced viewing the doctrine of Scripture through the lens of the doctrine of God. This demonstrates how reading lenses have the capacity to form and inform each other and not just approaches to the text.

In many respects it is unsurprising that the doctrine of Scripture is viewed through the lens of the doctrine of God, as the latter has always been central to a traditional Evangelical doctrine of Scripture. As the Bible is conceived as God's Word, its character and properties are corollaries of a particular understanding of God—it can't contradict itself, it can't lie, it can't be unauthoritative because God is consistent, truthful, and the ultimate authority, as was demonstrated in chapter 1.[12]

It has already been outlined that the doctrine of God was significant in participants' construal of the doctrine of Scripture, sometimes in this traditional

116   *Chapter 7*

sense, but more so in conceiving of the text as God's resource and its function in reader's lives. This nuances a conception of the doctrine of Scripture in the emphasis that is placed upon God's intention, action, or purposes in providing the texts. The text is conceived not so much in terms of its inherent properties, but instead in terms of the use to which God puts it and therefore how it functions in the life of the believer. The doctrine of Scripture is underpinned by an understanding of a God who wants to communicate, and effect change in the life of the believer.

The Doctrine of Scripture as God's Use of the Text

A first example of this can be seen from Amy (St.A's), who made several comments about her difficulty in understanding the Bible, which she always qualified with a version of the following statement about her understanding of the passage: 'It's in the Bible because God wanted it there'. This demonstrates how Amy's view of Scripture is primarily concerned with her understanding of God's intentions. Amy views God as someone who wants to teach her how to live and behave and uses the Bible to do this, and this dominates her understanding of the nature of the Bible.

Gina (St.A's) also demonstrated a view of the Bible that is primarily concerned with function. Her main focus when reading texts is to understand what it reveals about God: 'Well I think it's showing reflections of who God is. Actually, that's the most important thing, whether we individually believe bits of it and not other bits is irrelevant if we're taking on board the reflection of God.' In the same way that Amy viewed the Bible as God's medium for teaching her how to live, Gina views the Bible as God's medium for teaching her about God's nature. Both Amy and Gina's understanding of the Bible reflects their understanding of how God uses it, rather than particular attributes or beliefs inherent to the text. The doctrine of God is thus influential in forming participants' doctrine of Scripture which focuses on the text's function.

The Doctrine of Scripture as Content about God

However, Gina later elaborated on her statement about the Bible reflecting who God is (in the Genesis discussion), providing an example for further insight into how the doctrine of God informs the doctrine of Scripture:

> If we're looking at the Bible as telling us aspects of who God is and it's talking about the coming of his son Jesus Christ right from the very beginning, then this story to me talks to me about the obedience that you talked about and that he's a God of detail. That he does care but that there is judgement. Whether it's here

The Influence of Belief   117

on earth or in the next life after we die. But there is judgement and I think it's important that we know that.

This statement reveals not only that Gina conceives of the text in relation to its function or how God uses it ('telling us aspects of who God is'), but also that her conception of Scripture relates to an overarching theological understanding of its content or what it's about ('the coming of his son Jesus Christ right from the very beginning'). Such a theological construal of Scripture involves the determination of an overall narrative purpose, in Gina's case this is Christocentric. David Kelsey has demonstrated this practice in relation to how theologians use Scripture to authorise their theological proposals:

> Theologians do not appeal to Scripture-as-such to help authorize their theological proposals. In the concrete practice of doing theology, they decide on some aspect or, more exactly, some pattern in Scripture to which to appeal. That is to say that they decide on some one kind of unity to ascribe to the texts, and not some other kind. Not the text as such, but the text-construed-as-a-certain-kind-of-whole is appealed to.[13]

One such pattern that Kelsey identifies amongst theologians is Scripture construed as a unified narrative of 'a single, organic history of salvation',[14] in other words, a theological meta-narrative. This ties in with several of the interpretation movements outlined in chapter 4, particularly kerygmatic exegesis and strands of biblical thelogy. This way of construing Scripture does not seem too much of a stretch from Gina's assertion that the whole Bible is oriented towards the coming of Jesus—in other words, Jesus as the saviour of mankind is the pinnacle and overall point of the Bible. The theological meta-narrative of the Bible is ultimately about the history of salvation which reaches its zenith in Jesus. Gina's interpretation of the Noah narrative then, is offered in the context of her construal of the Bible's use by God and its content as being christocentrically oriented, closely linked with a view of the Bible as a meta-narrative of salvation history. This prioritisation of Jesus as the pinnacle of the Bible is unsurprising given that one of the hallmarks of being an Evangelical according to Bebbington's famous quadrilateral is cruci-centrism, a focus on the atoning work of the cross.[15] Indeed, Christian Smith has argued that a truly Evangelical reading of Scripture is Christocentric, prioritising the Gospel of Jesus Christ as the 'purpose, center, and interpretive key to Scripture.'[16] Gina's statement demonstrates how her theocentrism in relation to function, and her Christocentrism in relation to content, combine to offer an interpretation of the Noah story that is consistent with her understanding of God and God's purposes.

118 *Chapter 7*

Not all participants were explicit in revealing how they construe the text 'as-a-certain-kind-of-whole', but it is not too farfetched to speculate that their overarching conception of the narrative of the Bible would likely be closely related to the character and action of God reaching its height in the person of Jesus, especially given Evangelicalism's historical tendency to focus on the salvation of the cross. If this is the case, the doctrine of Scripture can be said to be construed through the lens of the doctrine of God on two fronts: first, in conceiving of the Bible's function, and second, in conceiving of the Bible's content.

Conclusion: The Doctrine of God Lens

In summary, this chapter has demonstrated that participants had a central cluster of prominent conceptions about the character of God, but these differed amongst participants as a result of the doctrine of God having multiple sources. Participants read through the lens of their doctrine of God when they brought these pre-existing ideas to the text and this resulted in the practices of producing tension, contextualisation, and extrapolating.

In these practices participants demonstrated that they were confident and clear in their core conceptions of the character of God, more so than the doctrine of Scripture, and that the doctrine of God lens had a parameter-setting function in relation to participant's interpretive conclusions.

Moreover, the doctrine of God lens also dominated in participants' understanding of the doctrine of Scripture, evidenced by their emphasis on God's use of Scripture and thus its function in believers' lives, as well as in conceiving of the Bible's overall content as being about God and God's revelation in the person of Jesus.

Having considered the doctrine of God lens and its relationship to the doctrine of Scripture, I now turn to a second lens that proved to be influential in my participants' readings—genre.

NOTES

1. Todd, 'The Talk,' 278.
2. Anna Strhan, *Aliens and Strangers?: The Struggle for Coherence in the Everyday Lives of Evangelicals* (Oxford: Oxford Scholarship Online, 2015), ch. 5, DOI: 10.1093/acprof:oso/9780198724469.001.0001.
3. Malley, *How the Bible Works*, 83–87.
4. Todd, 'The Talk,' 277.

The Influence of Belief 119

5. 'The Lord is not slow about keeping His promise as some people think. He is waiting for you. The Lord does not want any person to be punished forever. He wants all people to be sorry for their sins and turn from them.' NIV

6. Tanya Lurhmann has explored in depth how Evangelicals experience God and engage with God as a reality. See: T. M. Lurhmann, *When God Talks Back: Understanding the American Evangelical Relationship with God* (New York: Alfred A. Knopf, 2012); *How God Becomes Real: Kindling the Presence of Invisible Others* (Princeton, NJ: Princeton University Press, 2020).

7. Brother Lawrence, *The Practice of the Presence of God*, trans. E. M. Blaiklock (Chatham: Hodder & Stoughton, 1981).

8. Though not discernible from my participants, Village has identified how personality can play a role in conceptions of God: 'Created in the image of God, we recreate God in our own image. Empirical theology exposes a route whereby scripture reading might reinforce this idolatry. If we allow our innate psychological preferences too much sway in guiding our reading, we may hear only words that reinforce the notion of a God that is like us in every way. It is not that we reject other notions; we simply do not perceive them.' Village, *The Bible and Lay People*, 121.

9. Rogers, *Congregational Hermeneutics*, 120.

10. Roy Rappaport, *Ecology, Meaning and Religion* (Berkeley, CA: North Atlantic Press, 1979).

11. Malley, *How the Bible Works*, 137–40.

12. Within systematics, the anchoring of the Doctrine of Scripture in the Doctrine of God takes a different form; see: John Webster, *Holy Scripture: A Dogmatic Sketch* (Cambridge: Cambridge University Press, 2003).

13. David Kelsey, *The Uses of Scripture in Recent Theology* (London: SCM Press, 1975), 103.

14. Ibid., 101.

15. Bebbington, *Evangelicalism in Modern Britain*.

16. Smith, *The Bible Made Impossible*, 97.

Chapter 8

The Influence of Literature

Reading through Genre

In chapter 7, I demonstrated how reading the text through the lens of the doctrine of God had a parameter-setting function in relation to participants' interpretive conclusions. This chapter looks at the lens of genre, considering how this affected not only the way participants read the texts but also how the doctrine of Scripture functioned.

GENRE

Reading a text through the lens of its genre is not something specific to Bible reading, but all reading events. Humans seek to assign categories to the texts they encounter, usually on account of the text's context and content. Texts are therefore always assigned to some pre-existing category: fact, fiction, list, poem, tweet, headline, story, etc.[1] But literary theory has shown that genre isn't merely a classification tool but 'provides the *literary context* for a given sentence and, therefore, partly determines what the sentence means and how it should be taken. . . . Genre thus enables the reader to interpret meaning and to recognise what kinds of truth claims are being made in and by a text.'[2]

The significance of genre and its role in meaning-making is reflected in popular Bible interpretation guides which highlight the importance of understanding genre for effective interpretation, such as Gordon Fee and Douglas Stuart's *How to Read the Bible for All It's Worth*, now on its fourth edition, which is a genre-based approach to interpretation. Underlying this book is the assumption that different genres require different types of interpretative activity.[3]

One of the reasons that genre is so critical for Evangelicals, is its role in determining whether a text is to be read literally. Beynon and Sach write, 'When David says in Psalm 22 "I am poured out like water" . . . it's poetry,

121

122   *Chapter 8*

we're not supposed to take it literally. On the other hand, when the Gospels record that the tomb was empty, they mean that it physically was. The resurrection of Jesus is not a metaphor.'[4]

It is not surprising therefore that all my participants demonstrated an implicit recognition that the three texts were different genres, although an explicit exploration of genre did not always occur. Before turning to a discussion of their genre designations, it's worth considering in more detail how the question of genre is handled amongst commentators.

Genre of Genesis

A significant factor that determines whether Noah is read historically is how one approaches the genre of Genesis. What is the purpose of this book and what is it intending to do? Answers to these questions are by no means monolithic, particularly within Evangelicalism, and are connected to broader issues relating to the authority and inspiration of Scripture.

American Catholic biblical scholar David Pleins, who overviews the interpretative history of the Noah narrative, distinguishes between what he designates as 'exact literalists' and 'loose literalists', both of which could be considered an evangelical stance.[5] Pleins describes 'exact literalists' as those who read Genesis as a literal historical account, ignoring any extrabiblical evidence that might suggest otherwise. On the other hand, 'loose literalists' are much more likely to incorporate extrabiblical insight into their readings so that the genre is understood as historical in a modified manner: 'The story of Noah's food will thus be thought to correlate with some ancient catastrophe that changed civilisation in some decisive way.'[6] Pleins argues that this method often loses sight of the actual text so that it becomes a secondary concern.[7] Negotiating these approaches to genre and reading, that either hold too tightly or too loosely to the text, Pleins holds up the value of 'myth' as a genre that can socially construct and provide divine foundations to political circumstances.

Thinking about the Noah account in this light locates the text's meaning not in its historical factuality, but in its ongoing use in the present. This is somewhat similar to Rabbinic and Patristic readings of the text that can be quite creative in their understanding of the text's meaning for the present. For example, Jerome reads the dimensions of the ark typologically (300 x 50 x 30 cubits) seeing penance foreshadowed in the number 50 because of Psalm 50, the age of Jesus at baptism in the number 30, and 300 as the sign T, which symbolises the crucifixion.[8] This is not to say that such interpretations meant the text was not understood to be historical, but rather that meaning was continually readdressed in light of the present and the events of Christ. Whilst Evangelicals typically seek modern application from their readings of

The Influence of Literature   123

Scripture which often leads to christological interpretations, their understanding of the Bible as the Word of God limits the extent to which they would be comfortable 'overwriting' meaning found in the author's intention, to its continuing mythical use.

A much more typically Evangelical response to the problem of genre comes from Evangelical Calvinist and academic Vern S. Poythress, who determines genre according to that which the text claims for itself. Seeing Genesis as prose narrative covering generations and descendants,[9] Poythress turns to the issue of whether the text can be considered fiction or nonfiction and concludes that on its own terms, 'Genesis belongs to the same broad genre of narrative prose as does 1–2 Samuel and 1–2 Kings. Since there is no literary signal to tell us that it is fiction, and since, indeed, it belongs to a continual temporal development leading from creation to the exile, we conclude that it is nonfiction.'[10] For some adherents to the infallibility of Scripture therefore, the text's self-claim to be nonfiction must be upheld as true considering that Genesis is the 'Word of God' and therefore cannot be deceitful. As the Bible is authoritative, its self-claims must be taken seriously. Whilst Genesis does not explicitly claim to be nonfiction, according to Poythress there is no evidence to suggest otherwise, so it must be understood as nonfiction.

However, this does lead to the further question of whether the genre of nonfiction necessarily equates to accounts that are historically accurate. Methodist biblical scholar Lloyd R. Bailey focuses on this issue with regard to chapters 1–11 of Genesis, the 'primeval narrative'. This narrative is segmented from the following chapters in Genesis on various counts: first, the literature shares content and has parallels with material from across the Ancient Near East whereas the accounts of the Patriarchs are unique to the Israelites.[11] Second, from chapter 12 forwards, Genesis has a narrative form, whereas chapters 1–11 consist of a genealogy into which narrative material is inserted.[12] Third, the world of the primeval narrative is alien and strange to that of the known universe. What would typically be considered miraculous is considered the norm: snakes talk, the human lifespan is excessively long, etc.[13] Given all this, should Genesis be considered 'history' from chapter 12 with the beginnings of the accounts of the Patriarchs? Bailey claims that whilst cuneiform texts have confirmed some of the names and practices found in the patriarchal narratives, this does not necessarily confirm the historicity of the individual narratives.[14] Bailey concludes that history, in the modern sense of 'objective reporting' is not an appropriate category to which Scripture, and Genesis, can readily apply: 'By contrast with the modern concern for objectivity, the Bible was not concerned to distinguish "what really happened" from the impressions of the proper observer and recorder. It is overtly written from a theological point of view. Thus it speaks of God's involvement in a way that, even if it is true, could not be demonstrated to the

124   *Chapter 8*

impartial observer.'[15] This implies that the way in which to read Genesis is theologically, concerning oneself with the theological message of the narrative and secondarily with its historicity. This is in line with Protestant liberal Old Testament scholar Walter Brueggemann's approach who claims that the text should be read not as history or myth but as the proclamation of how God restores the fractured world: 'This story is not concerned with historical data but with the strange things that happen in the heart of God that decisively affect God's creation'.[16] This distinction however, between history and theology, discussed in chapter 4, is warned against by Poythress who claims that to read the Bible with a fundamental belief in the sovereignty of God over history is to expect the theological, historical, and literary to be integrated and that the presence of one does not outweigh the others.[17]

Genre of Psalms

When it comes to Psalm 44, the unique nature of the Psalms for believers who hold to an evangelical doctrine of Scripture is found in their dual nature of being human utterances to God, i.e., prayers, that due to their incorporation into Scripture, are equally considered to be God's utterances to humanity. When the poetic nature of the Psalm is taken into account, the picture is complicated further by metaphorical language. Is God really understood to be sleeping, or is that simply an expression of inactivity? This type of language in the context of poetry, rather than narrative or an epistle, creates an ambiguity of meaning such that interpretative options are often broader and harder to discern between.

Regardless of Christian denomination or evangelical identification, all commentaries take seriously the claims of the Psalmist and do not question the community's assertion of innocence. Whether this is because they are simply taking the text as it stands or because they are unwilling to question the claims of Scripture as God's Word is not made explicit. What is given attention, particularly as a consequence of genre, is the Psalm's structure and the patterns this produces. Commentators make note of the basic turn that occurs in the Psalm, from recollection of God's faithfulness in the past to God's current faithlessness experienced by the community. All commentators agree on the stark and transitional 'yet' of verse 9 that takes the Psalm into complaint followed by the striking repetition of the accusatory 'you' to begin each sentence of verses 9–14.[18] This 'yet' serves as the hinge for various oppositions that occur within the Psalm. For example, Bruggemann points out, 'It is exactly YHWH's military effectiveness that is celebrated in verses 1–8 and YHWH's military failure that is voiced in verses 9–16.'[19] This central section of complaint introduced by 'yet' forms the centre of a suggested

The Influence of Literature 125

chiastic structure. Psalm scholar Loren D. Crow puts forward the following pattern:

A — (1–3) Hymnic description of God's past aid
B — (4–8) Present community's faithful trust in God
C — (9–16) God's violence against this community
B — (17–22) Community's innocent contrast with God's action
A — (23–26) Petition that God aid in the present

Characterisation of the sub-genres of each section of the Psalm is also made difficult as a consequence of genre. Poetry leaves open the possibility of tone and meaning so that commentators vary between designating the first section of remembrance as either invocation or praise. The practice of recalling God's past deeds is commonplace in the Psalms and is easily seen as praise,[20] but the Psalm in its entirety suggests that this act of remembrance is one of invocation rather than praise. The author is not calling upon events from the past for the purpose of delighting in God's goodness, but rather in proving the existence of God's goodness. This is the common Greek rhetorical practice of hypomnesis—reciting past action as a reminder of the expectation for the present, it serves as a means to persuade God into action.[21] Old Testament scholar James Mays puts it succinctly: 'The recollection of the past and the confession in the present are ways of actualising and activating the reality of their content, a liturgical invocation of the work of God that is in such bitter and bewildering contrast with the present.'[22] This is why 'praise' is not the best characterisation of this section of discourse. This also sets Psalm 44 apart from other lament Psalms commonly structured as a movement from lament to petition to praise, or according to Bruggemann's cognitive pattern: orientation, disorientation, and reorientation. Yet Psalm 44 fails to reach reorientation and fails to end with praise.[23]

Whilst some of these challenges amongst scholars regarding structure and sub-genre are not obvious ones for the general reader, they highlight the complicated nature of poetry, which presents a multiplicity of interpretations and readings. As has already been mentioned, when the doctrine of Scripture plays a part in this dynamic, the waters become even murkier. As God's Word, the Psalm speaks truth, but as human poetry, the Psalm demonstrates textual practices that mean its truth might be more difficult to discern. A good example of this is verse 23 which accuses God of sleeping—'why do you sleep, O Lord? Awake!' An evangelical doctrine of God would affirm that God does not sleep as God is not human and bound to the necessities this entails. God not sleeping is attested to in Psalm 121: 'He who keeps Israel will neither slumber nor sleep' (121:4). What is to be made of this apparent contradiction? In order to preserve the consistency and divinity of Scripture,

126   *Chapter 8*

as well as the doctrine of God, Evangelical commentaries suggest that Psalm 44:23 is idiomatic, as a call to action and not a reflection of God's actual state.[24] Psalm 121's affirmation of God's vigilance is taken as normative, rendering Psalm 44 as metaphorical in order to be consistent. It is particularly interesting that these contradictory statements are both Psalms and therefore poetry, yet one is understood as being a factual statement determining the other as metaphor despite the fact that their genre does not indicate that one is necessarily more 'true' than the other. This is evidence of the way in which doctrine controls reading, in this instance, the doctrine of God. Because God is believed not to sleep, Psalm 121 is a straightforward statement of fact and Psalm 44 is a metaphor.

Genre of Ephesians

Amongst scholarship and commentators, the question of genre is minimally discussed with regard to Ephesians. This is because the internal features of the text clearly designate it as a letter or epistle and this isn't disputed. However, a connected issue does receive coverage amongst writers, which is the authorship of the letter—is Ephesians written by Paul?

The matter of authorship is significant for Evangelicals for whom Pauline authorship is the basis for claiming a text has apostolic authority and is therefore defined as Scripture. For those readers, to suggest that Paul was not the author of Ephesians is to question its fundamental designation as Scripture. As Catholic biblical scholar Stephen Fowl points out, for upholders of biblical inerrancy; 'the truthfulness of any of the text's assertions—and therefore its theological authority—depends on the truthfulness of the assertion of Pauline authorship.'[25] It is for this reason, and a context pre-critical scholarship, that Ephesians was traditionally thought to have been written by Paul to the church in Ephesus, as the letter itself attests in 1:1.[26] Generally speaking, this is still the view taken amongst more conservative Evangelical commentators, whilst more critical or liberal commentators claim the author of the letter is unknown. For all the reasons proffered as to why this is the case, there are counter-arguments refuting such claims: the impersonal tone that suggests Paul was not the author can be accounted for by its being intended as a circular letter. The predominantly unique language and style not found in Paul's other writings and therefore suggestive of a pseudepigraphic author cannot be adequately established given how small the undisputed Pauline corpus is. The close literary relationship to Colossians does not mean it is necessarily the work of a separate author using Colossians for reference. The theological differences present in the text and elsewhere in Paul's writing can be explained, etc.

The Influence of Literature 127

Stott settles the authorship issue in a particularly evangelical fashion by appealing to what the Bible claims for itself. When applied to the issue of the Pauline authorship of Ephesians, Stott looks to 1:1 and comments: 'For we must regard [Ephesian's] author . . . as "an apostle of Christ Jesus by the will of God", and therefore as a teacher whose authority is precisely the authority of Jesus Christ himself, in whose name and by whose inspiration he writes.'[27]

Stott is concerned to demonstrate the divine quality of the text which is attached to apostolicity. Whether this is Paul or not becomes a secondary question as to whether the author is an apostle or not, and this is what the text claims about its author and is therefore to be believed.

Responses to the authorship issue that are unconcerned with apostolic authority focus on the cultural practice of pseudepigraphy. For example, Fowl claims that the linking of authority with authorship reflects a modern concern, and that pseudepigraphy was an accepted practice in the first century and did not carry the connotations of deception we can attach to it today.[28] Similarly, Martin also suggests that the author of Ephesians was not Paul but a well-known disciple and companion of Paul who intended to summarise his teaching on the Church and Christian living for new pagan converts.[29]

The audience of the letter is a less-contentious challenge for evangelicals. Many scholars affirm that due to the fact that reference to 'Ephesus' in verse 1 is missing in many manuscripts and that the letter does not include personal greetings, it was intended for a wider audience than that of the city Ephesus.[30] Considering the letter's close affinity with Colossians, it is suggested that the region of Asia-Minor was intended for the circulation of this letter. Instances where interpretation of the text is based on extrabiblical knowledge of the city of Ephesus might be problematic for exegetes here.

Though not strictly a question of genre, these issues highlight important related issues, such as the role of the author and their intention when writing, as well as the intended recipients of the text, which we will explore further below.

Genre Classification

Amongst my participants, the genre of Genesis prompted the most genre discussion of the three texts with the following suggestions emerging (emphasis my own):

'Well I think when we look at the Old Testament, particularly passages like this—we're in the language of *myth* aren't we?'

'Again, it's historical in the sense of the materials that the ark was made of. Some of them were only available in northern parts of Turkey, which

128 *Chapter 8*

is where this has always been thought to be, so it's a very interesting mixture of what I think C. S. Lewis calls "*true myth*".'

'Well because this is an origin, this is part of the *origin story*, right? So I think it is history but it's. . . . it's not history in the same way that like, Samuel is history. In the sense that because it's an origin story actually you have to look far more for meaning than for detail I think.'

'I happen to think Genesis 1 to 12 is a *mythology* of the Christian beginning rather than a historical account of the Christian beginning.'

'I read this . . . and the way that the translations I read most of the time are written, I read them like *prose*, unless it's Psalms.

'something that kind of effects my reading of it is that I don't think Genesis 1 to 11 is a literal account of what happened . . . I think it's *poetic story*.'

'And also, looking at the stories, trying to examine what genre they are, trying to compare them to other ancient near eastern stories, I come away thinking "you know these are *reinterpretations* of stories that were current at the time when they were written".'

These genre designations were all offered by participants who indicated that the text shouldn't be taken as historical, as some of the quotes indicate. Those who opted for a historical reading did not designate the text as 'history' but rather specified the text should be read 'literally', which is a method of interpretation rather than a classification of genre.

The Psalm was described either as poetry, lament, or song (emphasis my own):

'People write *poems* like this which are, you know, "I'm going through a bad patch and so on"'

'they're *songs* and they're *poems* and were set to music but they still serve a purpose today'

'Yeah this is a *lament*, right?'

'I think many of the Psalms are just so honest, open *laments* or *praise*'

'this is a *song*'

The Influence of Literature   129

For Ephesians, participants were aware it was a letter and referred to it as such, but only one participant classified the text as anything other than a letter, referencing the passage as instruction (emphasis my own):

'when you interpret these New Testament *letters*'

'It was just a *letter* he wrote wasn't it? To a church.'

'Paul's doing something here in a whole *letter*'

'it's definitely direct kind of *instruction*'

It is likely that genre was considered in greater depth for Genesis because of the question of historicity that participants were tasked with, which naturally led to reflections of what type of text the narrative was intended to be. However, though explicit discussions of the genre of the Psalm and Ephesians were minimal, genre implicitly played a significant role in the way participants handled and approached the text. The following overview identifies three ways in which genre influenced reading and concludes that this lens has an important role to play in focusing participants' interpretive activity.

EXTRAPOLATING FROM GENRE

Chapter 4 analysed responses to Psalm 44 and highlighted the role that genre played in participants' decision about the truth of the psalmist's claims. Genre had a similar function to the doctrine of God in being used to establish 'what was really going on.' In the same way that the previous chapter demonstrated how participants started with the doctrine of God and used deductive reasoning to determine the historicity of Genesis, participants also began with the text's genre and using deductive reasoning established the extent to which the text reported reliable information.

This was demonstrated by Jake (St.A's) in relation to the Psalm: 'So I think we have to accept that this is a different kind of writing from history, it's not history, it's actually poetry . . . it's about people's feelings.' In this quote, Jake actively distinguishes between how one reads history and poetry and aligns the genre of poetry with 'feelings'. This suggests he associates history with objective fact and poetry with emotion and subjectivism, and thus the claims of the text need to be weighed in the light of genre.

The use of extrapolating from genre as a method to determine the reality or historicity of the text was also evident in discussion of Genesis. Participants used the genre of the text to determine the text's historicity. By doing this,

130   *Chapter 8*

participants were able to suggest that 'history' was not an appropriate designation considering what the text was intended to be. The text was never meant to be read as an accurate factual account of something that happened, and a historical reading is thus not respecting the inherent nature of the text. This can be seen by Sam (WO) in this extended quote of his genre designation cited above: 'But I think, for me, underlying my interpretation of the story, and this might be something that effects my reading of it, is that I don't think Genesis 1 to 11 is a literal account of what happened . . . what actually happened. I think it's poetic story, so I'm happy to almost ignore the problematic questions of "did God actually do this? Do I have to try and justify God in this?" Or do I just read it for what it is? As a story.' Sam evidences how Genesis's genre as 'poetic story' determines the appropriate questions that are to be asked of the text, which don't relate to implications of the account being 'real'. This extrapolating from genre to the reality of the text was closely linked with participants' assumptions about the text's author.

EXTRAPOLATING FROM THE AUTHOR

Contemplating the genre of a text requires examining the content of the text itself but also its historical context and origins. Who wrote this text and (to the extent that we can know this) what were they intending to communicate? Who were they writing to, and what were they hoping to accomplish by writing? Were they supposing themself to be writing a factually accurate account, or were they more concerned with making an ideological or theological point, or conveying their emotions? These types of questions about the author are part of the ways in which readers determine the genre of the text and, as a result, how it should be read.

Genesis, Psalm 44, and Ephesians provide three quite different perspectives on their (implied) authors. The author/narrator of Genesis does not identify themself or intrude upon the narrative. They recount the events of the flood without an obvious perspective or pejorative tone and have an omniscient quality—able to know everything that happened and God's response. This is the polar opposite to the author of the Psalm whose text expresses their personal grief and experience. Events are not being recounted from a future perspective but are being reflected upon from the midst of them. The author of the Psalm speaks to God rather than about God, revealing their lack of knowledge about God's reasoning, unlike the Genesis author who has privileged knowledge into the reasoning behind God's actions. However, what both authors have in common is their anonymity and ambiguity relating to when exactly in history their text was written.

In contrast, Ephesians offers (on the surface at least) more certainty as to the identity of the author and the time when the text was written. The involvement of the author in the text lies somewhere between Genesis and the Psalm. The use of first person midway through the text keeps the author in the reader's mind, but they are not nearly as prominent as in the Psalm and don't bring anything personal or emotional of themselves into the text. However, the text clearly addresses sets of people, which also serves to remind the reader of the dynamics of communication underlying the text. The author does not offer any particularly privileged insight into the actions or intentions of God but speaks confidently of Godly matters.

Amongst the focus groups, authorship was a topic of discussion. For example, at St.C's, Vanessa and Neil discussed the likelihood that the author of Genesis was prone to exaggeration or embellishment and Neil commented (erroneously) that scholars generally agree Moses is the author of Genesis, which would explain the anachronism of the distinction between clean and unclean animals in the text when the law had yet to be given which would inaugurate the clean/unclean distinction. This was deemed to be troubling because Moses was not present for the events of the flood thus leading the group to question his ability to report them, highlighted in the following exchange:

> Neil: He might have embellished it. Obviously Moses wasn't around when Noah was around was he?
>
> Stacey: We assume not!
>
> Neil: Fairly obviously . . .
>
> Michael: Unless he had a tardis or something. . . .
>
> Vanessa: Unless he was masquerading as Shem, or Ham or Japeth.
>
> Neil: Unless he had a tardis or a time macine . . . so questions arise from that too, certainly as far as question three is concerned.

Question three asked the participants if the text was historically accurate, so Neil's recognition that Moses wasn't offering an eye-witness account led him to further 'questions' about the text's facticity.

A further example where the author was considered in relation to the text's truthfulness, was Henry's proposal of the theory of accommodation. This theory assumes that the author of Genesis 7 was intending to truthfully convey an event that they experienced, but due to their limited knowledge, their understanding of what they experienced was incorrect. In the words of Paul Seely, 'It is thus perfectly in accord with an orthodox view of inspiration to

132 *Chapter 8*

recognize that the Flood account encompasses an accommodation to ancient cosmology. Yet that cosmology lacks any real existence, and therefore the literal history of a cosmic Flood that is dependent upon it is falsified.'[31] As the author had no concept of 'the world', vast flooding that went as far as the eye could see would have been considered to be the whole world. In Henry's words, 'it would make far more sense if it was a local area, which is their known world, which is all they've had known about . . . '. It's worth noting that for Henry, this characterisation of the author is formed from knowledge of how human understanding of the universe has increased exponentially since the time the text was written and a scientific conviction that a universal flood did not occur. In other words, Henry's assessment of the author of the text does not just derive from the content of the text itself but from non-biblical knowledge. This suggests that tradition, experience, and reason are also at work in the determination of who the author is and what they were trying to do with the text, discussed in the next chapter. This could also be seen in participants' reading of the Psalm. Their experience and knowledge of being emotionally distressed and traumatised had given rise to the understanding that 'objective' or 'factual' thinking is often obscured in this state.

The use of genre in determining the text's historicity outlined above is thus nuanced by the character and trustworthiness of the implied author. It is not simply that poetry equates to subjectivism or history equates to objectivism, but that the perceived character and agenda of the author contributes to how the genre of the text is construed. Identifying genre is thus not simply a matter of categorising what type of text is being read which leads ipso facto to a determination of the text's historicity or truthfulness, but rather an exercise in identifying what the author was doing in the writing of their text and given what can be gleaned about them from the text, whether they are to be 'trusted'.

In summary, participants read through the lens of genre when they let the text's genre, inclusive of its perceived author, function as a foundational consideration upon which to build a case for the text's factual accuracy and trustworthiness.

GENRE-BASED ENGAGEMENT PRACTICES

Whilst extrapolating from genre influenced what participants concluded about the text, a further significant practice when reading through the lens of genre related to how participants handled the text. It was the text's genre and content that largely determined what participants did with the text and how they engaged with it. Many of these ways of engaging with the text according to genre are to be expected. For example, Genesis elicited

The Influence of Literature 133

twenty-three instances of participants referencing either the chapter before or after the one read, whereas this only occurred three times in relation to the Psalm and once for Ephesians. This is unsurprising given that Genesis 7 is the middle section of a narrative, so references to the surrounding narrative are to be expected. Yet it is still evidence of the genre of the text influencing what engagement practices participants employed.

A further genre-based differentiation in engagement practices was reflections upon the society and culture from which the text arose, which occurred twenty-seven times in discussion of Ephesians, but only three times for Genesis and five for the Psalm. This is probably because participants simply had more knowledge about the Greco-Roman society behind the Ephesians text, as evidenced by Michael who confidently claimed in relation to Ephesians, 'like literally shocking at that time for him to say you can't go and do whatever you want with whomever.' In this, Michael evidences a seemingly confident understanding of the cultural climate surrounding Ephesians.

However, such societal and culture reflections are also likely to have been employed as a result of the epistle genre. Participants were more mindful that the text had original recipients and thus reflected on their culture and historical setting more than for the Psalm and Genesis where the intended audience is not clear or reinforced within the text. This can be a seen in a comment like Michael's above, or the following by Neil: 'I think that would have been quite explosive to some readers.' The participants were aware of an original audience due to the nature of the text as a letter and were therefore more inclined to consider their contextual situation.

Another example of genre-based engagement practices is reflections on the passage's 'textual history', which occurred ten times in discussion of Genesis but only four times for the Psalm and never for Ephesians. These 'textual history' reflections focused on the composition and transmission of the text to account for particular features of it. As Genesis was the oldest text and in a narrative style that was very different from contemporary stories, participants were inclined to make more comments about its style and history, reflecting on the oral tradition behind the text to account for these features. Vanessa provides an example:

> And it's interesting that it would have originally been an oral tradition, rather than written. Like, we speak very differently . . . than when we're writing. I take minutes a lot and interpreting what people mean from what they say, even in a business meeting, is actually quite a skill because people never say what they mean . . . I would know people who I take minutes of who make bold statements, like sweeping statements like 'the whole earth', they don't mean the whole earth, they are exaggerating to make a point. Being an oral tradition there's different rules to writing down.

134 *Chapter 8*

Vanessa's group were concerned by the concept of embellishment or hyper-bole in the text, but this was explained in terms of the 'oral tradition' behind it. Vanessa suggests that these practices are more obvious when said in person than when they're written down, and this might explain what would appear to be erroneous details (if one doesn't believe in a worldwide flood). The genre of the text as an ancient narrative prompted engagement practices relating to textual history.

These examples all serve to illustrate the point that the genre lens had a significant role in determining the practices that participants used to explore the text. However, though genre certainly played into the extent to which certain methods were employed, many ways of engaging with the text were demonstrated across all three texts, corroborating what was identified in chapter 6, that participants have a bank of hermeneutical practices that were deemed appropriate for the exploration of the text as a biblical text, as Scripture, rather than as a particular genre of biblical text. The extent to which these biblical practices were employed, however, was related to the content of the text. For example, all three texts prompted instances of participants comparing the text with other theologically similar biblical content, a result of their belief in the unity of the canon. However, the Psalm elicited slightly higher instances of this practice. Why might that be the case? I suggest it's because the Psalm raised the most complex theological questions for participants, as well as it being difficult to historically contextualise. As a result, the Psalm was contextualised theologically in light of the whole Bible. So, whilst this practice isn't unique to the Psalm, its contents will have likely affected the frequency with which it was employed.

In summary, though some reading practices were employed for all three texts as a result of them being biblical, the extent to which this occurred varied according to genre, and thus reading the text through the lens of genre largely determined what practices were used to explore the text.

THE DOCTRINE OF SCRIPTURE
THROUGH THE LENS OF GENRE

Having established the effect of participants reading through the genre lens, it is worth asking whether participants viewed the doctrine of Scripture through the lens of genre. If they did, how does the genre lens shape the doctrine of Scripture lens?

Whilst the genre lens didn't affect participants' perception of the Bible as the doctrine of God lens did, participants demonstrated that genre did influence how their Bible beliefs functioned. This is because participants' predominant belief about the Bible, that it is a vehicle of divine communication, functions itself as a genre—a textual category. This conception of Scripture has similarities with the prophetic genre with its emphasis on God's communication, albeit in different forms and with different content. Goldingay has highlighted how the prophetic genre is the truest locus of the inspiration of Scripture, and this category has come to be a model for an overarching conception of Scripture.[32]

The Bible's overarching genre as divine teaching then, also had to be married with the text at hand's literary genre—narrative, poetry, epistle. The process of marrying these two genres determined how exactly the text was conceived as God's teaching. Genesis and the Psalm taught the reader indirectly, in that the text's 'teaching' was not explicitly stated. Genesis was understood to be divine teaching in what the narrative shows about God (teaching theological truths) and in the example of Noah (teaching how to live). The Psalm was understood to be divine teaching in what the poem demonstrates about relating to God (teaching how to live). On the other hand, the teaching of Ephesians was explicit in what the text instructs, which was either taken as specific behaviour or underlying principles (teaching how to live).

What this meant was that a commitment to the doctrine of Scripture which centred on the Bible's teaching function, manifested itself in different forms according to the nature and content of the text being read. What it means for the text to be divine teaching for the majority of participants, is consequently genre and content related. The effective force of the doctrine of Scripture lens is determined by the genre lens.

What this ultimately means is that if the doctrine of Scripture lens sets the reading agenda in locating meaning in the text's teaching, the genre lens determines how that teaching is manifested and methods of discerning it. The genre lens can therefore be profitably seen as a focusing lens that sharpens the reader's interpretive focus both in identifying what form the text's teaching takes and prescribing what hermeneutical activity is appropriate for engaging with such teaching.

Conclusion: Genre Lens

In summary, reading through the lens of genre involved extrapolating from the text's genre and implied author to determine the factual accuracy of the text. Additionally, how participants handled the text was genre-dependent. As such, reading through the genre lens prescribed both interpretative conclusions and practices.

Most significantly, reading through the genre lens, in relation to the doctrine of Scripture lens, gives force and specificity to determining how the text functions as a teaching resource.

136   *Chapter 8*

These factors combine to give the genre lens the overall force of a focusing lens that hones the reader's understanding of the text as teaching and the practices to employ in relation to this.

So far, I have looked at the doctrine of Scripture as a lens that sets the reading agenda, the doctrine of God as a lens that determines interpretative conclusions, and the genre as a lens that establishes the form that the text's teaching takes. There is one other dominant lens to add to this emerging picture of the participants doctrine of Scripture and hermeneutical activity—experience, the topic of the next chapter.

NOTES

1. Fish, *Is there a text?*, 322–37.

2. Kevin J. Vanhoozer, 'The Semantics of Biblical Literature: Truth and Scripture's Diverse Literary Forms', in D. A. Carson and John. D. Woodbridge, eds., *Hermeneutics, Authority and Canon* (Leicester: Inter-Varsity, 1986), 80.

3. Gordon D. Fee and Douglas K. Stuart, *How to Read the Bible for All It's Worth*. 4th ed. (Grand Rapids, MI: Zondervan, 2014).

4. Beynon and Sach, *Dig Deeper*, 111.

5. Pleins, *When the Great Abyss Opened*, 17.

6. Ibid., 18.

7. Ibid., 18–19.

8. Andrew Louth, ed., *Genesis 1–11* (Oxfordshire: Routledge, 2013), 130–31, ProQuest Ebook Central.

9. Vern Poythress, 'Dealing with the Genre of Genesis and its Opening Chapters,' *Westminster Theological Journal* 78, no. 2 (2016): 224.

10. Ibid., 228.

11. Bailey, *Noah*, 118.

12. Ibid., 119.

13. Ibid., 120.

14. Ibid., 126.

15. Ibid., 129.

16. Brueggemann, *Genesis*, 74.

17. Poythress, 'Dealing with the Genre of Genesis,' 228.

18. Brueggemann and Bellinger, *Psalms*, 209.

19. Ibid.

20. Rom-Shiloni, 'Psalm 44: The Powers of Protest,' 686.

21. Loren Crow, 'The Rhetoric of Psalm 44,' 295.

22. Mays, *Psalms*, 177.

23. Rom-Shiloni, 'Psalm 44,' 689.

24. Mays, *Psalms*, 178; Eric Lane, *Psalms 1–89* (Fearn: Christian Focus, 2006), 204; Bruce Waltke, James Houston and Erica Moore, *The Psalms as Christian Lament* (Grand Rapids, MI: W. B. Eerdmans, 2014), 180.

The Influence of Literature 137

25. Fowl, *Ephesians*, 10.

26. 'Paul, an apostle of Christ Jesus but the will of God, To the saints who are in Ephesus and are faithful in Christ Jesus'

27. Stott, *Ephesians*, 21.

28. Fowl, *Ephesians*, 10.

29. Martin, *Ephesians*, 4.

30. Ibid., 5.

31. Seely, 'Noah's Flood,' 311.

32. John Goldingay, *Models for Scripture* (Grand Rapids, MI: W. B. Eerdmans, 1994), part 3.

Chapter 9

The Influence of Context

Reading Through Experience

So far, in chapters 3–6, I have explored how participants' doctrine of Scripture lens influenced their reading in setting the agenda and purpose of reading—to seek God's teaching in the text. In chapter 7, I added to this by showing how participant's doctrine of God lens had a role in determining their interpretative conclusions about what God's teaching *contained*, and in chapter 8, I identified how the genre lens had a role in determining *the form* God's teaching would take. This chapter looks at the final lens that proved to be prominent amongst my participants—context.

CONTEXT LENS

A person's context is their social environment and the culture in which they live. This context not only shapes an individual but also shapes their self-perception and experience of the world. As such, a person's context is not just what is external to them, but what is internal to them as an individual: their identity and experience of the world. A person's context is not a single entity, but the product of a number of interdependent sub-contexts or contextual paradigms of which they partake. For example, my participants all lived in Britain and were therefore living in a contemporary 'Western' context but within this culture are a myriad of sub-contexts relating to a variety of factors, for example, socio-economic status defining a person's context as 'middle class'.

Since the beginning of the 'reader-response' movement within biblical studies, the role of the reader and particularly the impact of their social location upon the making of meaning has been acknowledged. Readers were no longer considered to be passive, simply receiving a given meaning that the text puts forward, but they were actively involved in the construction of

140   *Chapter 9*

meaning. In Thiselton's words, 'reader-response theories call attention to the active role of communities of readers in constructing what counts for them as "what the text means."'[1] Part of this recognition involved acknowledging the ways in which one's social location impacts their making of meaning. Mark Powell's comparison of how different international readers interpret the reason for the prodigal son's poverty provides an excellent example.[2] The 'Bible in the Life of the Church' project from the Anglican Communion offers insights into the ways that context informs the interpretation of Scripture, with the project offering a window into the Bible reading of communities across the communion and the globe.[3]

In addition to one's geographical location are a myriad of factors that are now recognised as playing an active role in interpretation. Some were noted in chapter 1, namely, personality, place, and gender, but to add to this list, scholarship is now asking more context-based questions, such as what is the unique impact of reading Scripture from the perspective of being incarcerated,[4] from within the LGBTQI+ community,[5] and of being Black?[6]

Whilst my participants shared in many contexts, they also brought their own unique perspectives to the interpretation of the text. The following overview, however, considers broader contextual categories. For example, I have already conjectured that participants' secular scientific cultural context could have been a reason that defences for Genesis's historicity and Ephesians's relevance did not draw upon the doctrine of Scripture, in chapters 3 and 5, respectively. This is just one example of participants demonstrating their participation in a myriad of contexts by referencing societal norms and shared cultural knowledge and insight. This reflects Todd's findings, couched in reference to dominant 'voices', that his participants 'hold received notions of the text's authority in tension with aspects of their experience of contemporary culture, which questions that authority. The "canonical" voice co-exists and interacts with contemporary more contingent ones.'

However, two contextual paradigms in particular emerged in discussion: participants' Christian context and their personal context. The following sections explore instances of participants reading the Bible through their contextual lens.

Christian Context

All participants were Christians and shared in being part of Christian culture which was further specified by being Evangelical and Anglican. When participants read the text through the lens of their Christian context, they employed relevant knowledge and experience to elucidate the text and make connections to their lives. The Christian context thus established the parameters within which participants could identify the text's meaning. Though

The Influence of Context 141

closely related, the following sections reflect first on participants' use of their Christian knowledge and second, their Christian experience, gained from their Christian context.

Christian Knowledge

Participants' reading of the texts through the lens of their Christian context involved their drawing upon Christian knowledge. This knowledge took two forms: tradition and contemporary input.

The best example of drawing upon tradition as a form of Christian knowledge is Gina's (St.A's) assertion of the Bible's authority as the 'basic thing' to be trusted in for information and she states this specifically in reference to the issue of the existence of Satan. Her full quote is as follows: 'Because [God] allowed free will and he created angels and one of them decided he didn't like . . . he wanted to be God as well. I only go by what my Bible tells me Charles and I do believe most of it, maybe not always literally but if I don't believe it then what am I trusting in if I don't trust, to me, what is a basic thing?' This comment is somewhat unintentionally ironic as in claiming she trusts the Bible as an authoritative source regarding the existence of Satan, Gina actually details a prominent Christian tradition, rather than Scripture itself: that Satan was an angel who wanted to be like God and fell from heaven. The only explicit biblical reference to Satan falling from heaven comes from Luke 10:18,[7] but this does not mention the idea that Satan wanted to be like God as Gina declared. There are more complex scriptural passages that Gina could have been referring to—several prophecies addressing human figures have traditionally been interpreted as also speaking of Satan.[8] The association of these verses with Satan is the result of an interpretative tradition rather than a plain reading, though Gina claims her belief in the origin of Satan is a result of her trusting in 'the basic thing', the Bible. This demonstrates how tradition as Christian knowledge can operate largely under the radar. Gina did not differentiate between the Bible's content and traditional biblical interpretations.

Another example of the blurred lines between Scripture and tradition was also demonstrated in participants' false Noah narratives. Participants from both St.J's and St.A's incorrectly remembered that Noah either warned his contemporaries of the impending flood or was mocked by his contemporaries for building the ark. This does not occur in the biblical text. At a stretch, the idea that Noah interacted with his peers could be claimed as 'biblical' on the basis of 2 Peter 2:5 which describes Noah as a 'preacher of righteousness'.[9] However, this is a tenuous link and most likely itself the result of an earlier tradition attested to by Nadav Sharon and Moshe Tishel who establish several occurrences of this embellishment in second temple Jewish literature,

142   *Chapter 9*

showing it has been a persistent idea early in the history of interpretation.[10] Participants therefore demonstrated first, how tradition forms a part of their Christian knowledge as a result of their Christian context, and second, how Christian knowledge in the form of tradition is often confused with biblical content. This undermines the Evangelical Anglican belief in the Bible's sufficiency as a sole authority.

However, there were two notable explicit uses of tradition from the same participant, Sam (WO). In the discussion of Genesis, Sam stated that he was influenced by Jewish readings of the narrative, and in discussion of the Psalm and divine violence Sam stated that he reads the Old Testament acts of violence 'with the lens of the Church Fathers in terms of allegorical readings.' In both these instances Sam was aware and owned his interpretation as belonging to certain strands of historical tradition.

Sam's use of tradition was consonant with the second way in which the majority of participants read through the lens of their Christian knowledge: citing contemporary teaching, preaching, and scholarship. For example, Emma from St.J's explicitly stated that she now interpreted the Noah narrative in light of a book she had read by Rob Bell. Several explicit and implicit references were made to knowledge gained from books reflecting Bielo's finding from his fieldwork that 'books . . . have become the primary way that Evangelicals learn and reproduce core Christian doctrines, as well as matters of orthopraxy.'[11] This is just one example of many instances where participants referenced some form of contemporary input, often vaguely, as something 'read the other day' or 'heard.' These sources of input were all a product of participant's knowledge as a result of being engaged in a Christian context. Rogers explores how knowledge and hermeneutical practices are learnt by church members through such mediation (rather than direct Bible reading) as a result of the congregational horizon.[12]

When participants drew upon their Christian knowledge either in the form of tradition or contemporary external input, they were fleshing out the text through providing additional detail or background information. The text was then read in the light of this information. In other words, the traditions or teaching to which participants were exposed, whether this be explicitly or implicitly, framed and limited participant's understanding of the text. Understanding was therefore restricted to the parameters set for it by the participants' collective Christian knowledge. The false Noah narratives highlights this. Whilst the participants at St.J's checked their Bibles to confirm the entirety of the story and realised their mistake, participants at St.A's did not, and in fact, Amy formed a textual application on the basis of their false narrative:

The Influence of Context 143

I usually take from this that God asked Noah to do something that seemed ridiculous and everybody else was sort of making fun of him, 'why is he building this boat?' and I take it from this that sometimes God might want me to do something and I think 'really?' and other people . . . might say 'well that's ridiculous' and I then have to struggle and think 'well is it ridiculous or is this really the path that God wants me to follow?'

This demonstrates how a reader's Christian context and the knowledge this furnishes them with, both traditional and contemporary, has a direct impact upon the interpretations that participants were able to make. Where the false Noah narrative was not identified, Amy made an application from the text about remaining faithful to God despite opposition. Where the false Noah narrative was identified at St.J's, participants were unable to conclude about why there was seemingly no opportunity for anyone other than Noah and his family to be saved:

I also think that potentially if Noah had tried to intercede for someone or the people then God might have listened to that because he tends to. Or tends to at least extend the time that he gives people to repent. But maybe he wasn't moved to that because that wasn't God's plan in the first place. He really wanted to destroy everything. So maybe Noah just didn't think about it. Or that maybe he didn't like anyone either and so he was happy that they were all going to die. (Jane)

Jane's guessing as to why there was no intercession from Noah regarding his contemporaries was speculative. Having established the silence of the text, the groups' Christian knowledge set the scope of what they could conclude about the text, which was ultimately inconclusive.

Christian Corporate Experience

In addition to knowledge, participants also drew upon their experiences of Christian culture at a corporate level. For example, Anne (St.J's) contrasted contemporary Christian attitudes with that of the psalmist: 'It's very different to the way that we would pray. I think that most people, what would be most common, is that people feel distant from God because they're not spending enough time in prayer or they're not seeking God, rather than God is sleeping and not responding.' Anne offers her knowledge of how Christians tend to think about God. This knowledge was not predicated on a specific doctrine or source of external input but rather was offered anecdotally, presumably as something she had learnt and experienced from being a part of Christian culture. Participants often made such references to corporate Christian tendencies or proclivities, such as Taylor's (TO) comment that 'we expect God to be on our timeframe' or Jane's (St.J's) observation that Christian churches have an optimistic, positive outlook.

At times, participants showed self-awareness of the influence of their Christian experience and knowledge. For example, when reflecting at St.J's about their ability to understand Ephesians, the participants showed self-awareness about their own education, exemplified in Jane's comment:

> If a non-Christian reads this part of the Bible they can very much be like 'oh, so you agree with slavery then, the Bible says you can have slaves.' And you're like, 'no, it's cultural!', and they're like, 'so what about this part of the Bible?' . . . 'no, that's not cultural, that's for now!' That is quite interesting and it's really true that when you come from a Christian background, then there's certain things that you just hear over and over again and you're like 'ok that's what we believe'.

This quote demonstrates how participants realised that their reading of the text had been shaped by their Christian background. Occasionally participants would refer to their specific Christian experience, such as 'conservative' (Adam, GLC) or 'liberal' (Emma, St.J's), but on the whole Christian background experience was an implicit factor of reading the text.

Whereas participants wielded Christian knowledge in order to shed light upon the text, they used the text to shed light upon their corporate Christian experience. Participants sought to make connections between the text and their own lives (a consequence of the doctrine of Scripture, as has been seen) and therefore frequently contrasted the text with their corporate Christian experience.

In both these activities, reading through the lens of Christian context ultimately set the scope of what conclusions could be drawn from the text. This is reminiscent of Village's suggestion that one of the ways to think about how ordinary readers engage with the Bible is analogous to the parable of the talents. They read with the skills and background and experience and education they have at their disposal.[13] This ultimately is limiting. Interpretation is limited first by the available knowledge that participants had to expand their understanding of the text, and limited second, in the applications made according to their perceived corporate Christian experience. As Village recognised from his research, this highlights the difficulty of enabling readers 'to apply texts to their own world in a way that is not wholly dominated by that world or the assumptions they bring to the text.'[14]

The Influence of Context 145

PERSONAL CONTEXT

Very much connected to participants' Christian context is their individual, personal context. This incorporates facets of their personal identity, experiences, and knowledge. As no one lives in a vacuum, one's individual context is shaped by their broader context and culture and the following sections are thus mindful of the ways in which one's personal context is related to their Christian context.[15] The dominant ways in which participants read through the lens of their individual context included their previous encounters with the texts they were reading, their identity, and their personal Christian experiences.

Previous Readings

Participants had prior experience with the texts and referenced these when reading. Sometimes, this was simply acknowledging previous unanswered questions or notes a participant had made when reading the text in the past. On other occasions, participants offered their previous interpretations of the text, such as Amy (St.A's) commenting regarding Genesis, 'what I usually take from this . . . '. Amy then went on to offer a practical application from the text about obedience to God; she read the text in light of her previous application. A third type of reference to previous readings, was the acknowledgement of a change in the way the participant read the text. For example, Emma (St.J's) reflected on how her attitude towards the Ephesians text had changed over the years: '15 years ago, before I became a Christian, I would have been incensed by this passage. . . . because there's so much cultural oppression of women, that it taps into that kind of fire, and it took me a long time to get to where I could actually think about the whole bit, the whole passage, rather than just spluttering.' Emma reveals that her personal experience as a female and her knowledge and experience of the 'cultural oppression of women' had initially caused her to react strongly to the passage, such that she hadn't fully appreciated it.

These examples reveal two different ways in which previous readings can function. Amy's previous readings determined her present reading so that she was repeating what she 'usually takes' from the text, rather than exploring new avenues of meaning. In contrast, Emma's reflection reveals that she built upon her previous readings allowing them to grow and change. However, it should be noted that in both instances, previously held interpretations were offered; Emma's view of the text had changed in the past, not upon reading the text during the focus group. Indeed, it was difficult to discern the extent to which participants embraced new interpretations in the focus group

146   *Chapter 9*

discussions of the text. Though participants clearly did indicate that some
ideas they or others suggested were new to them, no one expressly stated a
strong conviction that they were adopting a new interpretation. The extent
to which participants were actively participating in a hermeneutical circle or
spiral was therefore difficult to discern.

What is of note, is that participants read through the lens of their previous
experiences with the text and so weren't beginning their interpretation from
a neutral or uninformed perspective. What they brought to the text, in terms
of their history with it, affected where they could go with it. Emma's journey
over several years with the text meant that she was highly unlikely to revert to
an interpretation that the text is sexist in the course of a single reading. Whilst
there is always a possibility of new and different interpretations, these cannot
emerge regardless of the interpretations of the past. Previous readings limit
the scope of interpretations that a reader makes. The influence of previous
encounters or experience of the Bible is explored on a broader level by David
Ford in his empirical research focused on the Bible reading of those outside
the church. Ford highlights how his participants' previous encounters with
Christianity and church affected their reading of the Bible.[16]

Identity

Emma's comment above demonstrates not only the tendency for participants
to read through the lens of their previous experiences directly with the text,
but also their personal identity and life experiences. Emma reflected on the
text in light of her identity and experience as a Christian, a female, and elsewhere, a wife. Other participants also referenced aspects of their personal
identity and these were both individual (as in the example above) and collective, such as references to participants being members of 'modern, western,
liberal society' (Christopher, TO) or simply 'contemporary readers' (Neil,
St.C's). Though Ephesians prompted identity reflections the most, they also
occurred in relation to Genesis and the Psalm, showing that reader identity
and context was a consideration even if the text didn't directly address questions of identity.

By commenting on their own identity, either personal or collective, participants showed an awareness of the subjectivity of reading; they understood
their response to the text in light of the influence of their experience. This
served both to highlight the difficulty of engaging with the text, as well as
prompted deeper engagement. By acknowledging the limitations of personal
identity in understanding and interpreting the text fully, participants were
prompted to attempt to engage with experiences beyond their own identity.
For example, at GLC, Martin as a married man wanted to hear how Adam
engaged with the text as a single man, and vice versa. They sought to expand

The Influence of Context   147

their own understanding from the identity perspective of someone different to themselves. In this way, the group offered a broader collective perspective for approaching the text than any single individual could have on their own. However, this perspective was ultimately limited by the members of the group. As Johnny pointed out at the beginning of the Ephesians discussion, 'I'm really aware that the discussion is being had by three men, so it would be good to have a female perspective.' The three male members of GLC couldn't engage with the text beyond their male perspective.

Christian Personal Experience

In addition to participants' identity and previous readings, their personal context also involved their individual Christian experience. This is very closely connected to, but not the same as, their corporate Christian experience. Rather than experiences of the Christian community or Christian tendencies on a broader scale, personal Christian experience involved participants reflecting on their own spiritual experiences and text applications.

References to spiritual experiences occurred amongst various participants, varying from implied visceral, charismatic experiences, to experiences of how God had been active in their lives.[17] For example, Henry spoke of God healing his heart and bringing transformation, and Dean spoke of having felt far away from God. Drawing upon personal spiritual experience was a way in which participants found connections between the text and their personal lives.

In addition to spiritual experiences, participants reflected on their personal experience of applying texts. This occurred predominantly in Ephesians, with some reflections prompted by Psalm 44 but none from Genesis. Closely aligned with previous encounters, participants related how the texts functioned in their own lives. In other words, their previous readings of the text did not just establish certain lines of interpretation, but certain lived consequences. In the Ephesians discussion married participants in particular reflected on their marriage relationship and how the text related to their experience and behaviour; for example, Henry (St.J's) reflected on his previous struggle to express his love to his wife. In the Psalm discussion, participants spoke about their experiences of being open and honest before God and of God's comfort when they're in a distressed place. For example, Dean (TO) spoke of the Psalms as being a 'go to' for his personal expressions of grief and frustration.

Participants thus drew upon their individual Christian experience to make connections between themselves and the content of the text. Participants saw the text as something that should actively relate to their lives, and they

148   *Chapter 9*

made this relation explicit in reflecting on their spiritual and applicatory experiences.

THE DOCTRINE OF SCRIPTURE
THROUGH THE LENS OF CONTEXT

Having overviewed how participants read the text through their context lens, in what ways did participants view the doctrine of Scripture through their contextual lens? How did readers' context shape their understanding of the doctrine of Scripture?

First, the doctrine of Scripture is a traditional doctrine of the Christian church and participant's beliefs about Scripture had thus come to be formed in relation to their Christian context. This was evidenced on a number of occasions. Most explicitly, Nick (WO) referenced his Anglican heritage that holds in belief to Scripture, tradition, and reason as an authority triad. More subtly, Neil's (St.C's) comments about the inspiration of Scripture reveal a traditional origin: 'Because I think with Scripture, if we believe Scripture is God-breathed, that's the word, the phrase in the New Testament: God-breathed . . . that is, we as Christians believe this is the Word of God'. Neil quotes a traditional interpretation of 2 Timothy 3:16 by assuming it applies to the entirety of the canon and his emphasis is placed on corporate belief ('we as Christians believe'). The nuance is subtle but significant, indicating that Neil, despite quoting the Bible, is actually drawing upon a traditional belief from his Christian context and using biblical language to underpin it rather than drawing upon the Bible to emphasise the scriptural origins of the belief.

A final example demonstrates some of the nuances involved in one's Christian context and how this shapes an understanding of the doctrine of Scripture. In response to Martin's suggestion that the psalmist is arrogant, Adam (GLC) replied, 'I try not to judge Scripture as such and I wouldn't want to say, "oh he's arrogant" because it's like "this is the Word of God" and that's partly my background of being fairly conservative and everything whereas you were saying you're from a . . . you have a more different approach to things and so when we come to certain issues I'm approaching from one angle, he's approaching from another angle.' Adam implicitly affirms that his understanding of the Bible as the Word of God does not allow room for the authors to be criticised in a negative fashion and this is a consequence of his 'conservative' background, which he contrasts with Martin's background. This quote affirms that the doctrine of Scripture is viewed through the lens of one's Christian context and this can differ amongst Christians depending on the specifics of their background, even within Evangelical Anglican parameters. One of the proposed answers to this issue is suggested by Rogers: 'it

The Influence of Context 149

is critical for churches to know their tradition, to be aware of their congregational horizons.'[18] Rogers in particular highlights how the church that one is a part of informs the traditions that are drawn upon in biblical interpretation.[19]

However, participants' Bible beliefs weren't just shaped by their Christian context but also their personal context. This is because the Bible is an experienced reality for Evangelical Anglicans. It's not just that readers let their personal experiences inform their reading, but that their reading itself is an experience.[20] Experience of the Bible informs readers' dispositions and beliefs about the Bible. What does it mean for the Bible to be an experienced reality?

First, participants experienced the Bible in the form of encountering the text, i.e., the actual experience of reading the text and the response that it evokes. This has three components: first, an emotional experience that the text evokes, such as Stacey (St.C's) claiming reading Genesis 7 made her 'uncomfortable'. Second, an experience of understanding or lack thereof. Participants' experience of the texts they read was closely related to their ability to understand and engage with the material. For example, Rose (St.A's) expressed not always being able to understand the message of a Psalm. The emotional experience and the experience of understanding may therefore be connected—the ability to understand itself evokes certain emotions. Third and finally, the event of reading the text might prompt the experience of divine communication—hearing God 'speak' or teach through the text or having an experience of God through the medium of the text. This third component is not a given of the reading experience and is partly determined by the expectation the reader places on the text.

This connects to the second way in which participants experienced the Bible—the experience of application, i.e., how the text makes a practical difference in participants' lives. This was the most common type of reflection participants made about their experience of the Bible, with contributions focusing on how texts function pragmatically. This was both specific, as has been noted in relation to the focus group texts, but also broad, such as Jane's (St.J's) comment about Romans 5:3–5 acting as a 'mantra in my head'.

What all of this highlights is that the act of reading the Bible is in itself an experience. This accumulation of experiences of encountering the Bible has a role in shaping the doctrine of Scripture. In other words, the doctrine of Scripture is not just an intellectual reality but an experienced reality through the event of reading. Experience of the Bible influences beliefs about the Bible but this is reciprocal; beliefs about the Bible equally influence experience of the Bible. For example, the experience of being taught by God through the text reinforces the belief that the Bible is God's teaching resource. But similarly, the belief that the Bible is God's teaching resource sets the expectation of being taught through the text. Beliefs about and experiences of the Bible are thus mutually reinforcing.

150   *Chapter 9*

Viewing the doctrine of Scripture through the lens of context therefore nuances individuals' doctrine of Scripture. As with the doctrine of God, a participant's personal background, membership in specific Christian communities, and experiences of reading the Bible contribute to a unique slant in relation to their doctrine of Scripture and how this plays out in the process of reading and interpreting.

Conclusion: Context Lens

In summary, participants' contextual lens was dominated by their personal and Christian context. Participants' reading of the Bible through this lens involved a variety of practices: drawing upon Christian knowledge in the form of tradition and contemporary sources of input to shed light on the text; letting the text shed light upon their corporate Christian experience; building upon previous interpretations; reflecting on the influence of their personal identity; and making connections between their personal experiences and the text. The overall force of reading through a contextual lens was setting the scope of what a text could mean. As the doctrine of Scripture lens determines the reading agenda in finding the text's meaning in the form of divine teaching, the contextual lens determines what that teaching could be. The text's meaning was thus identified within the matrixes of participants' personal and Christian context. In other words, what participants brought to the text, in terms of their personal and Christian experiences and knowledge, limited the scope of what the text could teach them.

Moreover, the contextual lens also had a role to play in participants' understanding of the doctrine of Scripture, evidenced by their references to the traditions and communities which formed their understanding of the Bible, as well as their experiences of reading and engaging with the Bible.

Before considering the four lenses that have been explored so far in this book and highlighting some overarching observations when placing these practices in conversation with hermeneutical theory (chapter 11), there is one more component of the research that has hitherto not been considered—the comparison of the formal and informal participants. The reader may have noticed or picked up from the quotes throughout the book that certainly in terms of language, but also knowledge, there were differences between informal and formal participants. Chapter 10 thus re-treads some of the ground that has been covered so far, but with a comparative consideration.

NOTES

1. Thiselton, *New Horizons*, 515.

2. Mark Powell, *What Do They Hear?: Bridging the Gap Between Pulpit and Pew* (Nashville: Abingdon Press, 2007), ch. 2.

3. Amos, ed., *The Bible in the Life of the Church*.

4. Bob Ekblad, *Reading the Bible with the Damned* (Lousville, KY: Westminster John Knox Press, 2005).

5. An early example of which is: Robert Goss and Mona West, eds., *Take Back the Word: A Queer Reading of the Bible* (Cleveland, OH: Pilgrim Press, 2000).

6. Esau McCaulley, *Reading While Black* (Downers Grove, IL: Inter-Varsity Press, 2020).

7. Luke 10:18, 'He said to them, "I watched Satan fall from heaven like a flash of lightning",' NRSV.

8. In Ezekiel 28:12–17, the Prince of Tyre is described as being in Eden with God and then subsequently cast out because of violence and a proud heart. In Isaiah 14:12–15, the King of Babylon is spoken against and referred to as 'Day Star, Son of Dawn' which in the King James Version is translated as the proper name Lucifer. Here, the Day Star's intention is in line with Gina's declaration, 'I will make myself like the Most High' and their subsequent fall is described.

9. 2 Peter 2:5, 'and if he did not spare the ancient world, even though he saved Noah, a herald of righteousness, with seven others, when he brought a flood on a world of the ungodly', NRSV.

10. Nadav Sharon and Moshe Tishel, 'Distinctive Traditions about Noah and the Flood in Second Temple Jewish Literature' in *Noah and His Books*, ed. Michael Stone (Atlanta, GA: Society of Biblical Literature, 2010), 156–58. Additionally, the persistence of this tradition has been propagated as a result of its reiteration in children's Bibles, documented by Russell Dalton's analysis of the story of Noah in children's Bibles throughout American history: Russell Dalton, *Children's Bibles in America: A Reception History of the Story of Noah's Ark in US Children's Bibles* (London: Bloomsbury, 2016).

11. Bielo, *Words Upon the Word*, 111.

12. Rogers, *Congregational Hermeneutics*, ch. 7.

13. Village, *The Bible and Lay People*, 167.

14. Ibid., 90.

15. Todd explores these paradigms in terms of 'domains' noting a difference between his participants' cultural domain, which was most dominant, and their modern confessional domain. See: Todd, 'The Talk,' 247–52.

16. David Ford, *Reading the Bible Outside the Church: A Case Study* (Eugene, OR: Pickwick, 2018).

17. For an empirical account of such spiritual experiences and how they can be learnt and associated with a broader Christian context, see: T. M. Lurhmann, Howard Nusbaum, and Ronald Thistead, 'The Absorption Hypothesis: Learning to Hear God in Evangelical Christianity,' *American Anthropologist* 112, no. 1 (2010): 66–78.

18. Rogers, *Congregational Hermeneutics*, 91.

19. Ibid., ch. 4.

Chapter 9

20. For research on Catholic experiences of the Bible, see: Tim Gorichanaz, 'Experiencing the Bible,' *Journal of Religious and Theological Information* 15, no. 1–2 (2016): 1–2, 19–31, DOI: 10.1080/10477845.2016.1168278.

Chapter 10

The Influence of Education

Comparing Responses

So far, I have examined my participants as a whole and any detections as to the differences between formal and informal participants will have been at the reader's own judgement. This chapter examines the conclusions of the previous chapters specifically in relation to whether there were any notable or significant differences between the two categories of participants. First, this chapter highlights some of the differences in participants' discussion of each text, both in relation to what they said about the text and what participants did with the text, concluding with some implications regarding the doctrine of Scripture. The chapter then goes on to consider any relevant differences between the lenses and lens usage of the two categories of participant, and then concludes with some reflections as to what all these differences might indicate about how theological education affects the doctrine of Scripture and its role in interpretation.

As was noted in chapter 2 but is worth reiterating here, formal participants were educated in a variety of theological institutions, both confessional and secular. Whilst the majority of participants had undertaken theological education for the purpose of going into ministry, some participants were in academia, and some were in roles unrelated to theology or ministry. This means participants' theological education not only varied but was also being 'used' in different contexts and for different purposes and therefore varied in terms of how much the content of their education was a part of their everyday lives. Though some differences could be seen between formal and informal participants, as will be elaborated, none were overwhelmingly stark, and this could likely be due to this breadth of theological education and current employment.

It is also worth owning that the analysis takes a somewhat statistical turn in this chapter, which differentiates it from those before. The interpretative conclusions and practices of the two categories of participants were compared

154 *Chapter 10*

for frequency to gain an overarching sense of significant differences, and the results are represented numerically.

THE BIBLE AND THEOLOGICAL EDUCATION

Before overviewing the differences found amongst my formal and informal participants, it is worth reviewing some important scholarship on the influence of theological education upon Bible beliefs. Though much is written on theological education and its value,[1] there are limited contributions within academia that specifically explore if theological education makes any difference to approaches to the Bible. In the UK, the work of Andrew Village is significant. His quantitative research consisted of 404 questionnaires completed by members of a range of churches and subsequently analysed for determinative patterns and correlations.[2]

The most important insights gained from Village's survey for my own purposes is the correlation of education with Bible reading attitudes and practices. He found higher levels of education are associated with a move away from 'conservative' to more 'liberal' beliefs about the Bible. As such, the practice of literalism declined with increasing education, even more so amongst those with theological higher education.[3] However, within Evangelicalism, education made no impact on the practice of literalism, something that Village suggests could be linked with charismatic experience: 'charismatic belief shapes both the way that Christians interpret their present-day experience and the way that they interpret the Bible. There is coherence between God experienced personally, God at work in the world, and God revealed in Scripture, but the key factor is personal experience.'[4] In other words, if one has experience of and belief in the extra-ordinary activity of God, one is more likely to maintain this belief in relation to the biblical text. An additional influencing factor in the choice of literalism as an interpretative strategy proved to be the doctrinal weight of the biblical material in question, explored in chapter 3.

Village also assessed his participants' use of biblical horizons in relation to a specific passage in the Gospel of Mark.[5] He found that those with higher education levels held a strong preference for the author horizon in opposition to the reader horizon. Yet in general, and as was established in chapter 5, relevance proved an essential feature of horizon separation and preference, with a tendency to avoid the author horizon for the sake of making meaning in the present. Village expresses concern regarding these findings that theological education brought the reader to the authorial horizon and 'left them there' but does not reflect on the doctrinal underpinnings of this horizon preference. Is it that theological education promotes particular hermeneutical activity, or

The Influence of Education   155

does such hermeneutical activity arise as a result of different beliefs about the Bible?

More recent research by Village has looked at the effect of higher education upon the faith those training for ministry[6] and found that the overall impact was minimal. As he caveats, this doesn't mean that theological education has no effect and indeed within ministerial training, character effects are increasingly valued above theological knowledge or positions. Harrison describes this effect of theological education:

> Nine qualities one might expect to see in the theologically educated: gratitude, joy, attention to beauty, responsiveness, humility, vulnerable learning, practiced listening, aware of the presence to God, and leisured diligence—not an exhaustive list and inevitably somewhat idiosyncratic. . . . The focus is less on knowledge and skills (important as these are) as on character, reflecting both the missional imperative to 'show the difference' following Jesus makes, and the assumption of the ancient world that education is inculturation ($\pi\alpha\iota\delta\epsilon\iota\alpha$) into a life of virtue ($\alpha\rho\epsilon\tau\eta$).[7]

Though such character might naturally have an impact upon engagement with the Bible, it is of note that there is no evidence that theological education has a specific outcome on Bible beliefs and practices.

Mark Powell's research involved a small-scale experiment explicitly contrasting the biblical interpretation of clergy and laity.[8] Though not overtly pinpointing the effect of education, the findings are indicative of the differences theological education might make to Bible reading, as a distinguishing factor between clergy and laity. Taking fifty clergy and fifty laity (from corresponding churches), Powell conducted two experiments. In both experiments participants read a Gospel passage and had to give a written response, but the prompt provided for their response differed. In the first experiment, participants were asked 'what does this story mean to you?' and in the second experiment they were asked, 'what does this mean?' Reflecting on the results from the first experiment, Powell notes 'most of the clergy responses indicate reader empathy with the character of Jesus, while most of the lay responses indicate reader empathy either with Jesus' disciples or with his audience (the Scribes and Pharisees)'.[9]

The findings from the second experiment are even more revealing. By removing the phrase 'to you', the types of responses varied. Powell found that a significant number of clergy referenced the author (Luke), whereas none of the laity did. This is in keeping with Village's findings above that show the theologically educated tend towards the author horizon. Another point of distinction was that in both questions nearly all the laity made some form of self-reference, but for the clergy self-reference was significantly lower for the

156   *Chapter 10*

question 'what does this story mean?' This might indicate that the laity readily apply the Bible to themselves, but clergy are less inclined to do so. Powell identifies a variety of understandings of where meaning is located across the range of responses: historically (the setting for the story), redactionally (the discourse setting of the narrative), and existentially (the setting of the readers). He concludes that laity always evinced a reader-oriented hermeneutic so that the question of meaning was always understood in terms of the reader. Consequently, in the case of the narrative genre, Powell suggests that the author-oriented hermeneutic may be less natural and has to be taught. How did my participants compare to these findings?

GENESIS

Interpretations

The points made by participants across all groups can be loosely categorised under six topics: (1) historicity, (2) narrative form, (3) moral challenge, (4) correct interpretation and/or implications/challenges, (5) story detail, and (6) meaning.

When looking at the points that were unique to informal and formal participants, the only topic with a distinct difference was number 6 listed above— statements of meaning relating to what the story is about, what can be learnt from it, and what it means for Christians today. Formal participants made significantly more points of this nature, with 27 percent of all the points made being about meaning, in comparison to 5 percent for informal participants. These additional comments about meaning were closely related to formal participants' engagement practices, which I discuss next.

Engagement Practices

Of all three texts, Genesis demonstrated the most disparity between how formal and informal participants handled the text.

Informal participants seemed to have a tendency to gather all relevant knowledge that they were able to and approach the text from a variety of angles: scientific, cultural, historical, literary, theological, and personal. For example, informal participants drew upon historical knowledge, scientific knowledge, and various resources and 'external input' in discussion of the plausibility of the events occurring. Additionally, they also drew upon their previous readings and understood the text through the lens of these experiences much more than formal participants. Informal participants also placed the narrative within the context of salvation history and discussed broader issues of sin and salvation in light of God's salvation plan.

Two other practices that dominated for informal participants included language analysis and imaginative speculation. These reflect two opposite ways of engaging with the text. The former, language analysis, looks closely at particular words or phrases of the text to ensure that the full depth of meaning has been discerned. The latter, imaginative speculation, engages on a creative level with the events of the narrative and suggests possibilities or potential consequences/details/circumstances that the text is silent about. These two practices, in combination with the others just listed, demonstrate the breadth of informal participants' engagement with this text.

This breadth is connected to informal participants' own recognition of both their limited understanding and more general limitations impeding their ability to understand. Several comments were made along these lines. It would appear that in light of these acknowledged limitations, the informal participants wielded all their available knowledge to shed light on the text and approach it from a variety of angles. In something of a 'kitchen sink' approach, they threw in all the relevant knowledge that they had about the text in order to understand better.

By contrast, formal participants were more confident in their ability to understand and interpret the text with no expression of limited understanding either inherent to the text or their own ability. Additionally, formal participants presented a more cohesive range of engagement practices than informal participants, one of which was demonstrating a stronger tendency to make links between Genesis and the rest of the Bible, with many of these intrabiblical references relating to Jesus' use of the Noah narrative. No informal participants referenced Jesus' use of the narrative and only one informal participant noted that Noah is mentioned in the New Testament. Similarly, formal participants were more inclined to reference other theologically similar biblical content and thus read canonically. They made more connections between the text and other biblical narratives, particularly within Genesis.[10]

Additionally, formal participants were also distinct in contrasting the narrative with non-biblical historical literature, specifically the Gilgamesh epic. Whilst one informal participant demonstrated knowledge of the Gilgamesh epic, this was only mentioned briefly and as confirmation of the existence of a flood, rather than a point of comparison to identify distinctive features of the Genesis text. This demonstrates more of a tendency for formal participants to consider the historical/literary context of the text. Taken together then, these insights suggest that formal participants are more inclined to read both canonically and contextually, in contrast to informal participants who embraced a variety of perspectives from which to understand the text.

Historicity and the Doctrine of Scripture

In terms of the historicity of Genesis, as a general tendency, informal participants showed more consensus in arriving at a hybrid understanding of the historicity of the narrative, believing it to contain both historical and non-historical components. The evidence or data that informal participants called upon in their determination of the text's historicity included scientific and historical knowledge. Additionally, informal participants were the only ones to raise the issue of the implications of historicity for the rest of the Bible. This indicated a concern for a consistency of approach to the biblical text as a whole, particularly the New Testament.

In contrast, formal participants demonstrated a broader range of opinions regarding historicity, from understanding the narrative as completely historical to largely fictional. In other words, formal participants demonstrated stronger views about historicity on either end of the liberal-conservative spectrum, whilst informal participants tended to occupy more of the middle ground. As stated above, Village's survey data found that amongst Evangelicals, theological education was found to have no impact upon levels of literalism, especially when combined with charismatic gifts.[11] Against this insight, my theologically educated Evangelical participants appeared to be both typical and atypical in demonstrating both literal and non-literal approaches to Genesis. This is likely because of the particular text in question—other Old Testament narratives outside of Genesis 1–11 might have rendered more homogenous results.[12]

The evidence or data that formal participants called upon in their determination of the text's historicity was much more text focused. This would suggest that interpretation for formal participants was conducted in relation to the text at hand, rather than the text in light of contemporary knowledge. However, as has been noted, formal participants also showed a greater awareness of other ancient flood accounts which was also a factor for some in their consideration of historicity. This shows a formal concern for historical context contrasting informal participants' use of knowledge from a contemporary context in determining historicity.

Formal participants did not reference a concern for what a non-historical reading indicates about the rest of the Bible. This could be because formal participants were more comfortable or familiar with the idea that Genesis 1–11 is differentiated from the rest of the text in terms of historicity, which was explicitly mentioned by a couple of participants. Or it could be that formal participants were equally more comfortable or familiar than informal participants with the idea that different texts require different interpretive strategies.

However, despite these differences, formal and informal participants showed no difference in their commitment to the truth of the narrative in a 'deeper' sense with no participants disregarding the text as being irrelevant or unimportant even if they deemed it to be unhistorical. Doctrinally speaking, therefore, both informal and formal participants were aligned in seeing the 'truth' and value of the narrative in what it teaches.

PSALM

Interpretation

Discussion of Psalm 44 tended to focus around five main topics: (1) author and events, (2) God's character, (3) the form of address, (4) human suffering, and (5) purpose or meaning. Naturally, several points intertwined several of these topics.

Whilst both informal and formal participants reflected on suffering, informal participants did so to a much greater extent, considering why suffering exists, if it has any purpose, and whether/what God's role is in it. Points about suffering accounted for 29 percent of all the points made by informal participants, as opposed to 14 percent for formal participants. The fact that a broader discussion of the topic of suffering was unique to informal participants corresponded with formal participants' tendency to stay closer to the text rather than venture into broader topics, suggesting that theological education could instil a sense of text-focus.[13] This was a general trend across the three texts, as was seen with Genesis, where several formal participants focused on the text for indications regarding the text's historicity as opposed to informal participants who drew upon scientific and historical knowledge.

As with Genesis, formal participants showed a preference to reflect on meaning and purpose accounting for 31 percent of all the points made, whereas only 18 percent of informal points reflected on meaning. This formal preference for meaning was very much linked with their increased practice of intrabiblical referencing and connecting the Psalm with the New Testament (another practice that was also demonstrated in Genesis). These connections were either relating the Psalm to Jesus or making reference to Paul's usage of the Psalm in Romans. None of these points were made by informal participants. Related to this, formal participants were the only ones to situate the text within a 'canonical trajectory' that sees a progressive development in an understanding of who God is, culminating in the person of Jesus. Meaning is therefore discerned from wider canonical context or frameworks through which the text is viewed. This focus on meaning also corroborates the

160   *Chapter 10*

suggestion above that formal participants are more text focused than informal participants.

Engagement Practices

For the Psalm, informal participants engaged in several practices more frequently than formal participants. Two such practices focused on understanding the Psalm in relation to the rest of the Bible. First, participants commented on theologically similar biblical content, where the Bible deals with similar themes or challenges that the Psalm deals with. Some of these instances were prompted by the specific context of the focus group, with links being made to Genesis, as a result of the group having just read that text. Second, informal participants also made more general points of comparison or similarity with 'biblical tendencies', i.e., things the Psalms 'tend' to do, or practices of the Israelites/God in general. In these practices, informal participants demonstrated much more specificity in the way they engaged with the text compared to the breadth of approaches employed for Genesis.

Informal participants also demonstrated some contextualising practices where they differentiated their theology with the contextual theology of the text. They recognised that 'the Bible' might conceive of God differently to themselves, but this was not framed as evidence of a developmental or progressive faith to which the Bible gives witness. The psalmist's thinking about God was attributed to them living in a more primitive time, but this was loosely alluded to and not fully explained.

Several informal practices centred around participants' personal response to the text including practicing empathy to relate to the experience of the Psalmist and in connection with this, drawing upon personal experience of the Christian faith when relating to the Psalm. Additionally, informal participants reflected upon their personal experience of 'applying' the Psalm, which predominantly took the form of emulation—sharing stories of their own honesty and outpouring of emotion before God. Informal participants stressed how they'd prayed in a similar vein to the Psalm or experienced what the psalmist had, and these experiences were placed in conversation with the text, rather than owned as something they bring to their understanding of the text.

In contrast, the contextualising practices of the formal participants were more specific than those of informal participants. Whereas informal participants drew upon anything similar or relevant from within the Bible, formal participants, as has been noted, showed more knowledge in making specific intrabiblical references and situating the Psalm within a canonical narrative arc. Several formal participants recognised that the Psalmist represents a particular point within a canonical trajectory and understood the psalmist's perspective and claims in light of that context, which none of the informal

The Influence of Education   161

participants did. The different ways in which formal and informal participants contextualised the text in relation to the rest of the Bible therefore suggests that theological education provides knowledge that enables contextual specificity but also provides a depth and richness to the canonical picture, which informal participants lacked. This is expanded upon below.

Formal participants, like informal participants, also demonstrated a personal response to the text, but they tended to reflect on their identity as a reader (English, a preacher, Charismatic) and how this shaped their approach, rather than their personal experiences. They therefore demonstrated an awareness of approaching the text from a specific context and how this impacts their understanding and response to the Psalm.

THEOLOGY AND THE DOCTRINE OF SCRIPTURE

In terms of the approach to the theology of the Psalm and what this indicates about the doctrine of Scripture, informal and formal participants showed little difference. The majority of participants across both categories dismissed the psalmist's claims about God on account of the psalmist's emotional state and desperate situation. The notable exception to this was formal participant Nick, but as the only one who upheld the claims of the Psalm, his view can't be taken as a representative of his category.

As has been noted, there were topical differences between the two categories and the points that were raised but these were not indicative of a substantial difference in terms of participants' doctrine of Scripture.

EPHESIANS

Interpretations

Discussion of Ephesians centred around five central topics: (1) culture, (2) meaning, (3) dynamics of interpretation, (4) relevance, and (5) irrelevance.

Though the smallest topic of discussion, informal participants made more points about the fifth topic, the irrelevance of the text to contemporary society. These accounted for 7 percent of the points made as opposed to just 1 percent from formal participants. This practice can also be seen as evidence of an informal tendency to fuse the text with contemporary society. As such, instances where fusion was difficult on account of cultural difference resulted in points about the text's irrelevance.

Informal participants also made several general reflections on topic 3 above, the dynamics of interpretation, which formal participants did not. Using the

162 *Chapter 10*

text as a jumping off point, informal participants reflected more broadly on the process of interpretation and their role as readers in this process.

Formal participants demonstrated more thorough knowledge of the first of these topics, the cultural context from which the letter came. It was only in formal groups that slavery was mentioned as potentially a positive and respectable form of 'employment' in Roman society, whereas the general sense of the way in which informal participants spoke of slavery was to equate it with the transatlantic slave trade of the sixteenth century and beyond. This shows greater knowledge and understanding of the context, which is likely a result of their theological education. Equally, formal participants tended to reflect on societal and cultural norms of the text's time in order to contrast the text against such a background. Though informal participants did this too, they tended to make more frequent moves between the culture of the text and contemporary culture, moving between topics 1 and 4 above. Formal participants were more focused on what light historical cultural insight sheds upon the text, rather than contemporary society, and they demonstrated more specific knowledge and confidence in their understanding of ancient culture.

Formal participants also demonstrated a tendency to reflect more specifically in relation to details of the text, rather than more generally about the dynamics of interpretation, evidencing again a formal preference to stay text focused rather than use the text as a launch pad to discuss broader issues.

Engagement Practices

In Ephesians, the informal participants showed preference for a variety of practices, three of which were in relation to the reader context. Though formal participants also engaged their own context in relation to the context of the text, informal participants did this to a much greater extent. Specifically, they reflected on their previous encounters with the text, their personal experience of applying the text, and general Christian tendencies as a context into which the text is applied. The other two predominant practices used by informal participants related to application, in particular discussing whether certain applications could or could not be made, and finally identifying the underlying meaning of the text. Informal participants were unique in considering what the text does and does not 'allow' and different ways in which it could be applied to today's context. Additionally, many informal participants stressed that the best method of 'application' was to identify the underlying meaning and principles of the text and apply those to today's context rather than simply take the instruction straight from the page—this often led to an understanding that the text should lead its readers to treat others with love and respect.

These two tendencies pose a curious but not unexpected tension for informal readers. On the one hand, discussion of the legitimacy of applications from the text demonstrates an instinct to follow the instructions of the text closely and discern exactly what they entail and what they do and don't allow. On the other hand, identifying principles beneath the text is a much more open approach that understands application to be broad and subject to discernment. This reflects the breadth of approaches to application and interpretation within the Evangelical community.

The formal participants only demonstrated two practices significantly more frequently than the informal participants in their discussion of Ephesians. The first was reflections upon the author's intention. Whilst both groups naturally referenced the author, the formal participants were the only ones to couch this in terms of the author's meaning or intention behind his writing. This could be due to theological education providing formal participants with the skills and knowledge to make more confident claims about authorial intention. Formal participants also evidenced a greater tendency to 'import' a theological concept to their understanding of the text. This was often repeated several times in different ways, demonstrating that the link between the text and the theological concept had been made in the past and was now a prominent paradigm or vantage point from which to understand the text. For example, Johnny (GLC) referenced husband and wife relations as being akin to the inter-trinitarian dynamic between Father and Son. This analogy isn't in the text, but was a theological concept that Johnny brought to the text. These practices are unsurprising, given that one would expect theological education to provide individuals with the knowledge and understanding to make such connections and understand texts in light of other theological ideas.

Relevancy and the Doctrine of Scripture

As with the Psalm, formal and informal participants were fairly equally balanced in their affirmation of the text's relevancy. Though informal participants tended to lean towards applying the underlying principles rather than specific applications, and formal participants were equally split between both, this did not signify anything conclusive about the two categories' doctrine of Scripture.

However, as with the issues of historicity, formal participants did evidence more extreme approaches to relevancy on both ends of the liberal-conservative spectrum. Sam expressed concerns about the relevancy of the text and claimed that if the author had been intending to promote unjust relationships, particularly the institution of slavery as anti-abolitionists claimed, then he felt the text should not be applied to contemporary life as it leads to 'un-Christly action.' On the other hand, Martin offered the most 'direct' application of the

164   *Chapter 10*

text to contemporary life, expanding upon his role as head of his family and what this means practically in relation to his wife and child. This continued the trend found in the discussion of historicity, that formal participants had stronger views both for and against literalism.

LENSES

Having considered some of the key differences in what formal and informal participants said about the texts, the practices they used to engage with them and their emerging doctrine of Scripture, it is worth summing up these trends in relation to the lens framework. What do these differences indicate about the way in which reading lenses functioned for the two groups?

Doctrine of Scripture Lens

Both formal and informal participants demonstrated a predominant view of the text as God's teaching resource from which to learn guidance for behaviour (application) and belief (knowledge). As was noted above, formal participants tended to make more meaning-related points than informal participants, which corresponds with a preference for learning outcomes; the meaning of the text was what could be learnt from it. In Genesis, 27 percent of all the points formal participants made related to meaning, compared to just 5 percent from informal participants. Similarly for the Psalm, 31 percent of points formal participants made related to meaning compared to 18 percent of informal participants' points. The discussion of Ephesians, however, was much more balanced with 37 percent of formal points and 33 percent of informal points relating to meaning.

The type of meaning made varied according to genre—for the Psalm and Ephesians, meaning was reflected on mostly in relation to behavioural application, but in Genesis meaning points were related to both behaviour and belief. Formal participants demonstrated a preference for finding meaning in the latter, making a total of thirty-six theological insights from the Genesis text compared to fifteen from informal participants. An example of meaning related to belief is the following comment by Jesse about Genesis: 'ultimately I think part of the narrative is that God is a God of justice and here are things that we need to be cognisant of and actually saying here are some of the reasons we need a redemption story, we need a redemption narrative.' This is contrasted to meaning in the form of application, exemplified by Jake: 'It's also about obedience and trust, isn't it? You know, are we actually going to obey when all the signs are that . . .'(unfinished comment).

The Influence of Education 165

In terms of the doctrine of Scripture lens therefore, whilst both groups saw the agenda of reading as being discernment of divine teaching, it would appear that formal participants have a broader understanding of this teaching in seeking theological insight (belief) as well as application (behaviour). This is to be expected considering their theological education: formal participants' study of theology will likely have made them familiar with the Bible as a source of theology. They therefore sought theological meaning in the text as well as meaning relating to life and behaviour. This insight reflects Powell's findings that the clergy he analysed (i.e., the theologically educated) were less likely to relate the text to themselves and instead focus on the text's meaning, whereas the laity were more inclined to orient meaning towards themselves in terms of the text's effect.[14]

Accordingly, that formal participants conceive of meaning more broadly might also be bolstered by the fact that many formal participants were actively involved in a form of ministry and therefore had responsibility in the areas of preaching and teaching. This means that many formal participants would have been in the habit of analysing a text to present several points of meaning to a congregation or audience. Indeed, some formal participants explicitly mentioned their response to the text in terms of how they would preach it.

The doctrine of Scripture's secondary role in determining the engagement practices of participants reflects the findings above regarding formal partici- pants' canonical tendencies. Bible-related engagement practices accounted for 30 percent of formal participants' overall engagement practices, with informal participants behind at 24 percent. The disparity here can be accounted for by formal participants' preference for intrabiblical referencing and canonically contextualising, practices they employed because of belief in the Bible's unity.

In sum, formal participants were more in tune with the conception of the Bible as a source of theology and informal participants were more in tune with conception of the Bible as a guide for life and behaviour and as such were the only ones to explicitly speak of the Bible this way. Of course, formal participants demonstrated their belief in the Bible as a guide for life and behaviour in their discussion of applications, but this was implied rather than explicit. The doctrine of Scripture lens therefore functioned slightly differently for informal and formal participants in their respective leanings as to the ultimate meaning of the text. Formal participants also evidenced a more dominant doctrine of Scripture lens in relation to the practices that they employed when engaging with the text.

Doctrine of God Lens

In terms of beliefs about God, informal and formal participants made a fairly equal number of assertions about God's character. Some aspects of God's character were asserted more by a particular category, depicted in table 10.1. Amongst informal participants, God's goodness and power were the two attributes mentioned most frequently, accounting for 14 percent each of all assertions made about God. In contrast, God's power accounted for only 4 percent of formal participants' assertions about God, and God's goodness only 6 percent. Instead, formal participants showed a strong preference to speak of God as loving, accounting for 21 percent of their assertions about God compared to 10 percent of informal participants'. Similarly formal participants also spoke more of God being just and sovereign.

These differences might tentatively suggest a potential variance in approaches to talking about God—informal language is reminiscent of the God of classical theism, whereas formal language is more typically biblical and specific to the Christian God. Additionally, only formal participants referenced the Trinity. It has also been noted in chapter 7, that two formal participants, Sam and Winston (WO), evidenced a Christocentric doctrine of God. Whilst two participants having a Christocentric doctrine of God can't be considered representative of their category, formal participants did demonstrate higher levels of christocentrism overall, which indicates something of a trend.[15] Taken together, these insights imply that formal participants appeared to be working with a slightly more complex and nuanced doctrine of God.

However, both formal and informal groups contained at least one participant who demonstrated evidence of incorporating judgement as part of their core comfortable conception of God. Moreover, Jane, an informal participant, expressed an openness to the idea that God can cause the seemingly negative. This suggests that whilst overall formal participants might have a more complex and biblical conception of God, theological education is not a dominant factor in determining core comfortable, periphery uncomfortable, and extrinsic intolerable layers of one's doctrine of God. Both formal and informal participants both included and excluded judgement as part of their core comfortable conception of God.

Table 10.1. Comparison of Theological Assertions about God

	Informal	Formal
God is good	14 %	4 %
God is powerful/omnipotent	14 %	6 %
God is love/loving	10 %	21 %
God is just	0 %	6 %
God is sovereign	4 %	8 %

The Influence of Education   167

Chapter 7 described the close relationship between the doctrine of God and the doctrine of Scripture and how the latter is looked at through the lens of the former to conceive of the Bible's function and content. It was noted how the Bible is a 'text construed as a certain kind of whole' and this can take the form of a unified meta-narrative of 'a single, organic history of salvation', as was the case for informal participant Gina (St.A's). Despite previously having illustrated this point with an example from an informal participant, it was actually formal participants who both demonstrated more defined theological meta-narratives that were closely tied to their conception of God, as well as more instances of employing these meta-narratives in relation to the text. Like Gina, salvation formed a part of their meta-narratives (9 percent of all the formal theological assertions made, compared to 2 percent from informal participants) as well as conceptions of the overarching trajectory of the Bible (9 percent compared to 1 percent). Winston (WO) provides a helpful example in relation to the Psalm:

> Don't you think that revelation is progressive in that God also worked with these people with revelation levels that were different in kind of getting to where we are today and understanding Christ, his character, his nature and just his fullness, the whole Godhead embodied in Christ himself. But in the olden days, in the previous dispensations, wars were part of their culture, were part of their tradition, were part of their lifestyle and so for them to see the victor of God they had to see their God defeating their enemy physically. They also had to see God giving them or granting them the victory in massacre, in so doing they saw the hand of God, purely his arm at work.

This higher tendency to employ meta-narratives is reflected in higher instances of formal participants' practicing of contextualisation. This is because, first, the more defined meta-narratives offered by formal participants suggest that they were practiced at integrating theological concepts into a unified whole, which they then sought to do in relation to the character of God through contextualising.[16] Second, a meta-narrative actually *requires* contextualisation for proper understanding by relating the part to the whole. It was not just that participants needed to contextualise the depiction of God in the text with their own understanding of God, but that participants were attempting to contextualise the depiction of God in the text with the overarching depiction of God in the Bible. As such, for formal participants, reading the text through their doctrine of God lens was more likely to take the form of contextualisation than tension because their doctrine of God was intertwined with their theological meta-narratives.

In sum, formal participants' doctrine of God appeared to be more complex and integrated with theological meta-narratives relating to salvation and a

168   Chapter 10

developmental understanding of the biblical narrative. This was connected to higher instances of contextualisation meaning that, generally speaking, for formal participants the role of the doctrine of God lens was predominantly to provide a background within which to understand the text, rather than informal participants' doctrine of God lens which provided a background against which to understand the text.

Genre Lens

Both informal and formal participants were equally balanced in their genre reflections and authorial reflections. Both categories practiced extrapolating and deductive reasoning by utilising the genre of the text as a starting point from which to discern the reality of the events within the text. Formal participants did this more for Genesis, most likely because their assessment of the genre of the text related to other ANE narratives, which only one informal participant mentioned, unconnected to genre.

Formal participants also demonstrated more differentiation across the three genres in their engagement practices. Of all the engagement practices employed by formal participants, a third only occurred in discussion of one of the texts, compared to a fifth of informal participants. This higher proportion suggests that the hermeneutical activity of formal participants was more closely related to genre; the employment of an engagement practice was specifically related to the genre of the text. Thus, the genre lens was more dominant in the process of interpretation for formal than it was for informal participants.

When it came to reflections on the author, the types of reflections the two categories made differed, with formal participants tending to speak of the author's intention and informal participants tending to reflect on the author's process or thinking. This is exemplified by contrasting Christopher's and Jake's reflections in relation to Paul and Ephesians:

I also think . . . Paul's doing something here in a whole letter so you know as quickly as I can, Ephesians 1:10—God is bringing everything back together including reuniting heaven and earth, in Ephesians 2:10 we realise he's done with Jew and Gentile, in Ephesians 3:10 the church is the manifestation of this incredible diversity brought back together. So, then Paul turns to talk about household codes, and I think he chose a line very Judaic in his thinking here which is a line against chaos right? If the church is to evidence the sense of God's working, it can't, in some sense he's instructing them to live in certain forms of togetherness and unity, so we can't have husbands and wives killing each other, we can't have disobedient kids, we can't have slaves fighting . . . I think you're seeing Paul trying to say, that you know, he thinks temporally about the world that we're in right now. . . . (Christopher, TO)

The Influence of Education   169

> I mean nobody is going to want to defend slavery but what Paul does is to accept it as part of the scene and try and make the best of it that he can so he says to slaves, 'when you're serving your master, do it willingly and not grudgingly' and he says 'masters don't threaten them and don't beat them unnecessarily'. (Jake, St.A's)

The slight nuance between these authorial reflections is significant. Formal participants were much more confident in proffering an intended purpose and their focus on authorial intention also connected with a higher focus on the text's meaning, as this was often discerned in terms of what the author was trying to communicate through their text. In contrast, informal participants' focus on the author's worldview and thinking/process in writing suggests more of a tentative approach to making overall claims about intention or purpose. Informal participants' reflections focused on the composition process and societal or cultural factors influencing the author, which are ancillary to, but not the same as, considerations of the author's intention or purpose. This is a subtle shift from Village's findings that 'the main effect of education was to shift interest away from the reader horizon towards the author horizon. This effect was heightened among those who had theological education to at least higher education certificate level. Such education tends to stress the historical background to biblical texts, so an increased awareness of the intentions or world of the author is not surprising.'[17] In contrast to Village, my formal participants didn't pay attention to the author horizon any more than the informal participants, but they did evidence an increase in focus on the author's intentions.

With regard to the function of the genre lens in identifying how the text's meaning as divine communication is manifested, both informal and formal participants were aligned, with the exception of Nick (WO) and the Psalm. Whereas for most participants the poetry genre of the text qualified how the text was understood as the 'Word of God', for Nick the text as the 'Word of God' qualified how the text should be understood as 'poetry'. As this was only one participant, it cannot be indicative of a formal tendency, but it is worth noting that the exception came from a formal participant.

In sum, formal participants tended to view the text through the lens of genre slightly more than informal participants on account of their genre-based hermeneutical activity, and the genre lens itself was slightly more focused in relation to the author's intention, most likely as a result of better knowledge. However, no significant difference was identified in the role of the genre lens determining how the text functions as the 'Word of God' and divine communication.

170   *Chapter 10*

Context Lens

Naturally, as a result of their difference in theological education, the participants were working from different contextual standpoints. This was evident when it came to their respective Christian context, specifically their Christian knowledge.

Formal participants demonstrated much more thorough historical knowledge particularly in relation to slavery, and ANE flood accounts. They also demonstrated more precise biblical knowledge in making increased intra-biblical references, compared to only a couple from informal participants. Informal participant's knowledge of the Bible appeared to be much vaguer with informal participants making more references to general 'biblical tendencies' compared to only a couple such references from formal participants. Additionally, formal participants were the only ones to reference Christian knowledge in the form of tradition. These references, however, demonstrated both respect and disregard for classical tradition and therefore in-keeping with overall findings that formal participants demonstrated stronger views on both ends of the spectrum. In terms of Christian knowledge from contemporary sources, both informal and formal participants called upon 'external input' in the form of teaching, preaching, reading, or scholarship to a similar extent.

In relation to corporate Christian experience, both informal and formal participants made a similar number of reflections about the contemporary church's response to the text. However, informal participants made over double the number of references to 'Christian tendencies' than formal participants, drawing upon perceived common Christian narratives or experience as a framework in which to explore the text. For example, Frank (St.J's) joked how the church would respond if someone prayed the Psalm at the front: 'If someone got up this Sunday and preached, and prayed 9 to 25, [our vicar] would be up there taking them off the stage wouldn't he? Probably.' Frank recognises in this jovial comment that accusatory language towards God is not something commonly found in church.

This higher tendency for informal participants to draw upon general Christian experience is reflected in their drawing upon personal experience. Informal participants demonstrated a much stronger preference for personal engagement practices, accounting for 12 percent of their engagement compared to 6 percent for educated participants, double the amount. These personal practices included relating the text to their personal experience of the Christian faith, sharing their personal experience of text application and previous encounters with the text, as well as practicing empathy in relation to the text. In particular, references to previous encounters with the text occurred sixteen times amongst informal participants and not at all amongst formal participants. This suggests that theological education could contribute to a less personal approach to Bible reading. Informal participants were much more open in bringing themselves and their history to the text, and frequently shared more personal anecdotes and stories, as well as their feelings about the text in general, but formal participants did not do this.

The only two experience-related engagement practices that formal participants exhibited more than informal participants were reflections on their identity and education. The latter is perhaps unsurprising as GLC participants were undertaking their focus group at their theological institution and during term time, so references to their learning and environment would be expected. For example, Johnny referenced a point about Genesis being 'in our church history paper'.

Additionally, all the participants were aware that the research involved a comparative factor in relation to education, which could also explain an increase in formal references to this.

What all this suggests is that not only is informal participants' context lens more dominant in their reading of the text, but that formal participants are also more acutely aware that they are reading through such a lens, particularly in relation to their personal identity. Informal participants also had moments of awareness, but formal participants showed more sustained awareness of how aspects of their personal identity inform their reading of the text. The overall outcome of a more dominant contextual lens, in combination with a preference outlined above for informal participants to view the text's meaning in terms of life guidance, was that informal participants made more specific reader-related applications from the text.

CONCLUSION

To repeat the caveat I offered in the introduction, my formal participants had undertaken their theological education in a variety of contexts and for a variety of reasons. As such, any reflections this conclusion makes on the effect of theological education cannot be specifically connected to particular types of theological education. However, some insights can profitably be noted.

Doctrine of Scripture

What difference does theological education make to an understanding of the doctrine of Scripture? Formal and informal participants were generally closely aligned in their beliefs about the Bible, but theological education seemed to prompt more 'extreme' views on both the liberal and conservative end of the spectrum in relation to historicity and relevancy. What this indicates overall about formal approaches to the doctrine of Scripture, is an

172 *Chapter 10*

increased confidence and certainty as to its nature. This was seen in formal participants openly disagreeing with one another, as well as more nuanced comments about the overarching narrative or trajectory of the Bible. In these types of assertions, formal participants demonstrated that they knew what they believed about the Bible and were set on this.

Theological education, then, can perhaps be said to fortify theological beliefs about the Bible. How might this happen? It could be that students are simply taught biblical beliefs which they then accept (either unwittingly or wilfully). Conversely, it could be that students strengthen and solidify their beliefs in reaction or opposition to the biblical beliefs they are taught. In these models the theological institution is conceived of as championing a particular theological standpoint. Alternatively, it could be that the process of theological education both introduces key ideas to students but also cultivates individual exploration and thinking so that students navigate themselves to their own strength of conviction. Village assumes that theological education 'increases the perception that certain biblical events are implausible and sets up a tension with doctrinal beliefs about the nature of scripture.'[18] Thus the retaining of a historical or literal reading amongst theologically educated Evangelicals 'is seen as a faithful and true belief that honours the power of God and the veracity of scripture, even if a modern Western perspective makes some events seem highly implausible. Education, and especially theological education, may offer the tools for interpreting parts of the Bible in a less literal way, but these are eschewed in order to maintain a relationship of trust and submission.'[19] This conclusion makes a number of leaps in assuming the nature, content, and force that theological education takes.

On the other hand, more recent research by Village has shown that generally speaking, higher education made little difference to the faith of those undertaking it.[20] Without having assessed my participants prior to their theological education, it is impossible to say whether this holds true for them and consequently whether it's the case that formal participants already had strong Bible beliefs prior to their education. Taking this into account, whether or how theological education has produced Bible readers with clearer and stronger views about the nature of the Bible and how it should be read, is difficult to conclude.

Role of the Doctrine of Scripture

What difference does theological education make to the role of the doctrine of Scripture in reading and interpretation? Though theological education provided stronger convictions about Bible beliefs, this didn't mean that the doctrine of Scripture had a more prominent role for formal participants in reading and interpretation. In terms of setting the reading agenda, the doctrine of Scripture lens was similar for both categories of participants, with slight preferences towards reading for theological insight (belief) for formal participants and reading for life guidance (behaviour) by informal participants. The doctrine of Scripture lens did, however, have slightly more prominence in terms of determining participants' engagement practices, with formal participants demonstrating more Bible-based practices in their preference for canonical considerations.

In relation to the other active lenses and how they affect the doctrine of Scripture lens, genre had a more significant impact for formal participants in determining what type of meanings might be taken from the text. This was evidenced in Genesis being the text where theological insight was sought more than application for formal participants. The two lenses were therefore closely connected, as the doctrine of Scripture's role in setting the reading agenda was qualified by the genre and content of the text. Moreover, the doctrine of Scripture and doctrine of God also appeared to be more closely related for formal participants in their more complex doctrine of God informing their understanding of the Bible's content: a theological meta-narrative spanning an overarching trajectory of the biblical canon. It could therefore be suggested that theological education affords a more complex integration of a reader's lenses. However, this is not accounting for the context lens, which was much less dominant for formal participants. Perhaps this is not unrelated to the close integration of the genre, doctrine of Scripture, and doctrine of God lenses. Theological education, though often with a focus on formation and reflection in some contexts, still exists within the rubrics of an academic approach. As such it promotes a more detached, critical, and objective perspective, even amongst confessional theological education contexts, as these are largely subject to the requirements of secular institutions with most courses being accredited externally. If theological education therefore affords its students with better knowledge and better integration of key facets pertinent to reading a biblical text, this could be at the expense of a more invested approach.

What this means for the doctrine of Scripture, is that whilst its role as a source of theology is reinforced through theological education, conversely its role in enabling the reader to be adequately addressed from beyond themselves is limited.

NOTES

1. For example: *British Journal of Theological Education* (Online) (London: Equinox, 1987).

2. Village, *The Bible and Lay People.*

174   *Chapter 10*

3. Ibid., 67.

4. Ibid., 149.

5. Ibid., 82–89.

6. Andrew Village, 'Does higher education change the faith of Anglicans and Methodists preparing for church ministries through a course validated by a UK university?' *Practical Theology* 12, no. 4 (2019) 389–401, DOI: 10.1080/1756073X.2019.1635310.

7. Mike Harrison 'What Do the Theologically Educated Look Like?' *Dialog* 53, no. 4 (2014): 345–55, DOI:10.1111/dial.12138.

8. Powell, *Chasing the Eastern Star.*

9. Ibid., 38.

10. Rogers found this to be a general feature of small group hermeneutics at one of the churches he researched, so not specific to the theologically educated, though he concedes 'the prevalence of text-linking at Holder required a high level of biblical knowledge . . . a point reinforced by the language of many group members being permeated with strong scriptural echoes.' Rogers, *Congregational Hermeneutics*, 107.

11. Village, *The Bible and Lay People*, 67.

12. Underscoring this point, Village found that 'there was a clear distinction in the Old Testament material between the sagas of Genesis and other stories such as Moses and Joshua. It seemed that some decision was being made as to whether an event was feasible and perhaps whether it was intended as story or history.' See: Village, *The Bible and Lay People*, 66.

13. Rogers calls this a 'multiple springboard style of hermeneutic' where the text is focused on but only briefly and then used as a jumping-off point to discuss a broader theme relating to the group. See: Rogers, *Congregational Hermeneutics*, 108.

14. Powell, *Chasing the Eastern Star*, 54.

15. It could be that christocentrism and therefore christological hermeneutics are predominantly caused by participants' 'congregational horizon' as Rogers suggests, rather than their theological education. See: Rogers, *Congregational Hermeneutics*, 87–88.

16. Walton also found that those in theological education undertaking theological reflection utilised theological themes as an interpretative tool for their experience. See: Roger Walton, 'Using the Bible and Christian Tradition in Theological Reflection,' *British Journal of Theological Education* 13, no. 2 (2003): 133–51.

17. Village, *The Bible and Lay People*, 88.

18. Ibid., 70.

19. Ibid., 70–71.

20. Village, "Does higher education change the faith of Anglicans and Methodists preparing for church ministries through a course validated by a UK university?" 389–401.

Chapter 11

The Influence of the Text

Reading for Transformation

Having outlined the dominant lenses that participants read the Bible through and considered these in comparison, I turn in this chapter to some final comments on this dynamic, before exploring the role of the doctrine of Scripture in relation to the transformational role of the text. This chapter thus turns to an overview of hermeneutical theory which posits that texts have the capacity to transform readers and I consider to what extent this occurred amongst my participants.

READING THROUGH LENSES: A SUMMARY

In addition to reading through their doctrine of Scripture lens, chapters 7–9 explicated a further three dominant lenses that participants read the text through, the doctrine of God, genre, and context. These chapters highlighted examples of reading through these lenses, the results of such readings, and therefore the general overall function of the lens in the process of Bible reading. It is important to stress that the lenses have a number of different functions depending on the text in question, but I have attempted to identify their most prominent role evidenced by my participants' conversations. Including the insights from chapters 3–6, the overall thrust of the lens dynamic can be described as follows.

The biblical text is read through a number of lenses, which are pre-existing frameworks of belief, knowledge, and experience that shape how one reads. Prominent lenses for my participants were the doctrine of Scripture, the doctrine of God, genre, and context. These lenses have an affective relationship both with the text and each other. As my focus is on the doctrine of Scripture, I have explored the God, genre, and context lenses in terms of these two

176 *Chapter 11*

relationships: how they shape the doctrine of Scripture and how they impact engagement with the text.

The roles of these lenses can thus be summarised:

1. Participants construed the Bible as God's teaching resource. The result of reading through the lens of this doctrine of Scripture was primarily setting the agenda or purpose of reading, why the text is read. The text was read to seek its ultimate meaning: divine teaching in the form of belief and behaviour.
   a. That the Bible was construed as God's teaching resource was the result of a dominant doctrine of God lens which understands the nature of the Bible in terms of its function by God and its content being about God.
   b. The ultimate meaning of the text was qualified by the genre of the text at hand which determines how the text functions as God's teaching resource.
   c. The belief in the Bible as God's teaching resource will be affected by the reader's Christian context and personal experiences of reading. Their beliefs about the Bible will therefore be individually nuanced.
2. Reading through the doctrine of God lens has a limiting function in setting parameters as to which meanings are valid, acting as a touchstone for interpretative conclusions.
3. Reading through the genre lens has a focusing function prescribing what hermeneutical activity is appropriate and thus how meaning is determined, as well as contributing to the interpretive conclusions drawn from the text.
4. Reading through the context lens sets the scope of what meanings are found: divine communication in the form of theological insight (belief) and life application (behaviour) is somewhat restricted to the knowledge and experience of a reader's context.

Combining Lenses

This book has framed the way in which participants engaged with the text through the metaphor of lenses, demonstrating the complexity of reading through numerous lenses at once. The way the four lenses I have outlined combine together in the process of reading is depicted in Figure 11.1. What this diagram demonstrates is that, depending on the emphasis or strength of each particular lens, participants have a myriad of approaches to the text.

It is worth reiterating at this point that many more 'lenses' could be added to this scheme, as well as be broken down into further sub-categories. The 'lenses' I have elaborated on in the previous chapters have been chosen for

The Influence of the Text

both their prominence identified amongst my participants but also because of the significance of their crossover with the doctrine of Scripture, my lens of interest.

In practice all these lenses are active at any given time just to different degrees of prominence. The lenses are not something that are 'put on' but are integral to perception, much in the same way that human beings have no choice but to see through their eyes.

At times, participants appeared to be constantly juggling the lenses through which they read, often trying to give due weight to each in their interpretative conclusions—this was seen most clearly in the discussion of Genesis where participants were torn between commitments to science, the omnipotence of God, the authority of the text, and the intentions of the author. At other times, participants appeared to be actively engaging one particular lens, making it more dominant. If all the lenses are active, but the reader has some control over the lenses they prioritise, what does this indicate about lens choice?

Lens Choice

Given that the lenses are always active, readers don't consciously 'choose' to read through them. However, as has been demonstrated, certain lenses were employed to a greater extent in relation to the text's content—the doctrine of God lens was more prominent in Genesis and the Psalm where the portrayal of God was somewhat problematic. This is the equivalent of a person's eyes

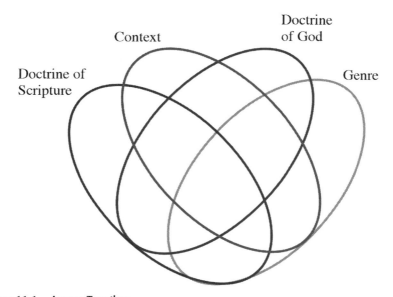

Figure 11.1. Lenses Together.

178   *Chapter 11*

adjusting according to the distance of the object being viewed. Depending on what is being looked at, and how far away it is, a person will naturally adopt either near-sighted or far-sighted vision. In the same way, depending on the text at hand, certain lenses will naturally be employed.

Additionally, participants did evidence both the ability to intentionally let a particular lens dominate or attempt to see beyond their lenses by disregarding them. These latter instances, however, were only ever 'attempts' because participants weren't able to ignore their lenses; they ultimately had to temporarily transform them. For example, when participants at St.J's speculated what non-Christians would make of the Ephesians text, they didn't eradicate their doctrine of Scripture lens; rather they transformed the lens into a non-Christian equivalent: 'religious text' rather than 'Word of God'. This transformation of the lens was wholly provisional; one can speculate how someone of different experiences or beliefs might respond to the text, but this will only ever be a speculation from within the limits of one's own lenses.

Having established how these lenses function, I now turn to consider the role of the text in relation to these dynamics.

THE TEXT'S TRANSFORMING CAPACITY IN THEORY

According to certain strands of hermeneutical theory, a text is not a passive object but an active subject and as such has the capacity to shape the reader and their lenses.[1] Lenses should therefore act as a provisional framework through which the text is viewed, as they are capable of being changed by the active agency of their subject, the text. It is in this respect that reading can be considered transformational for the reader, making the process of Bible reading dynamic and progressive. Ford evidences this with some of his non-Christian Bible readers who showed that interpretation was 'not limited by their preconceptions, assumptions, interpretive community, or particular theory they hold, for the transaction with the text was able to produce an atypical or unknown reading.'[2] The text has the power to change the reader.

But how does a text affect and transform a reader? According to Thiselton (whom I rely on heavily for the following overview), there are many ways in which a text can have a transformative effect: 'Because of their capacity to bring about change, texts and especially biblical texts engage with readers in ways which can productively transform horizons, attitudes, criteria of relevance, or even communities and inter-personal situations. In this sense we may speak of transforming biblical reading.'[3] This view isn't just held within the scholarly world of hermeneutics. Ford's previously mentioned non-Christian male readers of the Bible evidenced a belief in the Bible's active agency; 'even though most of the men indicated that they did not

The Influence of the Text 179

believe the Bible was true or divine, their responses show that they believed reading these texts, in this context, had the potential to be transformative.'[4] This view exists within popular thinking because it's also held within the Christian community. Within biblical scholarship, there have been many advocates for reading the Bible for transformation.[5] Kim identifies four different models of how transformation is conceived, advocating for a holistic model,[6] whilst popular literature might focus on a particular aspect of transformation.[7] Many scholars advocate for intercultural Bible reading as a key to transformation,[8] but fundamentally, however transformation is conceived, the uniting belief is that the Bible as a collection of texts has power to achieve it.

Within hermeneutical theory, various models of textual activity[9] are called upon to explore the transformational power of texts including speech-act theory,[10] projected narrative-worlds,[11] inter-personal understanding,[12] and changes in horizons of expectation.[13] In all these models, a reader has to be 'addressed' by the text 'speaking'. The text's address is only authentic when the distinctiveness of the text's voice is recognised in contrast to the reader's own voice. Being addressed therefore involves paying attention to the context of the text, it's author and recipients. To stretch the lens metaphor a little further, this attention to the text's context might be described as adopting the text's lenses in order to read the text on its own terms.[14] N. T. Wright frames this as the task of history, utilising what he calls an 'epistemology of love': 'The point of love is that it is neither appraisal nor assimilation: neither detachment nor desire, neither positivist objectivity nor subjective projection. When I love I am delightedly engaged with that which is other than myself. Part of the delight is precisely in allowing it—or him, or her—to be the "other", to be different.'[15] As such, 'Christians too, precisely because they are Christians, must humbly allow the sources to tell them things they hadn't expected.'[16] This involves asking questions such as, when the text speaks of God, what or who is it envisioning and how does that compare to my vision of God? When the text speaks of marriage, what social institution was in view and is this the same as the way I understand marriage today? Accordingly, by inhabiting the lenses of the text, a reader both views the text and themselves and sees both in a new light. Adopting the lenses of the text allows the text to speak authentically and thus for the reader to be genuinely addressed by an 'other' and not merely by the echo of their own voice. It is only by being properly addressed from outside of oneself that the text can be transformational.

If reading does reflect something of an echo-chamber of the reader's own perspective, readers are, according to Thiselton, prematurely assimilating. This is failing to read the text through its own lenses and only engaging with it through the reader's natural lenses. The results of this are described by Thiselton:

180   *Chapter 11*

In such a case the reader many stand under the illusion that the texts have fully addressed him or her. Still more significantly, interaction between the horizons [lenses] of texts and readers will, if premature assimilation has taken place, appear uneventful, bland, routine, and entirely unremarkable. Within the Christian community the reading of biblical texts often takes this uneventful and bland form. For the nature of the reading-process is governed by horizons [lenses] of expectation already pre-formed by the community of readers or by the individual. Preachers often draw from texts what they had already decided to say; congregations sometimes look to biblical readings only to affirm the community-identity and life-style which they already enjoy. The biblical writings, in such a situation, become assimilated into the function of creeds: they become primarily institutional mechanisms to ensure continuity of corporate belief and identity.[17]

This thesis has established how the reading process is governed by 'horizons of expectation already pre-formed', which has been framed as lenses. Participants' doctrine of Scripture set the expectation of how the text was meaningful ahead of reading. Does reading through the lens of the doctrine of Scripture therefore undermine the text's capacity to transform the reader? To answer this question, I will first consider the extent to which my participants appeared to be open to the text's capacity to transform the reader.

THE TEXT'S TRANSFORMING CAPACITY IN PRACTICE

In theory, the text's capacity to transform relies on the reader's engagement with the text's context, which I've termed 'adopting the text's lenses.' How far did this happen in practice? Assessing the extent to which participants adopted the text's lenses can be measured by identifying the engagement practices they employed that dwelt upon the text's context, which was noted in chapter 5. However, though this type of hermeneutical activity can be identified, it is difficult to determine the extent to which participants were being authentically 'addressed' by the text. What would this look or sound like? Were participants actually being changed as a result of engaging with the text's context? I will explore these questions below.

Of the seventy-eight engagement practices identified amongst participants, thirteen categories corresponded with contextual reflections: differentiating the reader's culture from the text's culture, considering the author's identity/intention/thought-process/worldview, reflecting on the circumstantial context that prompted the text to exist, the text's faith context, the recipients of the text, providing general historical societal and cultural information, exploring genre, cultural stylistic devices, and analysing language and translation. These contextual practices accounted for 24 percent of all engagement

The Influence of the Text 181

practices, but the majority (66 percent) were a product of the reader's context, depicted in table 11.1 below.

These statistics show that the majority of participant exploration of the text took place within the reader's natural lenses, rather than the text's lenses.

Further, it should be noted that participants did engage in a number of practices that showed they were aware of the text's lenses, but this awareness did not always result in an 'adoption' of such lenses. For example, George (St.J's) made the following comment about the Psalm: 'I guess British culture is quite reserved, but I feel like not all countries are like this and maybe that's coming through in this passage, it's like, extreme'. George does not dig further into Middle Eastern culture to reflect on the emotions of the psalmist, or consider whether the Psalm can really be considered 'extreme' if this is their cultural norm, or reflect on the appropriateness of reading the Psalm through a 'British reserved' lens. Instead, the style of the Psalm is accounted for as being 'cultural'. What George might be described as doing is noting that the text has different lenses to his own, but not actually adopting such lenses to see the text and himself in a new way.

Contrasting this is Emma's (St.J's) handling of the Psalm's affirmation of God's help in defeating the enemy:

> Emma: And more than that, we don't live in a tribal, warring society. So actually, the bit I find most difficult in this passage is verse 5, 'through your name we tread down our assailants' . . . I do not think of God as someone whose name is used as a way to tread down other people . . . that is the exact opposite of the God that I experience, who is about not oppressing, and freedom and . . . the reunification of all things. And that's where I'm like, 'but I don't live somewhere where there are people who are trying to kill me' . . . and if I did, I would definitely . . .
>
> Jane: . . . want them dead . . .
>
> Emma: yeah . . . I'd be focusing on the assailants bit of that rather than from my nice privileged luxurious place being like 'tread down? That's a heavy phrase.'

Emma engages with the text's lenses and rather than dismiss enemies as being irrelevant, she imagines how she would feel if her life were in danger from a

Table. 11.1. Engagement Practice Breakdown

Text Context	*24 percent*
Contemporary Culture Context	21 percent
Personal Context	9 percent
Belief/Doctrine Context	10 percent
Biblical Context	26 percent
Miscellaneous	10 percent

182 *Chapter 11*

known enemy. This leads her to reconsider her response to the idea that God 'treads down' the enemy, which didn't correspond with her previously held idea of God. Emma notices her own historical situatedness ('nice privileged luxurious place') thus seeing herself through the lenses of the text and by imagining herself in the context of the psalmist, hears the claims of God in a different way. It wasn't just that the text stated something about God that Emma was receptive to being challenged by (thus reshaping her doctrine of God lens), but that engaging with the text's lenses helped Emma to see how her own doctrine of God lens is shaped by her experiences of the world. As difficult as it is to identify exactly when someone is being authentically 'addressed' by the text, Emma's reflection does appear to be an example.

Contrasting George and Emma's comments provides nuance to the reality of exegesis. Whilst Evangelical Bible reading might profess to promote a contextual approach, and readers themselves know this, the extent and manner with which the text's 'context' is engaged with can vary wildly. This was established in chapter 3 where it was noted that exegesis can take two forms: either the applying of relevant contextual knowledge or personal involvement with this context through distancing. My participants tended to opt for the former form of exegesis, rather than the latter.

The fact that participants were less open to the address of the text and thus its transforming capacity is bolstered by recalling that on the whole, participants did not demonstrate a willingness for their doctrine of God to be challenged by the text. Where the text's portrayal of God and participant's own doctrine of God were in conflict, participant's own understanding prevailed and the text was interpreted in a way that upheld such preconceived conceptions of God. In other words, participants weren't open to the text changing the frameworks that they brought to the text and read the text through, which in this example, was the doctrine of God lens.

The Text's Transforming Capacity in Comparison

How does this conclusion stand when comparing formal and informal participants? Did they differ in their adoption of the text's lenses and thus their receptiveness to the transforming capacity of the text?

Formal and informal participants' exploration of the text's context accounted for almost the same percentage of their overall engagement practices, 14 percent and 13 percent, respectively. However, comparing some of their specific contextual engagement practices highlights areas of differentiation.

As was noted in the previous chapter, in relation to the author, formal participants focused more on intention, accounting for 16 percent of their contextual practices, compared to 2 percent for informal participants. Conversely,

The Influence of the Text   183

informal participants reflected more upon the author's thinking or process, accounting for 12 percent of their contextual practices compared to 6 percent for formal participants.[18] Formal participants' focus on intention reflects their better contextual knowledge, as has been noted. This is also reflected in 29 percent of formal participant's contextual practices involving sharing historical societal and cultural information, compared to 20 percent for informal participants. Formal participants actually knew more about the context from which the text came.

Though formal participants led in knowledge, informal participants engaged more personally with the text's context. Eight percent of their contextual practices were reflections on the text's recipients, compared to two percent of formal participants'. Moreover, 27 percent of informal participants' contextual practices were pointing out the difference between the text's culture and the reader's culture compared to 16 percent of formal participants'. These two practices present an interesting finding regarding informal participants' adoption of the text's lenses. As has been established, not all contextual engagement was equivalent to adopting the lenses of the text. In reflecting on the text's recipients, informal participants evidenced a stronger tendency to adopt the text's lenses by hearing it on its own terms. For example, Vanessa (St.C's) made the following point regarding Ephesians:

> When we read that first paragraph when it talks about wives submitting to their husbands, in a modern reading, we read that and go, 'not sure about that, that's a little bit close to the bone', whereas we read the bit about the husbands loving the wife and we're like, 'well of course, that's a marriage is not it? That's how everyone should behave in marriage in theory.' Whereas to them, they probably would have read the first bit and been like 'well of course the wife is going to submit to the husband but oh my gosh that's how you expect a husband to behave?'

Vanessa both recognises the effect of her natural 'modern' lenses and attempts to imagine how she would respond in a different context, with the outcome that the force of the passage is entirely different; she adopts the text's lenses effectively.

It could be that informal participants were better situated to do this because of their personal approach to the text. It has already been noted how informal participants engaged with the text much more personally, and in particular, the practice of empathy was higher amongst informal participants. This personal angle likely led informal participants to engage with historical societal and cultural information from a more invested perspective—placing themselves into the shoes and world of those in the text.

184 *Chapter 11*

However, whilst informal participants showed higher levels of lens adoption in their reflections on recipients, their higher levels of pointing out differences between the text's culture and the reader demonstrated the reverse. These types of reflections, whilst recognising the different contexts, rarely engaged to any depth with the text's context. For example, Terry's (St.A's) comment that the Ephesians text 'almost makes the male sound like a shrinking violet, doesn't it? You know, "for this reason a man will leave his father and mother", but it's more common for a daughter to leave a father and mother to marry the bloke, isn't it?' Here Terry makes a distinction between the text and reader context but fails to adopt the lenses of the text to explore the familial dynamic on its own terms.

What does this indicate about the ability of the two categories of participant to see the text and themselves through the lens of the text and thus be open to the text's transforming capacity? Whilst formal participants had better knowledge and were thus better situated to engage with the text's context, informal participants' personal approach to the text actually gave them the edge in adopting the lenses of the text. However, such a personal approach also had the opposite effect of centering informal participants upon their own context and situation. Strangely then, informal participants were both better and worse than formal participants at adopting the lenses of the text. As such, there was no overall distinctive difference in the extent to which formal and informal participants appeared to be receptive to being authentically addressed by the text.

In summary, overall participants did not evidence a significant proclivity to adopt the text's lenses and see the text, and themselves, through them. Instead, they tended to read the text through their natural lenses and these were fixed rather than provisional, and subsequently not open to being changed. Formal participants did not evidence any higher levels of being 'addressed' by the text and being transformed as a result; indeed they fared slightly worse than informal participants on this front by failure to consider the recipients of the text. This means that the text's transforming capacity, for my participants, was limited. What does this reveal about the role of the doctrine of Scripture in interpretation?

THE EFFECT OF THE ROLE OF THE DOCTRINE OF SCRIPTURE UPON THE ROLE OF THE TEXT

I have established that my participants predominantly viewed the Bible as God's resource and thus focused on the function of the Bible in their lives. This focus on the Bible as God's resource was conceived in terms of God's

The Influence of the Text 185

purpose of teaching and the corresponding reading approach was thus learning what God was intending to teach. A focus upon reading for learning ultimately locates the meaning of the text in its teachings about right belief and behaviour, which is essentially information. Participant's sought the information God wanted to teach. By contrast, the text's capacity to transform locates the meaning of the text in being authentically 'addressed,' in communication from the 'other.'

Information and communication are not mutually exclusive, but they are significantly different. Indeed, one communicates information; a reader who is 'addressed' may quite likely 'learn' something. The difference is found in the expectation of the reader. When a reader seeks communication, they expect to engage with an 'other' and as such, can't prescribe the form or content of the communication. By contrast, when the reader seeks information, the communicator fades to the background and the nature of the communication in the form of imparting information has already been determined. If the reader does not engage with the text's context, then an emphasis on information runs the risk that the information does not actually stem from the 'other' at all, but rather oneself.

This distinction is made clearer with reference to Rosenblatt's efferent-aesthetic reading scale. When a text is read efferently, 'the reader's attention is focused primarily on what will remain as the residue after reading—the information to be acquired, the logical solution to a problem, the actions to be carried out.'[19] This correlates with my participants' reading for the purpose of learning right belief and behaviour. By contrast, when a text is read aesthetically, 'the reader's primary concern is with what happens during the actual reading event',[20] 'the reader's attention is centred directly on what he is living through during his relationship with that particular text'.[21] Being 'addressed' by the text in authentic communication might not strictly align with a purely aesthetic reading, but it is much further towards that end of the scale than reading for learning and information, which is strongly efferent oriented.[22]

The location of meaning in information or communication is thus prescribed by a reader's expectation of the function of the text. As my participants largely seemed to understand the Bible as God's teaching resource, the reading task was therefore about learning, which locates meaning in gaining information. As a result, participants didn't seek communication in the text and thus engaged with the text through the text's lenses. A heavy emphasis upon learning meant participants engaged with the text predominantly in relation to their own context and read through their lenses (as has been seen), ultimately reducing the text's capacity to transform.

In summary, reading through the lens of a doctrine of Scripture that construes the Bible as God's teaching resource actually restricts the text's capacity

186   *Chapter 11*

to transform the reader. Whilst in theory the doctrine of Scripture prescribes that the text has an authoritative function in the reader's life, in practice the narrow conception of the Bible's divine communication as teaching actually diminished the text's capacity to be authoritative in the reader's life.

If the function of the doctrine of Scripture lens locates meaning in learning then this focus appears to have the effect of tunnel-vision at the expense of the text's meaning in communication. The participants' expectation that the text would communicate in the form of learning, clouded them to what Briggs describes as conceiving of Scripture as 'before' the reader: 'it precedes us and thus, in God's economy, the Word of God summons us to interpretive paths which it is not our job to delimit in advance; and it invites us to an attentiveness before what is actually said in Scripture which it is not our job to prejudge in advance.'[23]

In chapter 1, I outlined how Evangelical Anglicans posit that a commitment to the doctrine of Scripture was necessary for proper interpretation, determining both hermeneutical activity and interpretative conclusions. What this chapter has suggested is that reading within a commitment to the doctrine of Scripture that conceives of the Bible primarily as God's teaching resource, actually dulls the potential transforming role of the text and thus paradoxically undermines the reader's commitment to the doctrine of Scripture in the first place, which affirms the life-governing role of the Bible.

CONCLUSION

A Summary of the Book So Far

This book has presented the analysis of six groups' interpretation of three Bible passages that each present a challenge to the doctrine of Scripture. My Evangelical Anglican participants' responses to these challenges revealed both their dispositional beliefs about the Bible and their interpretative habits.

I have identified that amongst my participants a range of Bible beliefs exist corresponding to traditional doctrine of Scripture language. However, there was an overall preference to speak of the Bible in terms of function, and a general tendency for this function of the Bible to be couched as God's resource for teaching Christians what to believe and how to live. As a result, this view of Scripture led participants to read for the purpose of learning what the text said about what to believe and how to live. This is where the text's ultimate meaning was found.

The predominant role of the doctrine of Scripture in interpretation was thus setting the reading agenda or purpose—what the reader was reading for. In addition, the doctrine of Scripture also appeared to influence some of the

The Influence of the Text   187

interpretative practices that participants employed, and at times held sway in participant's interpretative conclusions. However, the bulk of both interpretative practices and conclusions were determined by other factors, namely, the text's genre and content and the reader's pre-existing beliefs about God and personal experiences. The role of the doctrine of Scripture was therefore diverse, though its primary influence related to the reading agenda and the location of meaning.

I have framed this role in terms of a reading 'lens' because it was not the only pre-existing framework that participants read the text through. Indeed, the other prominent lenses, which for my participants were the doctrine of God, their context, and the text's genre, had an impact upon both the overall conception and function of the doctrine of Scripture, as well as the interpretative practices and conclusions that participants employed and resolved, mentioned above. The doctrine of Scripture's primary role, then, cannot be isolated from other aspects of a reader's background, beliefs, knowledge, and experience. It is not the case that the doctrine of Scripture is the only aspect determining the purpose of Bible reading. Rather, the doctrine of Scripture's role in determining the reading agenda is filtered through and brought into connection with specific aspects related to the reader (doctrine of God and context).

Considering these findings in relation to the two categories of informal and of formal participants showed that theological education led to stronger beliefs about the nature of the Bible on both ends of the liberal-conservative spectrum, as well as a marginal preference for the reading agenda to be related to learning theological beliefs over behaviour.

Finally, this chapter has identified that one implication of reading through these lenses with the particular agenda of learning, was a diminishing of the text's capacity to transform. Participants wanted the Bible to be relevant to their lives and so dove into interpretation with fixed lenses that led to conclusions that fit within their pre-existing matrices of belief. By contrast, hermeneutical theory suggests that in order for the text to authentically communicate, one must actually step back rather than move closer, in adopting the text's lenses prior to the reader's own.[24]

Some Implications

The above overview of my research's key findings highlights several important implications about what this research has contributed to our understanding of the role of the doctrine of Scripture in interpretation.

First, issues in Bible interpretation are likely to be a result of conceptions of the Bible, rather than hermeneutical practices. This is because hermeneutical activity is ultimately oriented around one's reading agenda, and this is

188 *Chapter 11*

the result of beliefs about the nature of the Bible. In other words, particular conceptions of the Bible appear to result in particular reading agendas which result in particular hermeneutical approaches. My participants' view of the Bible's function as God's teaching resource led them to read for the purpose of learning, and this learning was construed as right belief and right behaviour. However, different conceptions of the Bible's function would most likely lead to different reading agendas. If the text was viewed as a medium of God's presence, for example, the purpose of reading would not be related to learning but rather to experience or transformation. This is the view of Thiselton who suggests: 'The question "what can I learn from this?" is not always the right one to ask. Some parts of Scripture serve not to speak about joy, but to give joy; some serve not to instruct us about reconciliation but to reconcile us. The Bible not only tells us about Christ, but also brings Christ to us'.[25] If my participants had a broader conception of Scripture related to the text's transformation, their reading agenda would encompass both learning and experiencing. The role of the doctrine of Scripture is still the same, it still sets the reading agenda, but that agenda will vary according to the view of Scripture held in view.

As a result of a different reading agenda, the hermeneutical approach employed will differ. For example, the belief in the Bible's function as God's resource and thus the participants' goal of learning right belief and behaviour oriented their reading towards their own context and themselves rather than the text's context. This instinct to apply the text meant that, on the whole, my participants did not adopt the text's lenses and were not authentically addressed by the text. A different conception of the Bible and thus agenda for reading would have an impact upon the reader's instinct to properly engage with the text's context, or text's lenses. One implication of my research is therefore that interpretation of the Bible should not be considered the concern of the field of hermeneutics alone, but actually that of systematic theology, in particular the doctrine of Scripture.

Second, the importance of one's conception of the Bible, needs to be considered in light of the doctrine of Scripture's connection to the doctrine of God, genre, and context. In particular, the doctrine of God and the reader's context and experience proved to be key factors that shaped views of the Bible. This is where individual nuance to the doctrine of Scripture is to be found. The doctrine of Scripture from a dispositional perspective is personal and construed differently according to different experiences and understandings of the character and purposes of God, as well as Christian context and tradition. If conceptions of Scripture are key to hermeneutical activity as I propose they are, then how these conceptions of Scripture are shaped by a reader's understanding and personal experience of God and the Bible is significant.

The Influence of the Text

Third, theological education had a disparate effect upon conceptions of Scripture. As the first two points have identified, conceptions of the Bible are key to hermeneutical activity in establishing the reading agenda. Theological education certainly appears to be effective at shaping understandings of Scripture, but with a variety of results, as my theologically educated participants evidenced views on the doctrine of Scripture from both ends of the liberal and conservative spectrum. If improvements or reform of interpretation start with conceptions of Scripture, then education can be a driving force for refining and shaping such conceptions. But how education works exactly is an area for further research, which I shall discuss next.

Limitations of the Research and Areas for New Research

There are many avenues for further exploration as a result of the findings of my research but also because of its limitations.

As was just noted, one of the limitations of my research was not being able to specify why theological education appears to result in stronger biblical beliefs at both ends of the liberal-conservative spectrum. A further avenue of research would be to explore in more detail how this occurs—is the resulting range due to differing theological contexts, teaching, or individual factors?

Moreover, this research is both too narrow and too broad in focusing upon Evangelical Anglicans. Whilst the denominational perspective is insightful for that particular group of Bible readers, my research would benefit from further exploration of other denominations to understand to what extent the dynamics witnessed are evidenced across other Christian groups. On the other hand, Evangelical Anglicans encompass a broad variety of views, and a focus upon either one of these traditions (non-Anglican Evangelicals or non-Evangelical Anglicans) might have produced more monolithic results.

Connected to this, with regard to the role of the doctrine of Scripture, further research into different conceptions of Scripture and the reading agendas they produce would add further insight into the role of the doctrine of Scripture and pave the way for constructive suggestions as to 'best practice' or rather 'best conceptions' of the Bible, for optimum biblical engagement.

How to Conceive of Scripture

This research has identified what role my Evangelical Anglican participants' beliefs about the Bible play in their reading and interpreting of Scripture. Such an insight is useful to anyone seeking to understand more about the dynamics of Bible reading, whether from an academic or ecclesial perspective. This book has not sought to assess my participants' conception of

190   *Chapter 11*

Scripture and how this functions in interpretation, other than to note that according to hermeneutical theory, a conception of the Bible as God's teaching resource can lead to a limited engagement with the reality of the text. In order to evaluate what has been outlined here, one has to return to systematics and ask what the Bible is, how it should function, and thus what the goal of Bible reading should be. This is the subject of numerous systematic treatises, and whilst I have not ventured to contribute a proposal in this book, I'll finish with a tentative suggestion implied from its findings.

What the Bible is, how it functions, and what the goal of reading is, should always be considered provisional and subject to the transformation of the text. Any conception of Scripture that is too rigid, narrow, or fixed has already decided in advance what the text is capable of saying and doing. But the text can say and do many things, it tells us so: 'All Scripture is inspired by God and is useful for teaching, for reproof, for correction, and for training in righteousness, so that everyone who belongs to God may be proficient, equipped for every good work.'[26] Whilst accounts of the doctrine of Scripture have typically been based on the first part of this verse, deliberating over the translation of 'inspired' and what this means and how this works, it might be better to base accounts of the doctrine of Scripture on the second half. The Bible has a variety of functions and thus can be conceived in a variety of ways with the ultimate goal of equipping those who belong to God. Perhaps the best conception of Scripture is one that, rather than limit such variety, recognises the limits of one's conception and thus lets the text determine how it will equip, rather than deciding for oneself in advance. Reading through the lens of this doctrine of Scripture broadens the reading agenda and makes the reader vulnerable to the power of the text, so that it can do all that it is capable of doing as the inspired, authoritative, sufficient, clear, and consistent Word of God.

NOTES

1. Dissenting voices in the belief of the autonomy of the text can be found in reader-response approaches like Fish, who claims that it is the reader alone who contributes to an interpretative interaction. See: Fish, *Is There a Text in This Class?*

2. Ford, *Reading the Bible Outside the Church*, 202.

3. Anthony Thiselton, *New Horizons*, 8. (emphasis Thiselton's own)

4. Ford, *Reading the Bible Outside the Church*, 175.

5. For example: Pauline Hoggarth, *The Seed and the Soil: Engaging with the Word of God* (Carlisle: Global Christian Library, 2001) ch. 1; Walter Wink, *The Bible in Human Transformation*, 2nd ed. (Minneapolis, MN: Fortress Press, 2010).

6. Yung Sun Kim, *A Transformative Reading of the Bible: Explorations for Holistic Human Transformation* (Eugene, OR: Cascade Books, 2013).

The Influence of the Text 191

7. Richard J. Foster, *Life With God: Reading the Bible for Spiritual Transformation* (New York: HarperOne, 2009).

8. Hans de Wit and Janet Dyk, eds., *Bible and Transformation: The Promise of Intercultural Bible Reading* (Atlanta, GA: SBL Press, 2015).

9. Thiselton, *New Horizons*, 32–35.

10. Richard S. Briggs, *Words in Action: Speech Act Theory and Biblical Interpretation* (Trowbridge: T&T Clark, Ltd., 2001).

11. Anthony C. Thiselton, *The Two Horizons: New Testament Hermeneutics and Philosophical Description, with Special Reference to Heidegger, Bultmann, Gadamer, and Wittgenstein* (Grand Rapids, MI: Eerdmans, 1980).

12. Dilthey and Betti are significant, summarised by Thiselton, *New Horizons in Hermeneutics*, 247–53.

13. Hans Robert Jauss and Elizabeth Benzinger, "Literary History as a Challenge to Literary Theory," *New Literary History* 2, no. 1 (1970): 7–37.

14. There are a number of complexities regarding the fact that the context of the author of the text, the recipients of the text, and/or the characters within the world of the text are not necessarily aligned. I do not have space to discuss the nuances of these different perspectives, but rather will refer to the 'text's context' or 'text's lenses' as a shorthand for all three of these perspectives, akin to 'historical context'.

15. N. T. Wright, *History and Eschatology* (Waco, TX: Baylor University Press, 2019), 125.

16. Ibid., 127.

17. Thiselton, *New Horizons*, 8. (emphasis Thiselton's own) ('lenses' added)

18. Village's horizon preference research found that higher levels of education engender more interest in the author horizon, which is reflected here in 22 percent of formal participants' reflections relating to the author, compared to 14 percent of informal participants'. See: Andrew Village, 'Biblical Interpretative Horizons and Ordinary Readers: An Empirical Study,' *Research in the Social Scientific Study of Religion* 17 (2006): 157–76.

19. Rosenblatt, *The Reader*, 23.

20. Ibid., 24.

21. Ibid., 25. (emphasis author's own)

22. It should also be noted that these two ways of reading are not mutually exclusive, either on the basis of the nature of the text or the proclivities of the reader, and my participants evidenced both.

23. Richard Briggs, 'Evangelical Possibilities for Taking Scripture Seriously,' in *New Perspective for Evangelical Theology: Engaging with God, Scripture and the World*, ed. Tom Greggs (London: Routledge, 2010), 19.

24. Thiselton, *New Horizons*, 34–36.

25. Thiselton, 'Understanding God's Word Today,' 105.

26. 2 Timothy 3:16, NRSV.

Bibliography

Adam, Peter. *Written For Us: Receiving God's Words in the Bible*. Nottingham: IVP, 2008.

Adams, Andrew. *Faithful Interpretation: Reading the Bible in a Postmodern World*. Minneapolis, MN: Fortress Press, 2006.

Alter, Robert. *Genesis*. London: Norton, 1996.

Alter, Robert. *The Book of Psalms: A Translation with Commentary*. New York: Norton, 2007.

Amos, Clare, ed. *The Bible in the Life of the Church*. New York: Morehouse Publishing, 2013.

Anglican Communion. 'Themes and Principles.' Accessed May 4, 2019. https://www.anglicancommunion.org/media/254164/2-Themes-Principles.pdf

Anthony, Francis-Vincent, and Hans-Georg Ziebertz, ed. *Religious Identity and National Heritage*. Boston, MA: Brill, 2012.

Arzt, Silvia. 'Reading the Bible Is a Gendered Act.' *Feminist Theology* 29, no. 10 (2002): 32–39.

Astley, Jeff. *Ordinary Theology: Looking, Listening and Learning in Theology*. Aldershot: Ashgate, 2002.

Astley, Jeff, and David Day, eds. *The Contours of Christian Education*. Great Wakering: McCrimmons, 1992.

Atherstone, Andrew. 'The Keele Congress of 1967: A Paradigm Shift in Anglican Evangelical Attitudes.' *Journal of Anglican Studies* 9, no. 2 (2011): 175–97.

Atherstone, Andrew. *An Anglican Evangelical Identity Crisis: The Churchman–Anvil Affair of 1981–1984*. London: Latimer Trust, 2008.

Atherstone, Andrew, and John Maiden, eds. *Evangelicalism and the Church of England in the Twentieth Century: Reform, Resistance and Renewal*. Woodbridge: Boydell, 2014.

Atkinson, David. *The Message of Genesis 1-11: The Dawn of Creation*. Leicester: Inter-Varsity, 1990.

Bacote, Vincent, Laura Miguélez, and Dennis Okholm, eds. *Evangelicals & Scripture: Tradition, Authority and Hermeneutics*. Downers Grove, IL: Inter-Varsity Press, 2004.

Bibliography

Bailey, Lloyd. *Noah: The Person and the Story in History and Tradition*. Columbia: University of South Carolina Press, 1989.

Ball, Imogen. 'Political and Religious Identities of British Evangelicals.' Theos Thinktank, August 15, 2017. https://www.theosthinktank.co.uk/comment/2017/08 /15/political-and-religious-identities-of-british-evangelicals

Bartholomew, Craig, Robin Parry, and Andrew West. *The Futures of Evangelicalism*. Leicester: Inter-Varsity Press, 2003.

Bartholomew, Craig; Stephen Evans, Mary Healy, and Murray Rae, eds. *'Behind the Text': History and Biblical Interpretation, Vol. 4*. Cumbria: Paternoster Press, 2003.

Baumert, Lisa. 'Biblical Interpretation and the Epistle to the Ephesians.' *Priscilla Papers* 31, no. 4 (2017): 28–32.

Bebbington, David. *Evangelicalism in Modern Britain: A History from the 1730s to the 1980s*. London: Routledge, 1993.

Bebbington, David, and David Jones, eds. *Evangelicalism and Fundamentalism in the United Kingdom in the Twentieth Century*. Oxford: Oxford University Press, 2013.

Belcher, Richard. *Genesis: The Beginning of God's Plan of Salvation*. Fearn: Christian Focus, 2012.

Bell, Rob. *What Is the Bible?* London: William Collins, 2017.

Bellinger, William, and Walter Brueggemann. *Psalms*. New York: Cambridge University Press, 2014.

Beynon, Nigel, and Andrew Sach. *Dig Deeper: Tools to Unearth the Bible's Treasure*. Leicester: IVP, 2005.

Bielo, James. *Words Upon the Word: An Ethnography of Evangelical Bible Study*. New York: NYU Press, 2009.

Boersma, Hans. *Five Things Theologians Wish Biblical Scholars Knew*. Downers Grove, IL: IVP, 2021.

Brierley, Peter. *Pulling Out of the Nosedive*. London: Christian Research, 2006.

Briggs, Richard. *Reading the Bible Wisely*. London: SPCK, 2003.

Briggs, Richard. *Words in Action: Speech Act Theory and Biblical Interpretation*. Trowbridge: T&T Clark, Ltd., 2001.

Brodie, Thomas. *Genesis as Dialogue: A Literary, Historical, & Theological Commentary*. Oxford: Oxford University Press, 2001.

Bruce, Frederick. *The Epistles to the Colossians, to Philemon, and to the Ephesians*. Grand Rapids, MI: W. B. Eerdmans, 1984.

Brueggemann, Walter. *Genesis*. Atlanta, GA: John Knox Press, 1982.

Brueggemann, Walter. *Texts Under Negotiation: The Bible and Postmodern Imagination*. Minneapolis: Fortress Press, 1993.

Brueggemann, Walter. 'The Kerygma of the Deuteronomistic History: Gospel for Exiles.' *Int* 22 (1968): 387–402.

Bunton, Peter. '300 Years of Small Groups: The European Church from Luther to Wesley.' *Christian Education Journal* 1 (2014): 88–106.

Carey, Martha Ann. 'Focus Groups: What is the same, what is new, what is next?' *Qualitative Health Research* 26, no. 6 (2016): 731–33.

Bibliography

Carson, D. A., and John. D. Woodbridge. *Hermeneutics, Authority and Canon.* Leicester: Inter-Varsity, 1986.

Chapman, Mark, Sathianathan Clarke, and Martyn Percy, eds. *The Oxford Handbook of Anglican Studies.* Oxford: Oxford University Press, 2015.

Chicago Statement. 'Chicago Statement on Biblical Inerrancy.' Accessed May 22, 2019. https://defendinginerrancy.com/chicago-statements/

Childs, Brevard. *Biblical Theology in Crisis.* Philadelphia: Westminster, 1970.

Church of England. 'Ministry Statistics.' Accessed May 31, 2020, https://www .churchofengland.org/sites/default/files/2017-11/Ministry%20Statistics%202016 .pdf

Clines, David. *Interested Parties: The Ideology of Writers and Readers of the Hebrew Bible.* Sheffield: Sheffield Academic Press, 1995.

Craigie, Peter. *Psalms 1–50.* 2nd ed. Nashville, TN: Nelson, 2004.

Crow, Loren. 'The Rhetoric of Psalm 44.' *Zeitschrift für die Alttestamentliche Wissenschaft* 103, no. 3 (1992): 394–401.

Dalton, Russell. *Children's Bibles in America: A Reception History of the Story of Noah's Ark in US Children's Bibles.* London: Bloomsbury, 2016.

deClaissé-Walford, Nancy. 'Psalm 44: O God, Why Do You Hide Your Face?.' *Review and Expositor 104* (2007): 745–59.

deClaissé-Walford, Nancy, Rolf Jacobson, and Beth Tanner. *The Book of Psalms.* Grand Rapids, MI: W. B. Eerdmans, 2014.

Ekblad, Bob. *Reading the Bible with the Damned.* Lousville, KY: Westminster John Knox Press, 2005.

Enns, Peter. *Inspiration and Incarnation: Evangelicals and the Problem of the Old Testament.* Grand Rapids, MI: Baker, 2005.

Fee, Gordon D. 'The Cultural Context of Ephesians 5:18–6:9.' *Priscilla Papers* 31. no. 4 (2017): 4–8.

Fee, Gordon D., and Douglas K. Stuart. *How to Read the Bible for All Its Worth.* Fourth edition. Grand Rapids, MI: Zondervan, 2014.

Feinberg, John S. *Light in a Dark Place: The Doctrine of Scripture.* Wheaton, IL: Crossway, 2018.

Finneran, Catherine, Rob Stephenson, and Cory Woodyatt. 'In-Person Versus Online Focus Group Discussions: A Comparative Analysis of Data Quality.' *Qualitative Health Research* 26, no. 6 (2016): 741–49.

Fish, Stanley. *Is There a Text in This Class?: The Authority of Interpretive Communities.* Cambridge, MA: Harvard University Press, 1980.

Ford, David. *Reading the Bible Outside the Church: A Case Study.* Eugene, OR: Pickwick, 2018.

Foster, Richard J. *Life with God: Reading the Bible for Spiritual Transformation.* New York: HarperOne, 2009.

Fowl, Stephen. *Ephesians: Being a Christian, at Home and in the Cosmos.* Sheffield: Sheffield Phoenix Press, 2014.

France, Richard, and Alister McGrath. *Evangelical Anglicans.* London: SPCK, 1993.

Fretheim, Terrence. 'The God for the Flood Story and Natural Disasters.' *Calvin Theological Journal* 45 (2008): 21–34.

Fulkerson, Mary McClintock. *Places of Redemption: Theology for a Worldly Church.* Oxford: Oxford University Press, 2007. https://hdl-handle-net.ezproxyd.bham.ac.uk/2027/heb.30685. EPUB.

Gadamer, Hans-Georg. *Truth and Method.* Translated by Garrett Barden and John Cumming. London: Sheed & Ward, 1975.

Geisler, Norman L., and William C. Roach. *Defending Inerrancy: Affirming the Accuracy of Scripture for a New Generation.* Grand Rapids, MI: Baker Books, 2011.

Goldingay, John. *Models for Scripture.* Grand Rapids, MI: W. B. Eerdmans, 1994.

Gorichanaz, Tim. 'Experiencing the Bible.' *Journal of Religious and Theological Information* 15, no. 1–2 (2016): 1–2, 19–31. DOI: 10.1080/10477845.2016.1168278

Goss, Robert, and Mona West, eds. *Take Back the Word: A Queer Reading of the Bible.* Cleveland, OH: Pilgrim Press, 2000.

Gregg, Tom, ed. *New Perspective for Evangelical Theology: Engaging with God, Scripture and the World.* London: Routledge, 2010.

Gregory, Jeremy, ed. *The Oxford History of Anglicanism, Vol. II: Establishment and Empire, 1662–1829.* Oxford: Oxford University Press, 2017.

Hailes, Sam. 'How Evangelicals Took Over the Church of England.' Premier Christianity, October 26, 2017. https://www.premierchristianity.com/home/how-evangelicals-took-over-the-church-of-england/3081.article

Hamilton, Victor. *The Book of Genesis Chapters 1–17.* Grand Rapids, MI: W. B. Eerdmans, 1990.

Harrison, Mike. 'What Do the Theologically Educated Look Like?' *Dialog* 53, no. 4 (2014): 345–55. DOI:10.1111/dial.12138

Hoggarth, Pauline. *The Seed and the Soil: Engaging with the Word of God.* Carlisle: Global Christian Library, 2001.

Houston, James, Erica Moore, and Bruce Waltke. *The Psalms as Christian Lament.* Grand Rapids, MI: W. B. Eerdmans, 2014.

Jauss, Hans Robert, and Elizabeth Benzinger. 'Literary History as a Challenge to Literary Theory.' *New Literary History* 2, no. 1 (1970): 7–37.

Jayasekara, Rasika. 'Focus Groups in Nursing Research: Methodological Perspectives.' *Nursing Outlook* 60 (2012): 411–16.

Kelsey, David. *The Uses of Scripture in Recent Theology.* London: SCM Press, 1975.

Kim, Yung Sun. *A Transformative Reading of the Bible: Explorations for Holistic Human Transformation.* Eugene, OR: Cascade Books, 2013.

Kings, Graham. *Nourishing Mission: Theological Settings.* Leiden, The Netherlands: Brill, 2022.

Kite, James, and Philayrath Phongsavan. 'Insights for conducting real-time focus groups online using a web conferencing service.' *F1000Research* 6 (2017): 1–6. DOI: 10.12688/f1000research.10427.1

Klink, Edward, and Darian Lockett. *Understanding Biblical Theology.* Grand Rapids, MI: Zondervan, 2012.

Krueger, Richard. *Moderating Focus Groups.* London: SAGE London, 1998.

Lane, Eric. *Psalms 1–89.* Fearn: Christian Focus, 2006.

Lawrence, Brother. *The Practice of the Presence of God.* Translated by E. M. Blaiklock. Chatham: Hodder & Stoughton, 1981.

Bibliography

Lawrence, Louise. *The Word in Place: Reading the New Testament in Contemporary Contexts*. London: SPCK, 2009.

Lewis, C. S., Arthur Greeves, and Walter Hooper. *They Stand Together: The Letters of C. S. Lewis to Arthur Greeves (1914–1963)*. New York: Collier Books, 1979.

Lindsell, Harold. *The Battle for the Bible*. Grand Rapids, MI: Zondervan, 1976.

Louth, Andrew, ed. *Genesis 1–11*. Oxfordshire: Routledge, 2013.

Lurhmann, T. M. *How God Becomes Real: Kindling the Presence of Invisible Others*. Princeton, NJ: Princeton University Press, 2020.

Lurhmann, T. M. *When God Talks Back: Understanding the American Evangelical Relationship with God*. New York: Alfred A. Knopf, 2012.

Lurhmann, T. M., Howard Nusbaum, and Ronald Thistead. 'The Absorption Hypothesis: Learning to Hear God in Evangelical Christianity.' *American Anthropologist* 112, no. 1 (2010): 66–78.

Lyon, Stephen. 'Mind the Gap!: Reflections on the "Bible in the Life of the Church" Project.' *Anglican Theological Review* 93, no. 3 (2011): 449–62.

MacDougall, Scott. *The Shape of Anglican Theology: Faith Seeking Wisdom*. Leiden: Brill, 2022.

Malley, Brian. *How the Bible Works: An Anthropological Study of Evangelical Biblicism*. Walnut Creek, CA: AltaMira Press, 2004.

Manwaring, Randle. *From Controversy to Co-Existence: Evangelicals in the Church of England 1914–1980*. Cambridge: Cambridge University Press, 1985.

Martin, Ralph. *Ephesians, Colossians and Philemon*. Atlanta, GA: John Knox Press, 1991.

Mays, James. *Psalms*. Louisville, KY: John Knox Press, 1994.

McCaulley, Esau. *Reading While Black*. Downers Grove, IL: Inter-Varsity Press, 2020.

McEntire, Mark. 'The God at the End of the Story: Are Biblical Theology and Narrative Character Development Compatible?' *Horizons in Biblical Theology* 33 (2016): 171–89.

McGrath, Alister. *The Genesis of Doctrine: A Study in the Foundations of Doctrinal Criticism*. Oxford: Basil Blackwell, Ltd, 1990.

McKnight, Scott. *Five Things Biblical Scholars Wish Theologians Knew*. Downers Grove, IL: IVP, 2021.

Merkle, Benjamin L. 'The Start of Instruction to Wives and Husbands: Ephesians 5:21 or 5:22?' *Bibliotheca Sacra* 174 (2017): 179–92.

Merkle, Benjamin L. *Ephesians*. Nashville, TN: B&H Academic, 2016.

Michaelson, Jr., Gordon E. Lessing's *"Ugly Ditch": A Study of Theology and History*. University Park and London: Pennsylvania State University Press, 1985.

Morgan, David. 'Focus Groups.' *Annual Review of Sociology* 22 (1996): 129–52.

Mowat, Harriet, and John Swinton. *Practical Theology and Qualitative Research*. London: SCM Press, 2006.

Noll, Mark. *Between Faith and Criticism: Evangelicals, Scholarship and the Bible*. Leicester: Apollos, 1991.

Osmer, Richard Robert. *Practical Theology: An Introduction*. Grand Rapids, MI: W. B. Eerdmans, 2008.

Packer, James. *God Has Spoken*. Fourth edition. London: Hodder & Stoughton, 2016.

198   *Bibliography*

Packer, James. *Truth and Power: The Place of Scripture in the Christian Life.* Wheaton, IL: Harold Shaw Publishers, 1996.

Park, David M. 'The Structure of Authority in Marriage: An Examination of Hupotasso and Kephale in Ephesians 5:21–33.' *Evangelical Quarterly* 59, no. 2 (1987): 117–24.

Perrin, Ruth. *The Bible Reading of Young Evangelicals.* Eugene, OR: Pickwick Publications, 2016.

Pleins, David. *When the Great Abyss Opened: Classic and Contemporary Readings of Noah's Flood.* Oxford: Oxford University Press, 2010.

Powell, Mark. *Chasing the Eastern Star: Adventures in Biblical Reader-Response Criticism.* Louisville, KY: Westminster John Knox Press, 2001.

Powell, Mark. *What Do They Hear?: Bridging the Gap Between Pulpit and Pew.* Nashville: Abingdon Press, 2007.

Poythress, Vern. 'Dealing with the Genre of Genesis and its Opening Chapters.' *Westminster Theological Journal* 78, no. 2 (2016): 217–30.

Rappaport, Roy. *Ecology, Meaning and Religion.* Berkeley, CA: North Atlantic Press, 1979.

Rogers, Andrew. *Congregational Hermeneutics.* Surrey: Ashgate, 2015.

Rom-Shiloni, Dalit. 'Psalm 44: The Powers of Protest.' *Catholic Biblical Quarterly* 70, no. 4 (2008): 683–98.

Rosenblatt, Louise. *The Reader, the Text, the Poem: The Transactional Theory of the Literary Work.* Carbondale: Southern Illinois University Press, 1994.

Sarisky, Darren, ed. *Theology, History and Biblical Interpretation: Modern Readings. First* edition. London: Bloomsbury T&T Clark, 2020.

Seely, Paul. 'Noah's Flood: It's Date, Extent, and Divine Accommodation.' *Westminster Theological Journal* 66 (2004): 291–311.

Sherwood, Harriet. 'As traditional believers turn away, is this a new crisis of faith?.' *The Guardian*, August 14, 2016. https://www.theguardian.com/world/2016/aug/13 /church-of-england-evangelical-drive

Smith, Christian. *The Bible Made Impossible.* Grand Rapids, MI: Brazos Press, 2012.

Smith, Greg, ed. *21st Century Evangelicals.* Watford: Instant Apostle, 2015.

Sparks, Kenton L. *God's Word in Human Words: An Evangelical Appropriation of Critical Biblical Scholarship.* Grand Rapids, MI: Baker Academic, 2008.

Sproul, Robert. *Ephesians.* Fearn: Christian Focus, 1994.

Stendahl, Kristen. 'Biblical Theology, Contemporary.' *Interpreter's Dictionary of the Bible.* Nashville: Abingdon Press, 1962. A–D: 418–32.

Stone, Michael, ed. *Noah and His Books.* Atlanta, GA: Society of Biblical Literature, 2010.

Stott, John. *Evangelical Truth.* Nottingham: Inter-Varsity Press, 2011.

Stott, John. *The Bible: Book for Today.* Leicester: Inter-Varsity, 1982.

Stott, John. *The Message of Ephesians: God's New Society.* Nottingham: Inter-Varsity Press, 1979.

Stott, John, ed. *Obeying Christ in a Changing World: Vol. 1, The Lord Christ.* Glasgow: Fountain Books, 1977.

Bibliography

Strhan, Anna. *Aliens and Strangers?: The Struggle for Coherence in the Everyday Lives of Evangelicals.* Oxford: Oxford Scholarship Online, 2015. DOI: 10.1093/acprof:oso/9780198724469.001.0001

The Bible in the Life of the Church. 'What the Anglican Communion has said about the Bible 2: Themes and Principles emerging from official and semi-official Anglican Communion documents.' Accessed April 23, 2020. https://www.anglicancommunion.org/media/254164/2-Themes-Principles.pdf

The British Academy. 'Theology and Religious Studies.' Accessed May 31, 2020. https://www.thebritishacademy.ac.uk/documents/288/theology-religious-studies.pdf

The Economist. 'Hot and Bothered.' Last modified March 10, 2012. https://www.economist.com/britain/2012/03/10/hot-and-bothered

Thiselton, Anthony. *The Hermeneutics of Doctrine.* Grand Rapids, MI: W. B. Eerdmans, 2007.

Thiselton, Anthony. *Thiselton on Hermeneutics: The Collected Writings and New Essays of Anthony Thiselton.* Aldershot: Ashgate, 2006.

Thiselton, Anthony. *New Horizons in Hermeneutics.* London: HarperCollins, 1992.

Thiselton, Anthony. *The Two Horizons: New Testament Hermeneutics and Philosophical Description, with Special Reference to Heidegger, Bultmann, Gadamer, and Wittgenstein.* Grand Rapids, MI: W. B. Eerdmans, 1980.

Thompson, Mark D. *The Doctrine of Scripture: An Introduction.* Wheaton, IL: Crossway, 2022.

Todd, Andrew. 'The Talk, Dynamics and Theological Practice of Bible-Study Groups.' PhD diss., Cardiff University, 2009.

Treier, Daniel J., and Douglas Sweeny, *Hearing and Doing the Word.* London: T&T Clark, 2021.

Treier, Daniel J. *Introducing Theological Interpretation of Scripture: Recovering a Christian Practice.* Grand Rapids, MI: Baker Academic, 2008.

Treier, Daniel J. 'Biblical Theology and/or Theological Interpretation of Scripture?: Defining the Relationship.' *Scottish Journal of Theology* 61, no. 1 (2008): 16–31. DOI:10.1017/S0036930607003808

Treier, Daniel J., and Kevin J. Vanhoozer. *Theology and the Mirror of Scripture: A Mere Evangelical Account.* London: Apollos, 2016.

Turnball, Richard. *Anglican and Evangelical?* London: Continuum, 2007.

UCCF, 'Doctrinal Basis.' Accessed April 1, 2019. https://www.uccf.org.uk/about/doctrinal-basis

Village, Andrew. 'Biblical Conservatism and Psychological Type.' *Journal of Empirical Theology* 29, no. 2 (2016): 137–59.

Village, Andrew. *The Bible and Lay People: An Empirical Approach to Ordinary Hermeneutics.* Hampshire: Ashgate Publishing, Ltd., 2007.

Village, Andrew. 'Biblical Interpretative Horizons and Ordinary Readers: An Empirical Study.' *Research in the Social Scientific Study of Religion* 17 (2006): 157–76.

Village, Andrew. 'Does higher education change the faith of Anglicans and Methodists preparing for church ministries through a course validated by a UK university?' *Practical Theology* 12, no. 4 (2019) 389–401. DOI: 10.1080/1756073X.2019.1635310

Village, Andrew. 'Biblical Interpretative Horizons and Ordinary Readers: An Empirical Study.' *Research in the Social Scientific Study of Religion* 17 (2006).

Waite, Hannah. 'The Nones: Who Are They and What Do They Believe?' *Theos* (2022): 29.

Walton, Roger. 'Using the Bible and Christian Tradition in Theological Reflection.' *British Journal of Theological Education* 13, no. 2 (2003): 133–51.

Ward, Timothy. *Words of Life: Scripture as the Living and Active Word of God.* Nottingham: IVP, 2009.

Warner, Rob. *Revinventing English Evangelicalism 1966–2001: A Theological and Sociological Study.* Milton Keynes: Paternoster, 2007.

Watson, Francis. 'Hermeneutics and the Doctrine of Scripture: Why They Need Each Other.' *International Journal of Systematic Theology* 12, no. 2 (2010): 118–43.

Webster, John. 'Hermeneutics in Modern Theology: Some Doctrinal Reflections.' *Scottish Journal of Theology* 51, no.3 (1998–2008): 307–41.

Webster, John. *Holy Scripture: A Dogmatic Sketch.* Cambridge: Cambridge University Press, 2003.

Wenham, Gordan. J. *Genesis 1–15.* Waco, TX: Word Books, 1987.

West, Gerald. 'Locating "Contextual Bible Study" within Biblical Liberation Hermeneutics and Intercultural Biblical Hermeneutics.' *HTS Theological Studies* 70, no. 1 (2014): 1–10. DOI: http://dx.doi.org/10.4102/hts.v70i1.2641

Westermann, Claus. *Genesis 1–11: A Continental Commentary.* Minneapolis, MN, Fortress Press, 1994.

Wink, Walter. *The Bible in Human Transformation.* Second edition. Minneapolis, MN: Fortress Press, 2010.

de Wit, Hans, and Janet Dyk, eds. *Bible and Transformation: The Promise of Intercultural Bible Reading.* Atlanta, GA: SBL Press, 2015.

Wright, N. T. *History and Eschatology.* Waco, TX: Baylor University Press, 2019.

Wolff, Hans Walter. 'The Kerygma of the Yahwist.' (trans. Wilbur A. Benware) *Int* 20 (1966): 131–58.

Yeager, Jonathan, ed. *The Oxford Handbook of Early Evangelicalism.* Oxford: Oxford University Press, 2022.

Index

accommodation, author, 50, 111, 131–32
address, of text, 10, 173, 179–89
application, 43–44, 74–78, 80–83, 100, 104, 142–49, 160, 162–65, 170–71, 176
atheism, influence of, 39, 47–48, 87, 140, 178
authority of scripture, 1, 5, 9, 80, 115, 126–27; challenges to the, 27, 39; historicity and the, 36, 50, 56; relevance and the, 74, 76, 85–86, 140; sufficiency and the, 7–8, 93–95, 141–42, 148
authors: Bible's, 6, 8, 27, 59, 67, 80–81, 101–2, 180, 182–83; historicity and, 130–32; horizon of the, 76, 154–56, 169; intention of, 36–38, 49–50, 75, 77, 123, 163, 168–69; relevancy/authority and, 85, 126–27

Bebbington, David, 92, 117
belief practices, 29, 100
biblical theology movement, 56–57, 94, 117
Bielo, James, 13, 58, 76, 142
Briggs, Richard, 7, 78, 186

canonical reading, 41, 51, 80–81, 96, 100, 134, 140, 157, 159–61, 165, 173; scholarship about, 56–60, 62
canonical trajectory, 97, 100, 159–60, 173
character of God, 40, 57, 63–64, 66, 68, 108, 114; contextualisation of the, 110–11, 167; doctrine of scripture and the, 97, 115–18, 188; education comparison of the, 166–68; historicity and the, 36, 45–46, 108–9; origins of the, 111–13; tension concerning the, 109–10
christological readings, 62, 111–12, 122–23, 166, 117
Church of England Evangelical Council (CEEC), 9, 36
clarity, 9, 97–98, 149, 157
communication, God's, 38, 42–44, 51, 77, 85, 91, 96–98, 103, 115–16, 134–35, 149, 169, 176, 186
consistency, Scripture's, 8–9, 51, 59, 69, 96–97, 112, 125–26, 134, 158, 165
contextual gap, 27, 75, 79–80, 160
context: Christian, 140–44; doctrine of Scripture, 148–50; personal, 145–47; reader's, 1, 22, 30, 65, 84–85, 112–13, 139–40, 153, 170–71, 176, 180–84

202   *Index*

dispositional belief, 20, 27, 186, 188

distancing, 38, 77, 105, 182

doctrine of God. *See* character of God

doctrine of Scripture: context and the, 148–50; doctrine of God and the, 115–18; education and the, 171–73; engagement practices and the, 10–11; Evangelical-Anglican, 4–10; function of the, 10, 44, 51–52, 101–14, 115–16; genre and the, 134–35; historicity and the, 50–52; relevance and the, 86–87; text and the, 184–86; theology and the, 68–69

engagement practices, 29, 99–101, 104, 180–81; education comparison of, 156–57, 160–65, 168, 182–84; genre and, 132–34, 168

Enns, Peter, 36, 38, 59

ethics, 50, 58, 77, 83

Evangelical Anglicans, 3–10

Evangelicalism: American/British, 92, 104n5; conservative/liberal, 20, 126, 144, 148, 154, 158, 163, 170–71

Experience: Bible, 149–50; Christian, 140–44, 170–71; God, 109, 111, 147, 154, 181–82; human, 65–67, 84–85, 132; identity, 146–47, 161, 171; personal, 48, 76, 100, 145–46, 160, 162, 170, 178, 183

external input, 142–43, 156, 170

focus groups, 19–29

Ford, David, 93, 146, 178–79

Gadamer, Hans-Georg, 11, 75, 102

Genesis 7: analysis of, 41–45; education comparison of, 156–59; overview of, 38–39; rationale for, 39; scholarship of, 40–41

genre, 28, 121–22, 176; doctrine of scripture and, 69, 93, 134–36; education comparison of, 164, 168–69, 173; engagement practices in relation to, 132–34; Ephesians,

126–27, 129; Genesis, 40, 122–24, 127–28; history and, 51, 129–32, 168; Psalm, 61–62, 124–26, 128; theology and, 67–68

Gilgamesh epic, 45, 49, 157

God's word, 1, 9, 98, 100, 148; authority of, 5, 76, 123; consistency of, 8, 97; genre of, 169, 135; historicity of, 36, 39, 45–46, 52; inspiration of, 6–7, 95–96; relevance of, 73–74, 76–78; theology of, 61, 64, 125

harmonisation, 40, 59. *See also* consistency, Scripture's

hermeneutics, 1, 4, 10–14, 37–38, 58–60, 76–78, 146, 178–80

higher criticism, 9, 10, 35–36, 56–57

historical-critical exegesis, 37–38, 59, 62, 77, 81–83, 99, 112, 133–34, 157–58, 162, 170, 180–83

historicity, 27–28, 39; doctrine of God and, 36, 45–46, 108–9; doctrine of scripture and, 44–45, 50–51; education comparison of, 158–59; genre and, 47, 51, 129–32, 158, 168; ordinary readers' approaches to, 37–38; relevancy and, 86–87; scholarship about, 35–37; science and, 46, 47–48; truth and, 36, 39, 41–50, 123–24, 131

Holy Spirit, 7, 9, 60, 74, 76–77, 85–86, 96

horizons: 101–2; congregational, 142, 148; distinction of, 75–76; education preference of, 154, 169; fusion of, 11, 77, 161; transformation of, 178–80

inerrancy, 1, 6–7, 36–38, 59, 92, 126

infallibility, 6, 123

inspired, 6–7, 9, 27, 35–36, 39, 45, 69, 74, 95–96, 115, 131, 135, 148, 190

Jewish readings, 56, 141–42

Index

kerygmatic exegesis, 56, 117

lenses, 102–3, 175–78; context/
experience, 139–50; doctrine of
Scripture, 103–4, 164–65, 171–73;
doctrine of God, 107–18, 166–68;
genre, 121–36, 168–69; text's lenses,
179–84
literal reading, 34, 42–45, 47, 56, 81,
94, 121–22, 128, 130, 141, 154, 158,
163–64, 172

Malley, Brian, 12–13, 57–58, 75–76,
109, 115
meaning, 74, 176; author's, 99,
122–23, 169; clarity and, 9,
124–25; education comparison of,
164–65; genre and, 121, 173; God's
communication as, 96, 185–87;
reader's role in making, 11, 139–40,
150; teaching as, 51–52, 68–69,
87, 94, 101, 115, 164–65. *See also*
application
meta-narrative, of Scripture, 117–18,
167, 172–73. *See also* canonical
trajectory; revelation, progressive
revelation
metaphor, 36, 41, 44, 45–46, 96, 122,
124, 126
myth, 40–43, 49–50, 53n32, 122–24,
127–28

Packer, J. I., 4, 10, 15n16, 36, 38
patristic readings, 55–56, 122, 142
Perrin, Ruth, 13, 19, 26, 37, 39, 50,
54n34, 58, 92, 104
Powell, Mark, 13, 140, 155–56, 165
practical theology, 3, 12
prayer, 61–62, 67–69, 124

reason, 7–8, 56, 86, 93, 109, 129, 132,
148, 168
reader-response, 11, 139

reading agenda, 51–52, 68–69, 91,
101, 103–4, 176, 186–90; education
comparison, 165, 173
relevance, 27, 73–74, 79–80, 92, 96,
100–101, 161, 178; doctrine of
scripture and, 86–87; education
comparison of, 163–64; hermeneutics
and, 76–78; ordinary readers'
approaches to, 75–76; reasons for,
83–85; scholarship about, 75
revelation, 7–9, 36, 41, 56, 76–77, 111–
12; progressive revelation, 8, 112,
167. *See also* canonical trajectory;
meta-narrative, of Scripture
Rogers, Andrew, 13, 71n38, 92, 115,
142, 148, 174nn10, 174nn13,
174nn15
Rosenblatt, Louise, 11, 185
rule of faith, 55, 61

salvation, 7–9, 66, 73–74, 117; salvation
history, 56, 100, 117–18, 157, 167
science, 39–40, 46–49, 132, 157–58
secular culture, influence of. *See*
atheism, influence of
Smith, Christian, 92, 117
social location, of reader, 12, 140, 146–
47, 161, 171
Sparks, Kenton, 6, 36, 56
Stott, John, 3–4, 6–7, 38, 77, 127
suffering, 61–62, 64–66, 159
sufficiency, 1, 7–9, 93–95, 142

teaching resource, Bible as, 44, 51–52,
68–69, 74, 78, 87, 91–95, 97–99,
101, 103, 116, 135, 149, 176,
184–88; context and, 150; education
comparison of, 164–65; genre and,
135–36
textual history, 47, 95, 133–34, 169
theological education, influence of, 21,
153–73
theological Interpretation, 43, 50–52,
55–60, 69, 87, 91, 93, 94–95, 104,
173; education comparison of,

164–65; scholarship movements in, 56–57

Thiselton, Anthony, 10–11, 20, 59, 76–77, 101–2, 140, 178–80, 188

Thompson, Mark D., 5–7, 10, 60

Todd, Andrew, 13, 43, 76, 92, 102–3, 108, 110, 140, 151n15

Tradition, 5, 7–9, 12, 75, 86, 93, 111, 132, 141–43, 148, 170, 188

Transformation, 77–78, 178–84, 188, 190

Transitivity, 57, 109

Truth, 10, 53n31, 58–59, 86, 159; genre and, 121, 125–26, 131–32; historicity and, 36, 39, 41–50, 123–24, 131; propositional, 74, 77–78

underlying principles, 80–83, 93, 100, 135, 162–63

unity, of Scripture. *See* consistency, Scripture's

Village, Andrew, 3, 13, 32n16, 37, 51, 76, 119n8, 144, 154–55, 158, 169, 172, 174n12, 191n19

Ward, Timothy, 6, 36, 77–78

About the Author

Dr Anna Hutchinson is a lecturer and tutor in Theology at St. Mellitus College, South West. Her main interest is in the Doctrine of Scripture and hermeneutics, but she previously specialised in Systematic Theology completing a Master's in Modern Doctrine from the University of Oxford, and her undergraduate degree in Theology was from the University of Durham.